D0640025

FABRIC OF FREEDOM
1763–1800

Books by Esmond Wright include

Washington and the American Revolution

The Making of America

The Formative Years: 1607–1763 by Clarence L. Ver Steeg
Fabric of Freedom: 1763–1800 by Esmond Wright
The New Nation: 1800–1845 by Charles M. Wiltse
The Stakes of Power: 1845–1877 by Roy F. Nichols
The Search for Order: 1877–1920 by Robert H. Wiebe
The Urban Nation: 1920–1960 by George E. Mowry

FABRIC OF FREEDOM

1763–1800

By

ESMOND WRIGHT

The Making of America

GENERAL EDITOR DAVID DONALD

American Century Series

HILL AND WANG · NEW YORK

A division of Farrar, Straus and Giroux

Copyright © 1961 by Esmond Wright
All rights reserved

Standard Book Number (clothbound edition) 8090-4355-6
Standard Book Number (paperback edition) 8090-0101-2

Library of Congress catalog card number 61-14479

Manufactured in the United States of America

FIRST PRINTING SEPTEMBER 1961
SECOND PRINTING SEPTEMBER 1963
THIRD PRINTING (FIRST AMERICAN CENTURY SERIES
EDITION) JANUARY 1964

13 14 15

For Olive

Foreword

ONCE IN a very great while there appears a historical work characterized by thorough research, fresh insight, and vivid writing. *Fabric of Freedom* is just such a rare book. In it Professor Esmond Wright of the University of Glasgow retells the story of the American Revolution, of the adoption of our Constitution, and of the establishment of the federal government.

Professor Wright's major theme is the slow and uncertain emergence of the spirit of American nationality under the stress of war and revolution. In 1765, he points out, "there was no 'nation' as yet." The War for American Independence was "in a sense thirteen revolutions rather than a single 'national' movement." Even by the end of the period the United States had not fully reached a sense of nationhood, but by 1783 *"country* was being used not for the little platoon one belonged to but for the whole, the new, the united nation." Intertwined with this theme of nationalism is that of democracy. At the beginning of the era aristocratic East and democratic West were so different that it was proper to speak of "at least two distinct societies in America," but the war was "productive of major social and political change." By 1800, though the United States was still in a "predemocratic" stage, the "fabrick of freedom" had been erected.

In Mr. Wright's pages these twin transformations are traced with the objectivity befitting an English author who teaches at a Scottish university and writes on an American subject. Neither an adherent of the Whig interpretation, which saw in the American Revolution the unqualified voice of freedom, nor a member of the Imperialist school of historians, who tended to view the Revolution as a disturbance of the best empire ever known to man, Mr. Wright views the conflict impartially. At the same time, his knowledge of British history has given him new insights into the American struggle. No previous writer has so completely integrated the scholarly researches of Sir Lewis Namier and his disciples and applied their findings to the American problem. Similarly, Mr. Wright brings a fresh understanding to the difficulties and vexations of British military strategy during the Revolution. Mr. Wright's British background also assists him in appraising the alleged economic motives behind the Constitution of the United States. Distant enough not to be involved in the acrimonious exchanges among American historians on this subject and informed by a European perspective, he is able to see merits in both sides of this heated historiographical argument. The Constitution, he concludes, "was at once the apogee of the Revolution and its Thermidor"—and he adds that it created a "strong government . . . made as weak and as divided as could safely be managed." Significantly he concludes: ". . . what Federalists and Anti-Federalists accepted as common ground was far more striking than the controversy between them."

Mr. Wright's writing is as witty as it is objective. The author of a biography of George Washington and of forthcoming studies of Benjamin Franklin and John Burgoyne, he has the rare ability to recreate a personality in a few carefully drawn sentences. His portrait of Alexander Hamilton, for example, is an adroit portrait in paradox. In a single sentence Mr. Wright says more than do most books about John Adams: "He carried his rectitude like a banner; and he stopped now and then to salute it."

An outstanding feature of Mr. Wright's book is his unusually thorough and elaborately annotated critical bibliography, which will henceforth serve as a standard guide for students of the Revolutionary generation.

In short, Mr. Wright's book is a vigorous and scholarly history of a crucial stage in American development. As such, it occupies a distinguished place in The Making of America, a six-volume series designed to bring the best of historical writing to a general reading public. Falling chronologically between Clarence Ver Steeg's study of colonial America and Charles M. Wiltse's *The New Nation: 1800–1845, Fabric of Freedom* is at once a spirited narrative of some of the most important years in the American story and a fresh interpretation of their significance.

DAVID DONALD

Contents

	Foreword	vii
1	The American Colonies in 1763	1
2	Parliament: Politics and Policy	22
3	Riot and Resistance: 1764–1774	51
4	Rebellion: 1774–1776	87
5	Revolution: Winning the War, 1776–1783	106
6	Revolution: the Home Front, 1776–1787	140
7	The Constitution	165
8	The First President: the Captive Federalist	188
9	The Second President: Federalism High and Low	217
10	What Then Is the American, This New Man?	237
	Bibliographical Essay	255
	Index	289

MAPS

The American Colonies in 1763	14
Military Map of the Revolution	114
The United States in 1783	158

Acknowledgments

I SHOULD LIKE to thank two of my colleagues in the History Department at Glasgow, Peter Parish and Peter Thomas, and Dr. John Woods of the Burke Papers in Sheffield, for reading parts of this book in manuscript, and for their wise and friendly counsel. They have done their best to save me from error, but I fear that errors, as I am sure some personal oddities of interpretation, will remain. For these I must accept full responsibility.

My major thanks, however, must go to two people: to David Donald of Princeton, formerly visiting Harmsworth Professor at Oxford, for the care with which he read the book in draft and for the excellence of his editorial suggestions; and to my wife, for her help and encouragement.

Acknowledgment is also made for permission to reproduce the maps in this volume: p. 14: drawn by Ava Morgan Weiss for *Rebels and Redcoats* by George Scheer and Hugh F. Rankin, © 1957 by The World Publishing Company, Cleveland and New York, and used by permission; pp. 114, 158: drawn by Vaughn Gray for *History of a Free People* by Henry W. Bragdon and Samuel P. McCutchen, © The Macmillan Company, 1954, 1956, 1958, 1960, 1961 and used by permission.

E. W.

FABRIC OF FREEDOM
1763–1800

1

The American Colonies in 1763

By the terms of the Treaty of Paris, signed on February 10, 1763, the North American mainland was shared between Britain and Spain. France retained only two small islands, Saint Pierre and Miquelon, off the coast of Newfoundland, at which her fishermen could dry their fish. She lost Canada and all her possessions east of the Mississippi River, as she lost also all but two of her stations in India and some, but not all, of her West Indian islands. There was a school of thought in the City of London that would rather have annexed wealthy and tiny Guadeloupe than vast but empty Canada. The arguments of the British sugar interest, of the fur traders, and of Benjamin Franklin in the end prevailed: Canada became British and Guadeloupe and Martinique, to Pitt's chagrin, stayed French. Britain returned the Philippines and Cuba, her conquests of 1761, to Spain, but exacted Florida in exchange; to offset this loss Spain was given compensation at the expense of France by the cession of Louisiana and the Isle of Orleans. The French possessions on the continent of North America were thus entirely and, as it proved, permanently lost.

British North America was a vast area, diverse in its people, in its many forms of government, and in its resources, geographically as ill-explored as it was constitutionally ill-defined. It extended, north to south, from the Hudson Bay Territory,

Newfoundland, and Nova Scotia (all won from France in 1713) and from Quebec (won in 1759) down to the Florida keys. From east to west it stretched from the indented coastal plains and the tidal rivers of the Atlantic seaboard to the Mississippi.

The importance of the Treaty of 1763 was at once American and Atlantic, continental and maritime. The French Empire in North America had come to an end; in Canada English culture and institutions came to dominate, but never quite to swamp, the French; and British North America was more than doubled in extent, although the *habitants* numbered only some seventy-five thousand. The removal of the French danger in 1763 transformed the situation of the British settlements from Massachusetts to Georgia; when the French reappeared, fifteen years later, the enemies of 1754 were welcomed as the allies and liberators of 1778. The military dependence on Britain that had lasted since the colonies were founded was now weakened. Not only was a new strategy necessary, the very extent of British success raised new political issues and set in motion new forces in the colonies themselves. Britain no longer needed to make concessions, and the colonies for their part developed wills of their own. The paths to the West now seemed open to them. Issues hitherto incidental to the French wars—fur trade, land policy, Indian relations—became intrinsically important. The American Revolution has its origin in the oversuccessful terms of the Treaty of 1763. "With the fall of Quebec," says Francis Parkman, "began the history of the United States."

Yet Britain's position as a naval and indeed as a world power was seen as beyond challenge in 1763. She controlled the North American mainland from the Atlantic to the Mississippi; she controlled the majority of the West Indian islands, from Bermuda to Jamaica, from Dominica and St. Vincent to Grenada; and she controlled also Belize and the Mosquito Coast. Although France held the sugar islands of Guadeloupe, Martinique and St. Lucia, and Cayenne in Guiana while Spain held Cuba and Hispaniola, Britain dominated both the Caribbean and the continent. She had eight thousand ships at sea, and seventy thousand sailors. Her policy, like her strategy, was neither unified nor consistent, but, as L. H. Gipson reminds us, it was never conceived solely for the mainland colonies. In 1763 there seemed ample justification for a mood of high imperialism in Britain.

The British colonies of the North American mainland extended for sixteen hundred miles along the seaboard, from the Isle of Demons in the Belle Isle Strait to the humid Okefinokee swamps. At either extremity there was a military or a naval outpost. Newfoundland had had a civil government since 1728 but almost half of its population of twelve thousand were summer residents only, exploiting the finest cod fisheries in the world. In 1763 the coast of Labrador was attached to the governorship of Newfoundland, but both areas were remote, foggy, and forbidding. Nova Scotia had been captured by Britain in 1710 and formally acquired by the Treaty of 1713. For fifty years it had been a weak imperial base against the French in Cape Breton. In 1749, Halifax was founded as a counterpoise to Louisburg. In 1755 the French were expelled from the Acadian settlements on the Bay of Fundy and the Annapolis River. Swelled by immigrants from New England, the British numbers in Nova Scotia grew to eleven thousand in 1766 and to twenty thousand in 1775. It was granted a representative assembly in 1758. Beyond on the St. Lawrence lay the province of Quebec, unripe as yet for representative government, French in character, with, Governor James Murray calculated in 1766, only nineteen Protestant families living outside Quebec and Montreal—as a group, "the most immoral collection of men I ever knew." Farther west, at Detroit and Vincennes, Kaskaskia and Fort De Chartres, were some fifteen hundred Frenchmen, the flotsam of France's failure in the West.

In the years after 1763 several military posts were established in the Floridas, the latest of the buffer colonies against Spain, and particularly in West Florida, that part of old Spanish Florida that lay beyond the Chattahoochee and Apalachicola rivers. It included most of the province of Louisiana to the south of the thirty-first parallel and east of the Mississippi, and the towns of Pensacola and Biloxi and Mobile. In 1764 the northern boundary of West Florida was moved to a line running east from the confluence of the Yazoo and the Mississippi, bringing in the fertile country around Natchez. Progress in East Florida was slower and, remote from the Mississippi, more deliberate. There was a regular parliamentary grant to encourage "Silk, Vines and other articles of beneficial produce"; experiments in colonization were begun; in 1767 a curious and ill-fated colony of fifteen hundred Greeks, Italians, and Minorcans under the leadership of Dr. Andrew Turnbull was settled at New Smyrna, sixty miles south of St. Augustine, to raise indigo and sugar cane. In 1781, two years before it ceased to be a British colony, East Florida acquired an assembly. The pattern set by the Carolinas and by Georgia was being followed.

The colonies that lay between the swamps of Florida and the high tides of the Bay of Fundy differed widely in their governments, in their economies, and in their populations. Despite their various origins, the Crown had gradually established direct rule over one colony after another, beginning with the "conversion" of Virginia in 1624. By 1763 only the proprietorships of Pennsylvania, Delaware, and Maryland and the self-governing or corporate provinces of Connecticut and Rhode Island remained outside royal control. Paradoxically enough, royal control was on the whole sought after by the colonists, for the very good reason that a remote Crown and a royal governor were often more tractable than a proprietor on the spot. Even Penn's benevolence availed him little; in 1765 Benjamin Franklin was sent to England to ask that the proprietorship be canceled and that George III assume direct control of Pennsylvania—a trip without result.

With the exception of Rhode Island and Connecticut, whose

governors and legislatures were fully elective, and of Massachusetts, where the council was elective, all the colonies had approximately the same form of government. The governor was
appointed by the King or the proprietor, and he in turn appointed the council—almost always from the wealthiest citizens—
and with their interests he normally identified his own. He was
usually, but not invariably, English, often a soldier, and frequently an absentee whose duties were carried out for him by a
lieutenant-governor—sometimes mistakenly described as "governor"—himself often a Scot. His powers were viceregal; he was
head of the colonial administration, supreme magistrate, and
commander of the military forces; some governors, Shirley in
Massachusetts or Loudoun or Amherst in Virginia, were also
Commanders-in-Chief of all the British forces in North America.
The governor granted pardons, enforced or vetoed the laws, summoned, adjourned, and dissolved colonial assemblies.

All the colonies had elective assemblies, which by 1763 had
established their right to initiate legislation, levy taxes, and make
appropriations, provided these were consistent with the colonial
charters and the laws of England. Just how binding these laws
were was coming to be a matter of debate. The French and
Indian War had been almost universally treated as an opportunity for wresting concessions from colonial governors. And Dinwiddie in Virginia was urging upon the home government the
need to tax colonists who were so obviously reluctant to make
the war their own. Until 1763 there prevailed in London a
timidity in this matter that in retrospect appears as wisdom.

The tradition of debate in the colonies was almost a century
old and took varied forms: the struggle for control of the
assemblies between great and small landholders or between
eastern and western counties; the struggle over quitrents, over
the right of the colonies to issue paper money or to win religious
freedom for minorities; or the struggle—everywhere in evidence
in the decade before 1763—between assemblies and governors for
control of the public purse. In most colonies, the governor's

salary had become dependent on an annual appropriation; hardly ever could he for long resist legislative pressure. "Every proprietary Governor," it was said, "has two masters; one who gives him his Commission and one who gives him his Pay."

Whatever the situation in Britain in 1763, the issues of 1688 were kept alive in the colonies, and many local situations—before as well as after the French and Indian War—were seen in terms of the stereotypes of the Glorious Revolution. For King read governor and for Parliament assembly, and invoke appeals not only to the Bill of Rights but also to the written charters as guarantees of colonial liberties, and one sees how close was the parallel between 1688 and 1766. It is true that the suffrage was limited, as in Britain, by property and religious qualifications, and that an office-holding class monopolized the most desirable posts; but elections were fought openly and often violently, and voting was oral; it was as easy to arouse popular excitement over the billeting of troops and the wickedness of taxation as it had been over Indian raids or proprietary interests. Moreover, through the parish vestries, the county courts, the town meetings and assemblies, there was abundant opportunity for participation in public affairs.

There is controversy as well as variety of view on the question of the relation of voting rights to property. Recent views have emphasized the extent of voting and the ease with which property restrictions were being overcome. Apportionment of seats greatly favored the older-settled areas at the expense of the newer—but less so than in contemporary Britain. The proceedings of assemblies were fully publicized—more so than those of Parliament in contemporary Britain. The variety of viewpoint reflects in fact the variety of the colonial situation. In Virginia a farmer could vote only if he owned one hundred acres of unoccupied land, or at least twenty-five acres on which stood a house twelve feet square—something larger, that is, than a cabin. In Massachusetts, a land of small and family-worked farms, the wide extent of property-holding made some 80 per cent of its male population eligible to vote. But among the artisans of Philadelphia the suffrage was a rarity. The pattern of government might appear to be royal; in some provinces, such as New York, it was oligarchic and in others, for example Rhode Island, exclusive; and many of the statutes, though thus far laxly enforced, were imperialist in intention. There was nevertheless a vitality in public controversy and in the election of representatives and selectmen in the colonies that belied, and was in the end to challenge, the authority of Whitehall.*

Generalization is more difficult about the colonial economies and societies. Although the social, like the political, implications of the settlement of America might be democratic, democracy came late on the scene. The mass of the colonists were far from being aristocratic; there was considerable social mobility, and the widespread ownership of property weakened the sense of class division. Yet the social structure was almost as aristocratic as that in contemporary Britain, which it reflected.

By 1763 there was a distinct upper class, composed of the large landowners, the wealthy merchants and lawyers, the governors and lieutenant-governors, the revenue officers, and "the friends of government." The basis of their prestige was land and, to a lesser but increasing degree, trade. The Granville tract in North Carolina covered one third of the colony; the Fairfax grant in Virginia ran from the Tidewater to the headwaters of the Potomac, wherever they might be; Maine was almost a private holding of Sir William Pepperrell, the conqueror of Louisburg; much of Georgia was owned by Sir James Wright.

If New England was by contrast an area of small, self-sufficient farms, and compact settlements due to the system of townships, there were, in the traditions of the Bible Commonwealth and of

* See C. S. Sydnor, *Gentlemen Freeholders: Political Practices in Washington's Virginia* (1952); Robert Brown, *Middle-Class Democracy and the Revolution in Massachusetts, 1691–1780* (1955); Philip S. Klein, *Pennsylvania Politics 1817–1832* (1940); J. R. Pole, "Suffrage and Representation in Massachusetts: A Statistical Note," in *William and Mary Quarterly*, Vol. XIV, No. 4 (October 1957). See also Leonard W. Labaree, *Royal Government in America* (1930).

Yankee thrift, forces making for similar social distinctions. They were seen in the seating of church members by "property, virtue and intelligence," from the brave coat lace-embroidered to the gray coat shading down, and in the listing of Harvard and Yale students by a "class" that revealed social rank rather than merit. Virginia's merchant-planter pioneers of the seventeenth century —the Byrds, Carters, Harrisons, Randolphs, and Lees—were now the colony's upper class. They were matched by the merchant-traders of New England—the Browns and Cabots, the Faneuils and Amorys—and by the merchant-financiers and fur traders of New York—the Phillipses, De Peysters, Morrises, and Franks. Newport was ruled by "twenty genteel families," not a few of whom prospered from the rum and slave trades. These men of property were "gentlemen" and "esquires," their property often buttressed by laws of primogeniture and entail.

In some colonies these family groups were seeking to be exclusive but they never were completely so. They could include an enterprising planter like George Washington, himself largely a self-made man and a protégé of the sixth Lord Fairfax; an enterprising privateer like John MacPherson of Philadelphia; a merchant-smuggler like John Hancock; a theater-owner like David Douglass; or an enterprising painter like J. S. Copley, who owed his status as much to his choice of a wife as to his skill as an artist.

Below the gentry was a large and fluid middle class, embracing clergymen, teachers, lesser merchants and lawyers, yeomen farmers, town craftsmen and shopkeepers, minor officials in government, plantation overseers, and skilled artisans, "the middling sort." This was a working middle class far more than a professional one, particularly strong in New England. Many a "goodman" and his "goodwife" claimed inclusion in it.

Below them in turn was a laboring force of mainly propertyless and therefore voteless workers, unskilled laborers, journeymen, or poor frontiersmen, many of them German or Scotch-Irish. Originally many of these, like many above them in the social scale, had been indentured servants working under a labor contract for a term of years, or convicts. Maryland alone received more than nine thousand convict servants between 1748 and 1775. *Convict,* of course, covered a multitude of sins, and some virtues; rogues, cutthroats and whores, Covenanters, Jacobites, and Quakers.

In the eighteenth century a new type of indentured servant appeared, the redemptioner. In the South, artisan and craftsman were harder to discover. By 1763 the Negro slave had almost entirely replaced the indentured servant as the South's labor force, although elsewhere white workers under contract continued to arrive. George Washington's first schoolmaster came under this system; one of the most interesting diaries of the Revolutionary period was that kept by an indentured servant, John Harrower; and one of the most interesting studies of early Maryland was a "dish of discourse" by an indentured servant, George Alsop. According to tradition, at least one signer of the Declaration of Independence, Matthew Thornton of New Hampshire, had been an indentured servant; so were William Buckland, who built Gunston Hall, and Charles Thomson, Secretary of the Continental Congress. To Alsop, Maryland was "a fertile and pleasant piece of ground." "You may depend upon it," said William Allen, "that this is one of the best poor Man's Country's in the World."

By the mid-eighteenth century there was a further labor force, owning no man master, coming into being in the high valleys of the Alleghenies and on the western fringe of society, from the Mohawk Valley to the pine barrens of Georgia. This was largely recruited from Germany, from Scotland, and from Ulster. But recruits for the West came from Tidewater America also. Native and immigrant alike sought in land ownership, and to a lesser degree in physical remoteness, a security and a freedom they had not enjoyed in the older societies, in Europe or in the Tidewater. In America itself this western migration not only settled the frontier but also released productive forces generally and kept wages high. "Labour will never be cheap here," wrote Franklin in 1751, "where no Man continues long a Laborer for others, but gets a Plantation of his own, no Man continues long a Journeyman to a Trade, but goes among those new Settlers, and sets up for himself." The Mohawk, Hudson, Susquehanna, and Shenandoah valleys, the Indian trails and wilderness roads became channels of traffic and of trade, and of economic optimism. They were channels of variety too, for frontiersmen were of many types: in the lush canebrakes of the western Carolinas they tended cattle, in the Cumberland Gap they were trappers and traders, in the northern timberlands they cut oak and white pine, from the Kennebec and Penobscot they went out to the Canso Strait, the Gulf of Maine, and the Grand Banks for cod and mackerel.

It was this force on the frontier that had precipitated clashes with French outposts and with Indians. Once its western enemies had been removed, it proved less amenable than ever to British —or Tidewater—control. It was hostile to all taxes to maintain others in an ease it did not share or to support institutions with which it had no sympathy. Although its "democratic" character has probably been overstated, it fought its own war against its own Establishment, whether it saw it as aristocracy, monarchy, or Episcopal Church, whether it was French, British, or American. By 1776 well over a quarter of a million people were in the back country, and in South Carolina four out of every five of the white population were on the frontier or in the Piedmont. Hard though Tidewater planters or Quaker merchants or Hudson Valley patroons might seek to maintain the culture of and the links with Europe, their influence waned with every step of westward advance; there was symbolism as well as utility in the deerskin of Daniel Morgan's riflemen and the coonskins of Daniel Boone. Behind the political challenge presented to Britain by colonial nationalism was the deeper and less tractable challenge of frontier protests to eastern merchants and planters.

Culture on the moving frontier might be basically English, as

Louis B. Wright has recently claimed, but it was unsophisticated and austere, a culture remote from Philadelphia or Charleston. There were few schools and churches, although the frontier had been swept as by a prairie fire in the Great Awakening, and some schools, churches, and colleges were that movement's curious legacy. This was a land of log cabins and small-scale subsistence farming, of linsey-woolsey homespun and a diet of "hog 'n' hominy." The economy was primitive, with a little tobacco or whiskey and perhaps a few furs to trade for essential manufactures; a land of poverty, violence, and opportunity, where politics was egalitarian and religion pentecostal.

This colonial society was increasing its numbers by its own fertility as well as by immigration: high birth rates and large families were the rule—the average number of children per colonial family was 7.5, and wives were exhausted by the constant childbearing. "An old maid or an old bachelor are as scarce among us and reckoned as ominous as a blazing star," wrote William Byrd. The Puritan code was strict. That aspect of it most scrupulously honored was the adage *increase and multiply*. The population was in fact doubling every generation, although more slowly in New England than elsewhere. In 1763 it was almost two million, of whom approximately one quarter were Germans and Scots-Irish and approximately one eighth Negro. By 1775 it was two and a half million; by 1790, at the first census, it was 3,929,214, of whom 757,208 were Negroes.

Preoccupation with the causes of the Revolution has led historians to exaggerate the extent of colonial tensions with Britain before 1763. They existed, of course, abundantly. But their basic cause until the middle of the eighteenth century was in fact political consanguinity. Colonies and home country were too much alike in political attitudes, with a mutual insistence on freedom of debate and on control of their own purses; and for a century and a half their economies were complementary and unconflicting. The tensions that had arisen repeatedly in the past were thus not fundamentally divisive. The uncertainty of Virginia's form of government in its early days, the quarrels with Governor Berkeley reflecting the quarrels at home, the experiments with the New England Confederation, and later the bolder absolutist plan for a Dominion of New England, arguments over land grants, head-rights, and charters, the petitions and counterpetitions of colonial agents in London throughout the eighteenth century: these were the stuff of colonial politics. All these issues produced situations of controversy and crisis, but none of them produced a revolution.

Far more striking than the differences with Great Britain were the differences between the sections. Sectionalism was deeply rooted, product of rock and soil, race and religion. From early days, the indented coastline and numerous harbors of New England encouraged maritime industries: the short but rapid rivers were a source of water power; cedar, spruce, oak, and pine for ships were abundant. By 1770 New England had almost one thousand vessels engaged in the cod and mackerel fisheries or in whaling; she built twice as many vessels as all other areas combined. And with shipyards went sawmills and wagons, barrels, furniture, and household goods, whale oil and spermaceti. Agriculture was important here as elsewhere. It was diversified, and free from the price fluctuations and overproduction that beset the South, but it was handicapped by rock and mountain, by short summers and long winters. This was a soil and climate unsuitable for tobacco, for plantations, and for slave labor; its farms were small and compact, tilled by an independent class of yeomen. Even these looked to the sea—Washington's "marines" and "commandos" were recruited from the fishermen-farmers of Gloucester and Marblehead, New Bedford and Nantucket. Captain John Smith, in his *Present Estate of New Plimouth*, 1624, had said "Let not the meannesse of the word Fish distaste you, for it will afford as good gold as the Mines of Guiana and Potassie with lesse hazard and charge, and more certainty and facility." New England's prosperity came from the sea; it is still

symbolized in the gilded codfish on the Speaker's desk in the
State House in Boston. There was a ready market for surplus
fish in the West Indies and in Catholic southern Europe. And
there flourished the triangular trade in rum, molasses, and slaves
between the West Indies, New England, and Africa.

What was striking about New England was its homogeneity
in race and religion and the dominance of the English and the
Puritan strains in church and state. There were few Negroes, almost all of them domestic servants or town workers. Here as
elsewhere fundamentalism and deism were making inroads, but
as yet they had not got far. To a South Carolinian like Edward
Rutledge, New England was peopled by men of "low cunning
and levelling principles." It was nourished by a strong current of
democracy and debate in congregation and in town meeting, and
by a well-organized system of education, evidenced in Harvard
(1636) and Yale (1701), Brown (1764) and Dartmouth (1769).
The Yankee virtues of industry and thrift, caution and esteem
for learning were to move west with the New England settlers
into the Ohio and upper Mississippi valleys. There, as well as in
New Haven and Boston, were to rise the little red schoolhouse
and the tall white spire.

> Clear, reticent, superbly final
> With the pillars of its portico refined to a cautious elegance.

The Middle Colonies—New York, Pennsylvania, New Jersey,
and Delaware—were very different. In the three great river
valleys, the Hudson-Mohawk, the Susquehanna, and the Delaware, there was abundant and fertile soil, and the Middle Colonies were the granaries of the rest. The governor of Pennsylvania
estimated in 1755 that the colony could export enough food each
year to feed one hundred thousand people. Navigation inland was
much easier than to north or south, and the West was first
reached along the Mohawk. This was Iroquois country, and it
was dominated by the Superintendent to the Northern Indians,

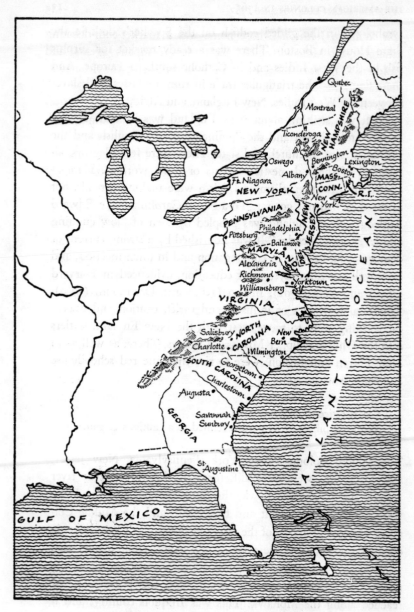

THE AMERICAN COLONIES IN 1763

Sir William Johnson, whose home was a market-cum-debating chamber for Mohawk chiefs, fur traders, company agents, and soldiers. The fur trade was still important and the Mohawk-Hudson junction at Albany was its pivot.

Both in New York and Pennsylvania, population was un-usually mixed. New York City was already cosmopolitan, with layers of New Englanders and Scotch-Irish, French Huguenots, Negroes and Rhineland Germans. Politics here were already coming to be a matter of fine calculation among Germans, Dutch, and Irish. With cosmopolitanism of population went a certain culture, a college (King's, now Columbia, founded 1754), a theater and two newspapers, and a tradition, thanks to John Peter Zenger, of free and frank comment. Dutch influence had left its mark on the Hudson Valley in a distinguished upper class of *Vans* and *velts:* government was distinctly less democratic up the Hudson than in Manhattan; the Van Rensselaer manor cov-ered an area two thirds the size of Rhode Island; this was a region of tenants rather than freeholders. But New York, colony and city, lived also by trade. The city was freer and more mate-rialist than Boston, a place of *nouveaux-riches*. "With all the opulence and splendor of this city, there is little good breeding to be found. . . . At their entertainments, there is no conversa-tion that is agreeable; there is no modesty, no attention to one another. They talk very loud, very fast and altogether." But John Adams was a prejudiced observer.

Pennsylvania, with which were linked the "lower counties" of Delaware and west New Jersey, was the most tolerant and in many ways politically the freest of all the colonies. To it had migrated many Rhinelanders and many Scotch-Irish; by 1776 at least a third of its population was German, and Franklin had fears that German would become its principal language. The rest of the population tended to be either Quaker or Scotch-Irish. The Germans and Quakers were pietist, industrious, and frugal. They made good husbandmen, and the Germans were also among the leaders in all the colonies in glass, brick, and iron production. Peter Kalm, the Swedish traveler in 1749, was lyrical in his praise:

> Again and again as we traveled through the forests of Pennsylvania we saw at moderate distances little fields which had been cleared of wood. Each of these was a farm. These farms were commonly very pretty, and a walk of trees frequently led from them to the highroad. The houses were all built of brick or of stone which is found here everywhere. Every countryman, even the poorest, had an orchard with apples, peaches, chestnuts, walnuts, cherries, quinces and such fruits, and sometimes we saw vines climbing in them. The valleys were frequently blessed with little brooks of crystal clear water. The fields by the sides of the road were almost all mown.

By 1763, however, the Quaker and pietist elements were a source of weakness as well as strength. They were both conservative and pacifist. They had consistently refused appropriations for the colony's defense and Pennsylvania had been saved in Braddock's day only by Franklin's exertions. The Scotch-Irish frontier, menaced by Indians, became hostile both to Quakers and proprietors; their easy affluence, business acumen and, it seemed, inveterate meanness seemed to imperil the existence of the colony. This clash between west and east was to store up problems for the future, as it had in the past. Meanwhile the colony prospered. Its best index was its metropolis, Philadelphia. In 1763 it had twenty-three thousand people and was the largest city in North America, with the first circulating library and the first fire company, a flourishing theater, secular university, gazette, and a distinguished "first citizen" and "man of business" —his own and other people's—in Benjamin Franklin. The Scots traveler Dr. Alexander Hamilton found the City of Brotherly Love much to his taste in 1744:

> They have that accomplishment peculiar to all our American colonys, viz., subtilty and craft in their dealings. They apply themselves strenuously to business, having little or no turn towards

gaiety (and I know not indeed how they should since there are few people here of independent fortunes or of high luxurious taste). Drinking here is not att all in vogue, and in the place there is pretty good company and conversation to be had. It is a degree politer than New York tho in its fabrick not so urban, but Boston excells both for politeness and urbanity tho only a town.

The South was still more distinct. Settled early by English trad-ers or landowners, it developed along its slow-moving, wide-mouthed tidal rivers along novel lines. Here as elsewhere the majority of free men were small farmers, and many of them earned a living by producing grain, fruit, and pork. But the tone of society was set by the plantation. John Rolfe's "discovery" of tobacco made it, despite the fulminations of James VI and I, the staple crop of the Chesapeake Bay region; in South Carolina and Georgia the basis was rice and indigo; in both, the planta-tion quickly evolved. During the eighteenth century the price of tobacco became steady, but the costs of production inexorably in-creased, partly because of the heavy charges imposed by trans-porting it to Britain—for which the factors and agents at home were often blamed—still more because of soil exhaustion. The reliefs sought by the planters—crop restriction, lower import duties, reduction of debts, curtailment of the slave trade—were opposed by British interests. An energetic planter like Washing-ton sought to diversify his crops or to speculate in western land.

A plantation economy demanded a large labor force; four fifths of the Negro population were south of the Mason-Dixon line. They represented 40 per cent of the population of Virginia, 60 per cent of that of South Carolina. Many planters—among them William Byrd—wanted the abolition of the slave trade and eventual emancipation of the slaves. Many, like Washington and Jefferson, willed freedom to their own slaves when they died. But, despite its qualms, the South took no legal action against slavery; nor was such action feasible. The peculiar institution—and the fear of slave uprisings—promoted self-sufficiency, executive ability, and the habit of command among its masters; Washington had a larger staff to direct at Mount Vernon than when he assumed the presidency in 1789. The South preserved the class distinctions, the Episcopalian Church, the parish and county government, and the *mores* of an older England. From Britain it was largely recruited; to Britain it sent its crops and from it bought its goods; and to Britain also came its sons for education —although as often to Edinburgh and the Inns of Court as to the older universities.

The South was rural. The big house of the plantation was workshop and mill, tannery and hotel as well as home, and it could occasionally be a cultural center, like Westover on the James, Robert Carter's Nomini Hall, or Bermuda Hundred. But so sympathetic an observer as Chastellux found Virginians "ignorant of the comfort of reading and writing." There was only one college in the colonial South, William and Mary. The leisure of the planter was active rather than contemplative: he turned to horses and hunting, cockfights and cotillions, gossip and hospitality rather than books. His ways were gregarious, not solitary. "He who rides his horse alone can catch his horse alone."

The traditions of the Tidewater South were as well established as those of New England or Philadelphia, but very different. This was a society warm and convivial, quick to anger, sensitive to injury, open, unshrewd and feckless. Yankees found it not to their taste: South Carolina was, to Josiah Quincy, a land of "opulent and lordly planters, poor and spiritless peasants and vile slaves." Samuel Bownas, the Quaker preacher who visited Virginia in 1727, thought that "the intemperance of the people was shortening their days." John Woolman found "a Dark Gloominess hanging over the land." For, tied to the soil, the inefficient colored labor force was almost completely without initiative, and the plantation economy was draining the land of its vitality. The indebtedness of the South to England was not only social but also economic. Jefferson bluntly described his fellow planters as "a species of property annexed to certain mercantile houses in London." Virginians owed British creditors at least two million pounds sterling by 1775.

Moreover, there were differences and tensions within each section. Almost all colonies had boundary disputes with each other; all were slow to help each other against French and Indians. New England was sharply divided by the conflict between frontier and coast; eastern Connecticut quarreled with western; Massachusetts was contemptuous of Rhode Island, and Newport and Providence were contemptuous of each other. Pennsylvania was torn apart by such crises as the march of the Paxton boys. North Carolina, lacking ports and towns, roads and specie, did not fit the southern stereotype. Its chief product was naval stores, not tobacco like Virginia or rice like South Carolina. Its social character reflected this. In 1763 it had just under a hundred thousand inhabitants, only sixteen thousand of whom were Negroes. Its scattered lumbermen, planters, and Indian traders were a turbulent community; one visitor called it bluntly "a hell of a hole." Like sentiments, a little more decorously expressed, recur in William Byrd's *History of the Dividing Line* and *A Journey to the Land of Eden.* "To speak the Truth, tis a thorough Aversion to Labor that makes People file off to N. Carolina, where Plenty and a warm Sun confirm them in their Disposition to Laziness for their whole Lives." In 1771 there was an ugly civil war between western and eastern North Carolina. Georgia, with five thousand whites and two thousand Negroes, was more frontier than colony. In South Carolina the western frontiersman had less influence than anywhere else, and Charleston became in the mosquito season a center of gracious living, seeing itself as a would-be Athenian state. But Gideon Johnston thought the South Carolina people "the Vilest race of Men upon the Earth . . . a perfect Medley or Hotch potch made up of Bankrupts, pirates, decayed Libertines, Sectaries and Enthusiasts of all Sorts . . . the most factious and seditious people in the whole World." Well might James Otis predict in 1765: "Were these colonies left to themselves tomorrow, America would be a mere shambles of blood and confusion."

As a result of such contradictory estimates, one of the foremost students of the South in the colonial period, Carl Bridenbaugh, distinguishes among three Souths: Chesapeake society, Carolina society, and the back settlements. And if we add this same writer's insistence on the growing importance of craft skills and urban life in North and South, it is clear that there was little uniformity inside either section or state. When the Revolution came, it took a different form in each section—indeed, in each colony. There were in a sense thirteen revolutions rather than a single "national" movement.

For there was no "nation" as yet. The French and Indian War of 1756–63 had been fought as a series of distinct operations by each colony and had been won by British rather than by colonial troops. Virginia, which (like New Jersey) failed to attend the meetings held at Albany in 1754 to discuss a possible union of the colonies for defense, was left to fight its own wars with little aid from the Carolinas or from Maryland in 1756. Of the five colonial assemblies that voted on the Albany plan, four rejected it. The Boston Town Meeting thought it a danger to the liberties of the people. None of the colonies was ready to agree on a common defense; indeed, except during Pitt's ministry, each was slow to defend even its own territory. They rejected a common policy and vociferously rejected all schemes whereby they could tax themselves for defense purposes. So vigorous a soldier as Washington had strongly opposed using the shortest route to Fort Duquesne in 1758 since it lay not through Virginia but through Pennsylvania. As late as 1781 all that could be agreed upon was a loose confederation, not a union of states.

These colonial prides and jealousies were notorious. They were economic as well as political, and quite as much geographic as psychological. Communications were still difficult; as late as 1801, Jefferson as President lamented that of eight rivers between

Monticello and Washington, five had neither bridges nor boats. Franklin's labors to produce a plan of union at the Albany Congress in 1754 were less successful—and perhaps less important— than his role as postmaster and builder of postal roads; the high- way, then as now, has been the cement of the common life.

2

Parliament: Politics and Policy

THE WORK OF Sir Lewis Namier and his associates in recent years has revised all prevailing views on the structure of British politics in the age of the American Revolution. George III, it is now clear, was not a tyrant seeking to destroy the constitution; he did not destroy the party system, for there was no system to destroy and little as yet that was recognizable as party. The government was royal and was produced by devising links between various "connections"; and in the eighteenth century, it was the government that made majorities, not majorities the government. Ministers were responsible not to Parliament but to the King, and they managed Parliament on his behalf. The King himself, unlike his Hanoverian predecessors, was genuinely interested in Britain; he was strong-willed and hard-working, young and sincerely patriotic; but he was also obstinate, short-sighted, and unforgiving.

From the moment of the King's accession in 1760, American affairs played a major part in British politics. For the first sixteen years, questions of American defense, American taxation, and American "rights" were among the chief topics of parliamentary debate. Inevitably they became involved with all the other controversial issues: the wisdom or otherwise of the peace settlement with France in 1762–63; the liberty of the subject and the free reporting of parliamentary debates, raised by the career of John

Wilkes; the heavy cost of government and, especially as it seemed in a Parliament of landowners, the heavy burden of the land tax; and the "rights" of the King-in-Parliament to be the supreme lawmaking authority in the Empire. American questions could rarely be considered in and for themselves, but they were discussed almost as thoroughly in Britain as in America.

Central though American affairs were, however, any consistent approach to them by the government of the day was all but impossible. Government was too fluid, too mixed and broad-bottomed, to allow any consistent policy to emerge on any issue. All the Whig groups, whose composition was very fluid, supported the 1688 settlement; by 1763 this had involved them in the support of the *status quo* and in strong views on the sanctity of Parliament. They were worried by the American problem, but they were worried more by its disruptive effect on British politics than by any other aspect. They were often therefore short-sighted in their estimates of it. "The seditious spirit in the colonies owes its birth," said Grenville, "to the factions in this House."

One of the Whig groups, the Old Whigs, has normally been excepted from any such indictment, largely because of the role of its spokesman, Edmund Burke, the exponent of party government in its modern sense, and in his speeches of 1774–75 the exponent of a liberal imperialism toward the colonies. The researches of Professor Namier and of Professor Pares have reduced the importance of this group and of their spokesman. Their leaders were not distinguished. Rockingham was young, wealthy, honest, and of sound judgment, but no speaker and no fighter for causes; he was, says Mr. Christie, "the pilot who shunned rather than weathered the storm." The fourth Duke of Devonshire was popular and equable in manner but of mediocre talents. They were not particularly skillful in parliamentary management; they refused to establish an American secretaryship, although this had long been discussed; Burke's eloquent justification of party, however prescient, was in some measure an elaborate and rather stagy defense of the Whig families, "the great oaks that shade a country." Even Lord Rockingham's administration of 1765-66, so often thought of as liberal, was a coalition government that had to include three of the King's Friends.

Nevertheless, alone among the Whig groups, the Old Whigs had something that approached a policy for America, and it had a certain discernible consistency. They opposed the taxing of the colonists not on grounds of principle but for reasons of a political tact that Burke elevated into wisdom: "things that are lawful are not always expedient"; "magnanimity in politics is not seldom the truest wisdom and a great Empire and little minds go ill together." They opposed the Stamp Act not as a measure that was illegal but as one that was unwise.

Similarly, Lord Chatham, who denied that Parliament had any power to tax America, had to head mixed administrations, and, however liberal on some issues, it was Chatham in 1766 who proposed a bill "declaratory" of Parliament's "high rights and privileges" over America. The liberal was also the imperialist, and did not see the terms as antithetical. Pitt, who became Lord Chatham in 1766, was himself in no small way responsible for the confusion of politics in the early years of George III's reign, partly by his understandable but impulsive resignation in 1761, still more by his unpredictability. Like all politicians of the day he had a following, though it was small and powerless—"square pegs who could not fit into round holes" as Dr. Brooke describes them. Pitt wielded an influence, however, that could have made, as it helped to destroy, governments. He was popular in the City and had the support of Beckford and Wilkes. If he had combined with the Whigs he could have destroyed Bute in 1762 or Grenville in 1765. But he declared himself against any combination with the Whig families who had refused to destroy French trade and seapower in 1761-62; he declared himself indeed against all connection, and particularly against its high priest Newcastle, his uncongenial bedfellow of the years of victory. For

Pitt's Whiggism, like his grandfather's before him, was born of respect not for gentry but for trade; he spoke for the rising commercial classes.

He saw himself, however (in his own phrase), as "a man standing single," and this was as anachronistic in the 1760s as was Burke's apologia for party. He played fast and loose across the political checkerboard, the vain, theatrical victim of gout and of his own temperament, seeing himself, in the 1760s as in the 1750s, as the figure to whom in the end all would have to turn. There seems no reason to reverse Winstanley's judgment of some forty years ago: "Pitt failed as a domestic politician, and the early years of the reign of George III constitute the record of his failure." The latest detailed study of his 1766–68 administration, that of John Brooke, attributes its failure not to his illness nor to the weakness of his Cabinet, but to deeper political causes. "He looked with contempt upon cultivating a majority in the House of Commons. . . . He cared neither for the friendship nor enmity of politicians who thought in terms of places and patronage. . . . It was not his illness alone that wrecked the Administration; it was the mixture of grandeur and aloofness which made so great a statesman so poor a politician."

The same doubts hung at the time over Shelburne, lacking though he was in Pitt's flamboyance. "The Jesuit of Berkeley Square," he was seen by colleagues as a "secret enemy" and was never trusted, in part because of his early association with Bute; no group grew up around him. His manner was both obsequious and sarcastic; he was jealous and suspicious; he had no skill in the management of men; he had all Pitt's faults and few of his virtues; and, where India was concerned, he seems to have been open to the charge of directing his activities to the ends of personal financial gain. But of all the major politicians of his day, Shelburne alone was well informed on the American question. And he was perhaps the most consistently liberal figure in Parliament, on economic and parliamentary questions, on Wilkes, free trade, and religion. He served for a few months in Grenville's ministry as President of the Board of Trade and formulated an intelligent and coherent western policy. And in 1782 it was through his contacts with Richard Oswald and Franklin that the peace was at last signed.

It was therefore impossible for any one group to allow the American question to become the key question of policy. In any event, any such assumption would have been false to eighteenth-century politics. The task of government was administrative, not legislative. No group other than the Rockinghams had anything resembling a party "program." In a real crisis, as in 1775, parliamentary opinion tended to rally behind the King. When it finally broke with him, as in 1782, the government came close to paralysis and the King himself thought of abdication. As a result, no agreed solutions could emerge from Parliament for the baffling problems of the New World, for its frontier security, for its native population, for the financing of its defense, or for guiding its growing trade along new lines.

Only three men showed genuine concern for those problems at the legislative level: Rockingham, who held office for only one year; Pitt, whose illness deprived his country of its one possible political savior; and Shelburne, who came to power only in time to make a peace of surrender. Whatever the reason for it—an unimaginative King, an unrepresentative House, or mere faction —during the years from 1760 to 1784 Parliament was complacent about and indifferent to the American problem. The colonies, their sugar and tobacco, furs, fish and timber, their governorships and tax collectorships, their stamp distributors and Indian agents, their markets for London, Bristol, and Glasgow agents, were the spoils not of an imperial system gone awry or of a despotic King, but of a parliamentary and largely aristocratic battleground in which only a handful of men knew or cared about them. And until 1782 the association of the American cause with radicalism, with "Wilkes and liberty," and its exposition at home mainly by merchants and dissenters, by London aldermen or by somewhat suspect Irish carpetbaggers, did not enlist particular sympathy in a Parliament that was still the preserve of the Duke of Omnium.

Moreover, at a time when politics was relatively unaffected by public opinion but greatly affected by pressure groups, when West Indian planters and Indian "nabobs" were peculiarly powerful, there was no sustained American pressure group in Parliament at all. Only on repeal of the Stamp Act was there temporary accord between the West Indian and the American merchants: it did not last. A few individuals were interested in the American problem; and there were two ex-colonial governors, Thomas Pownall of Massachusetts—on this issue the ablest and most experienced of all members of Parliament, although regarded as a "wild man" and, worse, a bore—and George Johnstone of West Florida.

But they were a handful only, and they were not a united group. Those of them who showed independence and had posts to lose—like Conway and Barré—lost them in the war, to be regarded as heroes in America. By no means all Americans living in London shared their sentiments; former colonial agents as often as not came in the end to support Britain, among them Richard Jackson and William Knox. Between 1763 and 1783 only five Americans sat in the House of Commons, and of these never more than three sat at any one time. Of them, one—Paul Wentworth—was a loyalist, and another—Henry Cruger of New York—was by no means consistently pro-American. Only Barlow Trecothick, who helped to have the Stamp Act repealed, was of real help to the American cause. What was needed was a Virginia or Massachusetts cousinhood to offset Jamaica and India House. The absence from Parliament of an American "interest" in these years was the most serious political fact of all.

The role of government in the eighteenth century was thus—of necessity—small. And its powers of law enforcement were, it should be remembered, very limited. Mobs and riots were frequent occurrences. This explains much of the Revolutionary period: the ineffectiveness of the mercantile system before 1763 and the bitterness aroused by the law once its enforcement was

effective; the power of mobs, whether of transient soldiers and
sailors in New York, angry at British press gangs, or of those who
wrecked the Stamp Act and the tea duty of 1773; the effect on
civil government of groups like the Sons of Liberty or the
Mohawk River Indians, and the powerlessness of authority to
curb them; the danger implicit in any meetings under the Liberty Pole; and the fear of a standing army and the invitation to
belittle its garrisons. In the eighteenth century the line that separated a snowball fight from an outbreak of civil war, or even a
revolution, was a narrow one. Violence was never far below the
surface in eighteenth-century society, whether at home or over-
seas: except in the most disciplined or sophisticated societies it
never is. And when authority is weak or hesitant, it is natural to
see the right of assembly, the right of vigilante justice, and even
the right to riot as expressions of a natural right.

In the circumstances of eighteenth-century parliamentary politics,
then, a policy for the colonies was hard to manufacture. It was
not indeed felt to be needed, except in a crisis. The administration of the colonies was the responsibility of the Privy Council
and primarily of the Secretary of State for the Southern Department, acting on the advice of the Board of Trade and Plantations. The Board, which consisted of eight active and eight
honorary members, examined all laws passed by the colonial assemblies and occasionally imposed a royal veto on them. Of
8563 laws submitted to it, 469 were disallowed. It drafted instructions to colonial governors, recommended appointments, and
gave advice. None of its members had had colonial experience,
and they invariably and exclusively reflected mercantile opinion.

In the early part of the eighteenth century the Board had declined in influence, and the Duke of Newcastle in particular had
been jealous of its allegedly wide powers of patronage. There
was no consistency of opinion as to its powers. The Earl of
Halifax, on becoming its President in 1748, had sought to extend its authority, and began a campaign for the creation of a

specifically American department. From 1752 to 1761 it had the right to appoint colonial governors and to control all ordinary correspondence with them. In 1757, with Pitt's support, Halifax was admitted to the Cabinet. He was a clear-headed imperialist and wanted the colonists taxed for their own defense. This new efficiency, again antedating 1760, along with Pitt's zest and success as Secretary of State, brought Parliament into the day-by-day matters of administration; increasingly the Commons took an interest and at times an initiative, rarely unselfish or high-minded, in colonial patronage, in the workings of the laws of trade, or in curbing American manufactures. And this parliamentary curiosity, which at home appeared a guarantee of liberty against royal or bureaucratic power, appeared in colonial eyes at best as meddling interference, and in the end as a new species of tyranny.

The Board of Trade was then intermittently powerful, but its power again declined after Halifax's retirement in 1761. The Board was never an effective and not always a sympathetic colonial office, close though its contacts were with merchants and colonial agents; whenever it proposed major expenditure, particularly for colonial defense, it met opposition from Parliament and the Treasury; it could in the last resort only advise and recommend, not enforce. "The Lords of Trade," said Governor Belcher, "are not very mighty lords; nor are they able to administer life or death."

Nor did the creation in 1768 of a third secretaryship of state, designed to be a Secretary for American Affairs, improve matters. Hillsborough was quite unqualified for the post and his powers were never precisely defined. When the office had been first proposed, Newcastle spoke of a "Secretary for the Indies." Although by 1768 it was concerned with the American colonies, it was not until Germain became its holder in 1775 that it came to rank as equal to the two existing secretaryships. What vigor there was under Hillsborough (1768–72) and Dartmouth (1772–75) came from the office of its permanent secretary. This post was held by John Pownall as Secretary of the Board of Trade from 1748 to 1768, and then as Under Secretary for the Colonies (1768–70). Unlike his brother, an ex-governor of Massachusetts, John Pownall knew of the colonies only at second hand, and he favored a policy of coercion toward them. Pownall was succeeded by William Knox, who served until the department was abolished by Rockingham's reforms in 1782. Knox had estates in Georgia as a rice-planter; he had been an agent for Georgia in London from 1762 until 1765, but lost his post because of his advocacy of the Stamp Act. He favored the creation of a colonial aristocracy and the inclusion in Parliament of representatives from the colonies. It was from Pownall and from Knox that the first drafts of bills came. The frequent changes of ministry and their fluctuating membership gave these permanent officials considerable influence.

There was, however, even after 1768, no one single agency in London wherein lay exclusive responsibility for the colonies. The Secretary of State and the Board of Trade, the Treasury, and the Surveyor and Auditor-General of the colonies, the Commissioner of Customs, the Secretary-at-War, the Admiralty and the Admiralty Courts, the Surveyor-General of the King's Woods, the Postmaster-General, the Bishop of London—all were involved. Much time was spent in consultation and discussion among them; still more was wasted in the physical effort of reaching the appropriate authority. The Admiralty alone had fifteen branches scattered in all parts of the town, from Whitehall to Cheapside; the Board sat in Whitehall, but the Navy Office was in Seething Lane, the Victualling Office in East Smithfield, the Ordnance in the Tower. Any rapid dispatch of business was unusual, almost impossible, in London, and it took a further five weeks at best, and ten weeks as normal, to pass the results on to the colonies; a similar period followed in waiting for a reply. "Seas roll and months pass between the order and the execution," said Burke.

And the documents that were dispatched were bureaucratically standardized. The instructions issued by the Board of Trade were not changed in essentials throughout its existence, from 1696 to 1782. Hillsborough, as American Secretary, insisted that all applications from any colony should come direct from the governor to him, and not through a colonial agent in London, even though that agent was Franklin. Governor Sharpe similarly told Maryland to avoid modes of transmission that were "disrespectful to the Crown." There was small awareness of the colonial growth in population, of their sense of being, in Governor Bernard's words, "perfect states, not otherwise dependent on Great Britain than by having the same King."

The result of this was that the British government was parliamentary and—as it saw itself—free at home but bureaucratic and royal abroad. Indeed, at a time when separatist feeling in the colonies was very strong, and the political structure and societies of the colonies varied, centralization was increasing—not decreasing—in London. More and more colonies were coming under the control of the Crown, even if in one or two cases governors were not appointed by the Crown. In 1752 colonial governors were reminded that they must abide by their instructions and that all colonial laws should be brought into conformity with royal instructions. The more daunting the colonial problems and the more extensive the territory to be administered, the more the need grew for plan and pattern. In the new areas acquired in 1763—Canada, the Floridas, the trans-Allegheny country—there were no representative institutions, and little information available; here was no local opinion to conciliate, and politics could be discounted. It was all too possible for Americans, for whom the pattern of government had not changed since 1660, to see themselves as protesting against a tyranny like that of Charles I; the Burke-Whig view of George III has some validity when the King is seen in an American rather than a British context. When after 1763 Parliament increasingly associated itself with the King in colonial matters, it appeared in American eyes as remote and unrepresentative, not the guardian but the enemy of liberty. The

Declaration of Independence was America's Grand Remonstrance.

Before 1763 Parliament had played small part in colonial rule, either in theory or practice. There is hardly a single Act of Parliament for the colonies before 1763 that is not a trade bill. At various times, however—1701, 1706, 1715, 1722, and again in 1744 and 1748—the Board of Trade, in its efforts to establish a homogeneous system of administration, tried to extend the royal prerogative in the colonies, and brought in measures to make the private proprietary colonies royal. Parliament was slow and reluctant to interfere with colonial charters or to tighten the system, but it did authorize the transfer to the Crown of the rights of the Carolina proprietors in 1729, and it appropriated considerable sums to help establish Georgia in the 1730s. For the rest, it confined itself mainly to trade regulation. The administration of the colonies was left to the executive. It was of course more powerful in theory than in fact; the years from 1733 to 1763 were years of administrative laissez faire that came close to destroying the mercantile system.

Then why, after 1763, did Parliament suddenly concern itself, not merely with the trade, but with the actual ruling of the colonies? In part, the answer is constitutional. The departments responsible for America were now headed by members of ministries based on parliamentary combinations. Such combinations were held together by patronage, and the colonies were a rich field. For their part, too, the colonies maintained agents in London, and sometimes these agents were themselves members of Parliament, like Richard Jackson or Burke himself. Even when they were not, they brought what influence they had to bear on Parliament.

But it seems also to be true that in the years from 1756 to 1774 Parliament was becoming remarkably self-conscious. There was at last an end of Stuart threats, and an end of the reversionary problem that had bedeviled the monarchy. The winning of America and India brought more than pride; it brought to a

head both a sense of the importance of the colonies and a sense of
their absolute dependence on the mother country—distressingly
true in the light of colonial hesitations to help the campaign
against the French. The Wilkes case, the attempt to suppress the
printing and reporting of debates, the concern with privilege—
due as much to a parliamentary as to a royal sensitiveness—indicate the mood. In 1763 there was a new consciousness of victory
and of Empire, of which Pitt was the symbol. For the first time
the colonies were valued not merely for their trade or as coun-
ters in European diplomacy but as possessions; there was glory
in their mere extent, and their administration could no longer be
ignored. And there was, in all the factional politics of the eighteenth century, no serious questioning of the legislative authority
of Parliament. Some, like Pitt, might with baffling logic hesitate
to admit that the legislative power included the right to tax. But
few had his doubts, even on this. The year of the Stamp Act saw
the publication of the first volume of Blackstone's *Commentaries
on the Laws of England.* "There is and must be in every state a
supreme, irresistible, absolute and uncontrolled authority, in
which the *jura summa imperii,* or rights of sovereignty, reside";
"this supreme power is by the constitution of Great Britain vested
in the King, Lords and Commons."

Parliamentary sensitiveness to its own rights was very evident
in Grenville's attitude to the American problem. After the repeal
of his own Act, he consistently opposed all suggestions for a return to the old system of requisitions or for a revenue derived
from quitrents, on the ground that all such funds would be
Crown revenues, beyond the control of Parliament. British parliamentary imperialism was born in 1763. This was a different
species, of course, from the jingoism that had to wait for widespread literacy and a popular press. It was in fact more dangerous
because less responsible. Power over remote territories and increasingly alien peoples was now to be political as well as economic; trade could flourish by means of war; Oceania would

now give law to the sea, even if those giving it were in fact a small group of men in a faction-ridden Parliament.

This imperialism had three elements: mercantile, strategic, and political. The first of these is familiar enough, and was in a measure inherited. Britain, like all other European powers, expected her colonies to serve as sources of supply for articles which could otherwise be obtained only from foreign rivals, and she expected them to purchase manufactured goods from the mother country. The colonies had been founded expressly for profit, either for those who settled the land, for the proprietor to whom a charter was granted, or for the company under whose direction the whole venture was risked. Few companies ever transferred their headquarters from London (Massachusetts Bay was exceptional) and this link between the City and Westminster was close. The objective of the state was that of any other merchant— profit and a favorable balance of trade, the excess to take the form, where possible, of imports of gold or silver. The laws that systematized these developments, insofar as they ever were systematized, were enacted over a century. They were built around the Navigation Acts of 1651 and 1660, given a comprehensive form in 1696: they confined the carrying trade within the Empire to British or colonial ships; they listed or "enumerated" the commodities that could not be shipped to foreign countries (sugar, cotton, tobacco, indigo, wool, and [later] naval stores, rice, furs, copper); the Staple Act of 1663 required that all exports from Europe to the colonies be shipped *via* England; and a number of restrictions, to prevent competition with Britain, were laid on colonial manufactures—on woolen yarn and cloth (1699), beaver hats (1732), and iron manufactures (1750)—which could not be exported outside their locality of production.

There can be no denial that the economic subordination of the colonies brought great advantages to Britain. As the *London Magazine* of 1766 put it, "The American is apparelled from head to foot in our manufactures . . . he scarcely drinks, sits, moves,

labours or recreates himself, without contributing to the emolu-
ment of the mother country." By 1772 Britain's exports to the
colonies equaled her entire exports in 1704. The colonies were
coming to be important as markets, as well as the suppliers of
raw materials. Her merchant marine flourished. The adverse balance of trade in the colonies led to dependence on the British
merchants or factors for credit; and shippers, shipbuilders and
ship factors, ship and freight insurance firms, British merchants
and manufacturers—often, as the colonists believed, the manufacturers of the shoddier articles—lived off the system.

Equally there can be no denial that the colonies were seriously
affected by the system; indeed, their economies were permanently
shaped by it and in some measure their expansion hindered.
They were a debtor community. Paper money was banned from
circulation lest they pay their debts with depreciated paper, yet
a sound currency was unobtainable. The diversity of colonial
currencies in itself handicapped local economic development. The
iron industry of the Middle Colonies was curbed, and the South's
concentration on tobacco led to periodic overproduction and a
slump in prices. The New England colonies could produce none
of the staples for which the system was devised; when they
turned as they did to fishing and commerce, they became in some
degree competitors with Britain. Having no commodities to send
to Britain in exchange for manufactures, New England tried to
encourage local industry and to develop her own trade with the
West Indies, exchanging timber, fish, beans, and shoes for sugar
and molasses. Since the British West Indies were not large enough
to absorb the products of New England and the Middle Colonies,
the surplus lumber and fish were sold to the French West Indies.
This was illicit, and the British West India interest demanded the
cessation of a trade that might be ruinous to their already peril-
ous sugar economy. For this reason the Molasses Act of 1733
was an attempt to put a prohibitive duty on colonial imports of
French and Spanish West Indian sugar and molasses. Had it
been enforced, it would have ruined the New England traders

for the sake of the British West Indies. When it was not enforced
it brought the law and its officials in the colonies into contempt.
There was much bitterness in Britain that this illicit Yankee
trade between the French islands and Boston, Newport, and
Providence flourished even more during the Seven Years' War
than in the years of peace, and that it was due to the collusion
of customs officers as well as the cupidity of colonial importers.
By 1763 it was thought of not merely as illicit but as treasonable.

Nevertheless, the Navigation Acts were neither mischievous
nor wicked. Indeed, the system was much less oppressive than
that of France or Spain, and it brought some important advantages to the colonies. Tobacco and coffee had a monopoly of the
home market. There were bounties for the production of indigo,
lumber, and naval stores that totaled some sixty-five thousand
pounds sterling a year for the thirteen colonies by 1776. New England's shipbuilding industry flourished; in 1775 approximately
one third of all the ships employed in the total British carrying
trade—estimated at seventy-six hundred—had in fact been built
in New England yards. And in Chesapeake Bay clipper-schooners
were being built and used. Here at least defense was compatible
with opulence. Despite the Iron Act of 1750, the expansion of
the iron industry continued; by the outbreak of the Revolution
there were more furnaces and forges in production than there
were in England and Wales, producing pig iron and bar iron of
excellent quality. If this was in part due to the availability of supplies of iron ore and charcoal, it was due also to the availability of
capital. The colonies were prosperous and were being encouraged in their prosperity by long credits from home. Moreover,
the plantation colonies fitted into the mercantile system admirably: the economies of the South and of Britain were in large
measure naturally complementary. The system benefited both
parties until 1763. Where there was discord, the casualness of
administration, the charter privileges of the colonies, and even
the shoals and sandbars of their coasts combined to make enforcement of unpopular laws obligingly difficult. And until 1763

Britain carried the burden of colonial defense and gave colonial goods and ships protection abroad. Indeed, it is now clear that this was fully realized in the colonies. Systematic smuggling was confined mainly to two articles, tea and molasses. For the rest, the system brought prosperity, assured markets and easy credits. Where it hurt, it was tacitly evaded.

As a result, historians have now some hesitation in accepting the indictment of mercantilism that it was fashionable to make in the free-trading nineteenth century, which paid as much respect to Adam Smith as to Edmund Burke and which condemned the running of great nations "by the maxims of the counter." Bancroft's simple view of it as a basic cause of the Revolution is no longer tenable. While there was clearly much that was irksome in the Trade and Navigation Laws, in the heavy drain on colonial specie that drove them to do business in foreign territories, and in the heavy indebtedness, the colonies had come into existence not for political but for economic reasons, "for England's profit, not her glory." Colonial prosperity had been largely the consequence of the laws of trade. "The Act of Navigation," said Burke, "attended the colonies from their infancy, grew with their growth and strengthened with their strength. They were confirmed in obedience to it even more by usage than by law."

There is now abundant evidence that it was not primarily for mercantilist reasons that the Americans revolted. Much can be made of Virginian indebtedness to Britain, but Washington expressly countered the proposal made in 1774 to withhold remittances due from Virginia to merchants at home: "Whilst we are accusing others of injustice, we should be just ourselves, and how can this be, whilst we owe a considerable debt, and refuse payment of it to Great Britain, is to me inconceivable. Nothing but the last extremity can justify it." This factor did not weigh with him, or his planter friends, as a reason for separation; even in crises planters lived by a code. As late as 1775 Franklin, whose code of conduct was always more adaptable, was willing to have the Navigation Acts re-enacted in each and every colony if Britain would only drop her claim to the right to tax. The first Continental Congress accepted the Acts of Trade.

Such later historians of the navigation system as L. A. Harper and O. M. Dickerson agree that the Acts presented no great impediment to colonial trade, but they do argue that real bitterness was felt after 1764 toward British customs and revenue collectors, stamp officials, and enforcement agents. It was distaste not for the old mercantilism but for the new imperialism, for its overzealous officers and what seemed to be their "racketeering," for the many seizures that followed the new and irksome bonding regulations, that produced the clashes of 1765 and thereafter. The correspondence of Washington with the Hanburys and of Hancock with the house of Harrison and Barnard suggests that it was the sharp practice of the factors in Britain that angered the colonists; it was shoddy goods and querying the bills that produced tension. It was not the system but the ways in which it was abused that brought hostility.

For in 1763 the failure of the mercantile system seemed to the British government far more striking than its merits. Ever since the emasculation of the Molasses Act, Yankee traders had ignored the law. Colonial governors had long complained; as early as 1743 Governor William Shirley thought the whole system was in danger of collapse and pleaded for the trial of offenders against the Acts of Trade in the courts of Vice-Admiralty. By 1750 the trade was averaging five hundred thousand pounds sterling in American exports. During the Seven Years' War trading with the enemy flourished even more, and Pitt instructed governors and naval officers to stamp it out. This prompted an inquiry into the colonial customs service, which revealed that it cost far more to maintain than it collected, and confirmed that it was both inefficient and corrupt. This Treasury memorandum was the basis of the Order in Council of October 4, 1763, and of the subsequent policy of a succession of ministries. Customs officers were ordered to their posts in America and forbidden to carry out their duties by deputy; they were promised one half of the proceeds of all ships and cargo condemned after seizure; colonial governors and military and naval officers were ordered to help them in enforcing the law. The real answer, it was thought, lay in the strengthening of the courts of Vice-Admiralty in the colonies. The Revenue Act of April 5, 1764, set up a new Vice-Admiralty court at Halifax, Nova Scotia, to which a seizer or informer could, if he chose, take his case, and where it would be tried without benefit of jury. Customs officers were freed from civil suits for damages in colonial courts. A new apparatus of officialdom and, it was hoped, of efficiency was set up. All the evidence before Parliament suggested that it had long been overdue.

In keeping with this came the Revenue (Sugar) Act of 1764, a reinvigoration of the Molasses Act. It had been discussed in the Board of Trade since 1750, but the colonial agents had managed by concerted action for thirteen years to block it. The new vigor swept away their protestations; the Act of 1733 was confirmed and extended. The duty on foreign molasses was lowered from sixpence to three pence a gallon, but that on sugar was increased; heavy duties on French West Indian products were imposed and were to be enforced; importation of rum or spirits from foreign colonies and trade with the French islands of St. Pierre and Miquelon were forbidden. Smugglers were hit by it; Yankee distillers were given a monopoly at home—for which they showed no gratitude; there were some concessions to South Carolina's rice exports which compensated New England not at all. And it was ominously stated in the preamble to the Act that these duties were designed to raise a revenue to meet the costs of colonial defense and that such a policy was just. It was accompanied by a Currency Act prohibiting the use of paper money as legal tender, a sore point in a debtor society always chronically short of hard money. This was aimed chiefly at Virginia.

The Sugar Act could be opposed on economic grounds. Frank-

lin put this colonial case forcibly and well in a letter to Peter
Collinson from Philadelphia in April 1764:

> I think there is scarce anything you can do that may be hurtful
> to us, but what will be as much or more so to you. This must be
> our chief security, for Interest with you we have but little: the
> West Indians vastly outweigh us of the Northern Colonies— What
> we get above a Subsistence, we lay out with you for your Manu-
> factures. Therefore what you get from us in Taxes you must lose
> in Trade. The Cat can yield but its Skin. And as you must have
> the whole Hide, if you first cut Thongs out of it, 'tis at your own
> Expence. The same in regard to our Trade with the Foreign West
> Indian Islands. If you restrain it in any Degree, you restrain in the
> same Proportion our Power of making our Remittances to you, of
> course our Demand for your Goods—for you will not clothe us out
> of Charity, tho' to receive 100 p. Ct. for it in Heaven— In time
> perhaps Mankind may be wise enough to let Trade take its own
> Course, find its own Channels and regulate its own Proportions
> etc. At present, most of the Edicts of Princes, Placeats, Laws and
> Ordinances of Kingdoms and States, for that purpose, prove politi-
> cal Blunders. The Advantages they produce not being general for
> the Commonwealth, but *particular* to private Persons or Bodies in
> the State who procur'd them, and at the Expence of the rest of the
> People.

This expression of Yankee laissez faire was to be repeated
through the next decade. It was a *cri de cœur* from the new economic forces in the Northern and Middle Colonies. They no
longer fitted the British system but were now themselves part
of an American system that had grown up around shipbuilders
and smugglers, traders to Africa and the Caribbean, iron manufacturers, and sugar importers. If Britain proposed to enforce
mercantilism, there was a competing mercantilism arising now in
America itself.

The second element in the shaping of British policy in and after
1763 concerned colonial defense and the frontier. This is indeed
a field that needs very much more careful scrutiny than it has

had thus far, and which probably appeared the most baffling problem of all in the eyes of the home government. Its financing was not its most difficult, although it became its most controversial, aspect. George Grenville has been presented as the major culprit, as tactless, pedantic, and mean, a Chancellor of the Exchequer preoccupied with economy. Whatever his rigidity of mind and manner, there was certainly a serious financial issue here. In 1763 Britain had emerged from the most expensive war in its history; despite unprecedented wartime taxation, the national debt stood at £133,000,000, an increase of £60,000,000 since 1755.

What is often forgotten, however, is that the method of financing the colonial wars had long been a subject of debate; Dinwiddie as lieutenant-governor of Virginia and Halifax as President of the Board of Trade had both urged a tax on the colonies. In the years 1754 to 1756 the Board had discussed this and other schemes. By 1763 it was urgent. The public debt, Lord North estimated, fell on the Englishman to the extent of eighteen pounds per person per year, but only to the extent of eighteen shillings on the colonist. The American paid on the average sixpence per year in taxes; his counterpart in Britain paid twenty-five shillings. And the size of the national debt was in some degree Pitt's responsibility. He had in 1757 destroyed the extensive civilian powers conferred on Braddock and Loudoun, the commanders-in-chief 1755-57, and substituted the old requisition system: he asked for men from the colonial governors; the colonial assemblies voted them and were then granted a reimbursement of part of, often most of, the cost by Parliament. That there were few difficulties in this system was not due to Pitt's planning or choice of commanders but to the simple fact of Britain's generosity: the five campaigns after 1757 cost Britain the sum of £866,666 sterling. The colonies offered high rates of pay and high bounties to recruits, and the specie or credit they received helped them in the process to wipe out their own debts. Nor, as Stanley Pargellis has shown, was this reckless expendi-

ture necessary: the bulk of the fighting was still done by regulars; it was the regulars who suffered the casualties; Maryland
and Pennsylvania were still slow to furnish men and supplies.

Pitt, it is usual to say, was no financier, like many another
imperialist since; he left the menial task of postwar budgeting
to others. Ironically enough, this fell to his brother-in-law, Grenville. British taxes were themselves increased, and the new cider
tax produced riots in southern England. Even so, there was no
intention of transferring the burden of the debt after 1763 to the
colonies.

There was however a belief, implicit in mercantilism, that the
colonists should, as in the past, contrive to bear the main weight
of their own defense. But that defense, now involving the protection of a vastly extended Empire, could no longer be left to
colonial militia or volunteers, supplemented by major expeditions
from home in every crisis. Such methods were cumbersome, slow,
ineffective, and very expensive. Moreover, the new and little-
known territories in Canada and Florida had few white inhabitants, and those of doubtful loyalty, to call on. They could only
be controlled, or for that matter surveyed, by garrisons of regular troops. A permanent British army must be maintained in the
colonies, stationed at strategic points.

On this there was small divergence of view among Pitt, Bute,
Newcastle, and Grenville. Grenville's own ministry was, indeed,
little different in composition from its predecessor. Plans were
being discussed and prepared long before he took office; it was
the Albany Congress that suggested a line of defense at the
Appalachians; it was a succession of commanders-in-chief and
colonial governors who insisted on the unreliability of colonial
militia even for garrison duties; it was the Newcastle-Bute administration of 1762 that decided to retain in the colonies a
garrison of ten thousand men and to tax the colonists to help
maintain it. The cost of the new garrisons in Gibraltar, Minorca,
and America was estimated at £372,774; of this, £100,000 should
be raised in America. Finance, much as it interested Grenville,

seemed the least contentious aspect of this new burden. And the policy was being prepared by men other than Grenville.

The frontier problem in 1763 was composed of many strands: the protection of the Indians and the honoring of treaties with them, particularly the Delaware and the Cherokee; the importance of the fur trade; the disposal of land if and when it was bought from the Indians; the claim of colony against colony and of one land company against another; the siting of forts and garrisons; the relationship of the new territory to the older settlements, some of which had claims from sea to sea; and not least the character of its government. None of these issues could be seen in isolation; a working solution had to be found for all of them; they continued to baffle Americans after 1783 as much as they baffled British officials in 1763. And significantly they were baffling in the American colonies in 1763, but not in Canada. There was infinitely less trouble in the newly acquired Quebec, where the fur traders were powerful, where white settlers were few, where government was completely autocratic—and where (as a consequence perhaps?) there was no revolution. The defense of the frontier was quite the most intractable problem of all, and one where Americans, then and later, were quite as hesitant, selfish, and culpable as British officials.

The great debate had been proceeding since Halifax took over the Board of Trade in 1748, and it went beyond both administration and finance, and beyond the question of sugar islands *versus* Canada. Indeed it is going on still, for the acquisition of Canada and of the trans-Allegheny country by Britain in 1763 posed for the first time the issue of native *versus* settler, a problem nineteenth- and twentieth-century British imperial administrators met repeatedly in South and Central Africa. Fur trade and humanitarianism together demanded the protection of the Indian in his hunting grounds, extensive and mobile though they were. Inevitably this ran counter to the frontier expansion and land hunger of the settlers thrusting north up the Kennebec, west along the Mohawk and Monongahela, south along the Allegheny mountain valleys toward the Cumberland Gap and the Clinch and Holston country, with speculators not so far behind them. The frontier represented America's own imperialism and, like all settler imperialisms, it was rough and ready in its methods, antinative in its essence, and scornful of the liberal but remote control of London. The liberty it sought in the West was liberty to take Indian property in land without too much fuss, an imperialism that did not cease with 1776.*

In 1754, on the failure of the Albany Plan, the British government had put Indian political relations under the direction of its American commander-in-chief, Braddock; it created two superintendencies divided by the Ohio, appointed Sir William Johnson to the northern superintendency in 1755 and to the southern, first Edmond Atkin and, on his death in 1761, John Stuart. Johnson and Stuart were outstandingly able. They held some of the Indians in line with Britain throughout the war, whereas in earlier conflicts all but the Iroquois had supported France. But they could not maintain frontier peace indefinitely: treaties were hard to enforce; frontiersmen were aggressive for land; each colony competed with its neighbor; traders were greedy for furs and generous with firewater and firearms; Indians were debauched, deceived, and deceitful; all parties were quick to anger—and to practice brutality. There was an ugly war with the Cherokees from 1759 to 1761.

Three months after the signing of the Treaty of 1763, and after the decision was taken to retain Canada and the Floridas, came the rising of the northwestern Indians under Pontiac, the Ottawa chief. Pontiac feared British rule, and feared much more the encroaching settler. Although Henry Bouquet defeated the rebels, every western station except Detroit and Fort Pitt had been captured by them, and some two hundred settlers and traders had been killed. Only four colonies—New York, New Jersey, Connecticut, and Virginia—gave any aid against them. It

---

* For a fresh view of this, see R. W. Van Alstyne, *The Rising American Empire* (1960).

was three years before there was real peace in the new territory between the Ohio and the Great Lakes, and it was almost entirely the work of British regulars.

The Pontiac conspiracy appeared to confirm the wisdom of decisions already taken in London in 1759 and communicated to all colonial governors in 1761. Egremont, Secretary for the Southern Department to both Bute and Grenville, told the two superintendents to reassure the Indian tribes. Frightened by the Pontiac rising, the Grenville ministry issued a proclamation in October 1763, forbidding colonial governors to authorize surveys or grant patents for any land beyond the "sources of any of the rivers which fall into the Atlantic Ocean from the West or Northwest." The new West was closed to settlers and to speculators. It was to be an Indian reserve under military control and with free access for traders under careful regulations. And separate governments were established for Quebec, for East and West Florida, and for Grenada.

This was as complete an administrative revolution as the revision in trade regulations. Although issued hurriedly, it too was the work of years, and of the back room rather than of Parliament. The proclamation of October was based on "Hints relative to the Division and Government of the conquered and newly acquired Countries in America," whose author was probably Henry Ellis, a former governor of Georgia and Egremont's "man of business" on colonial topics. It drew also on a report of 1761 and on the opinions of Dinwiddie and Knox. These "hints" were used in the summer of 1763 by John Pownall as the basis of the report he drafted for the Board of Trade, with the added suggestion that New England's territorial claims to the West should particularly be curbed, lest they pull away the French settlements on the Mississippi from their "motherland," Quebec. To this problem the Board was to return, with grievous result, in the Quebec Act of 1774. Indeed, Egremont in 1763 wanted the whole area then put under the civil control of Quebec. Shelburne, the new and young president of the Board, demurred and won the day. Responsibility was handed to the military.

There was much to be said for this policy, revolutionary though it was. Until the Seven Years' War, land settlement had been encouraged and such governors as Spotswood themselves led their expeditions over the mountains. But bulwarks against the French were needed no longer, even if French incursions could not be entirely ignored. The fur trade was now safely in British hands and land settlement would destroy its profits. The farther west the settlers moved, the harder control over them would become. The settlement of the West would draw labor from the East, and could only be done at the expense of the Indians and economically perhaps of the Tidewater. And unless defense was to be still more burdensome, the Indians must clearly be pacified. Halifax, colleague of Egremont as Secretary of State, thought the Indians unduly neglected. They had been promised security in their land titles by wartime treaties; they supplied the furs which were seriously overvalued as a commodity; they were thought of as a potential market for manufactures. The line protecting them would divert white settlement, it was hoped, to Canada, to Georgia, and to Florida and thus renew the steady onward development of the Tidewater areas. Nor was the line of demarcation immutably fixed. The decision, Egremont stressed, was made "for the present." Limited settlement was to be permitted at the discretion of colonial governors, particularly in the bitterly contested reaches of the Upper Ohio, but the land was to be fairly bought. It was a worthy blueprint devised by worthy men, placid and passionless.

Yet it is easy to see how unpopular the Proclamation Line appeared in colonial eyes, especially to frontiersmen eager for land and security, to land speculators, and to colonial governments with western claims. It is equally easy to say that it was never fully honored, that no civil government was provided until 1774, that the line was steadily pushed back, by settlers and companies, by methods more dubious than fair, and that successive admin-

istrations were obliged to recognize the fact. Moreover, governors as well as planters and merchants combined to flout the law.
What is not always fully appreciated is that while the administrations did in the end accept the changing line of advance
as a result of the pressures brought on them in London by agents
and merchants, they were now being advised also by a new element, the military and the Indian Superintendents who came to
form a new imperial bureaucracy on the frontier. It was well
informed, simple-minded, practical; these were the men on the
spot, to whom the problems could be neither placid nor passionless.

They were British regulars or, like Johnson, British-Indians,
drawing their pay and their status from Britain; they were remote from Tidewater and not very amenable or sympathetic to
it; some of them were Swiss *condottieri* like Bouquet and Haldimand, doing a job for pay, and doing it well; they distrusted the
land companies and their coterie of rascally agents, like Cresap
and Connolly, the most Scotch-Irish and least scrupulous group
in the colonies. From sad experience they dismissed colonial
fighting qualities. They had only a little less contempt for many
of the instructions they received from Whitehall. They were a
military caste whose first and major task, as with all responsible
soldiers, was to prevent war ever breaking out. They represented a new pressure group, remote from London, but a group
which was at last directly in touch with the frontier and able
to report all too authentically on conditions there.

To the men of experience now living in London as ex-
governors or as agents, like Pownall and Bollan, the home government listened; but after 1763 it listened still more carefully to
the soldiers on the spot. The colonists of course distrusted a
peacetime standing army, and feared that it might be used whenever there was local trouble. It was "a rod and a check over us,"
said Eliphalet Dyer of Connecticut. The picture of the colonies
furnished to London after 1763, and still evident in the pages of
the Bouquet and Haldimand Papers in the British Museum or in

what survives of the Johnson Papers, would have given the colonists still more reasons for alarm. For to these men the frontier was the scene of a cold war—fought between agent and agent, Indian and white, settler and trapper, colony and colony. In such a cold war the peace of the frontier, they thought, was too important to be left to civilians. Part of the responsibility for the consistency of the British determination after 1774 to impose its will on the colonies rests with the dispatches received from Commander-in-Chief Gage, who held the post from 1763 to 1774, and whose pleas, like those of all commanders-in-chief, were for still more troops. If London grew more rigid and in the end, after all the to-and-fro, quite adamant by 1774, this was not just the obstinacy of weakness but also the reflection of the judgment of Britain's own frontiersmen, its soldier-governors and Indian administrators.

The third element in the pattern of parliamentary imperialism was the most dangerous of all. By 1763 a doctrine of explicit sovereignty was emerging, prone now and then to take the form not merely of parliamentary supremacy but of personal superiority of British over colonials it was to feed hungrily on the events of the next decade. Stimulated by the war and by the evidence of colonial half-heartedness and dealings with the enemy, there now ran through the writings and reports of a number of officials a recurring emphasis: let the law be enforced. Blackstone and Mansfield had their precursors in writers like the economist Malachi Postlethwayt, in *Britain's Commercial Interest* (1757), or in Soame Jenyns. The indolence of Walpole had ceased to appear a virtue.

A succession of governors had recommended taxing the colonies, Shirley and Dinwiddie among them. Otis had already described the group around Shirley and Bollan as authoritarians, "full as high in their notions of prerogative as the churchmen." Under the Duke of Cumberland's stimulus, the powers of commanders-in-chief had been increased and strongly centralized,

almost making of the office a captaincy-general for the colonies.
There were blueprints from Shirley and Halifax, Knox and
Pownall, pointing to similar civil plans. Pownall's *The Administration of the Colonies* was a liberal sketch and saw the
Empire as "a grand marine dominion"—with the colonists represented at Westminster; but after the Albany failure, it seemed
clear that such plans would have to be drawn up in and enforced from London. Shirley criticized Franklin's *Plan of Union*
of 1754 because it followed too closely "the old charter form of
government" and was unsuited to an "Imperium over all the
Colonies." The union of the colonies would need to be established by act of Parliament. The strengthening of the executive
by freeing royal officials from the control of colonial assemblies
was the single consistent theme in the political career of Charles
Townshend.

There was in 1763 no respect for American fighting qualities.
Amherst and Forbes, Loudoun and Gage were unanimous in
their scorn for colonial troops. There were frank sentiments being voiced on assemblies and freedom of debate. "The British
Form of Government, transplanted into this Continent never
will produce the same Fruits as at Home . . . ," wrote Carleton
as early as 1768. "A popular Assembly, which preserves it's [*sic*]
full Vigor, and in a Country where all Men appear nearly upon
a Level, must give a strong Bias to Republican Principles." Out
of this mood was to come the Quebec Act. By 1769 Parliament
regarded Boston as a city where contention too rapidly became
treason. What the colonists saw as a clash of sovereignties was
not viewed so sympathetically in London. North condemned the
Massachusetts constitution because of its dependence on "the
democratic part." Germain went further. "I would not have men
of a mercantile cast every day collecting themselves together and
debating on political matters."

In all their differences of emphasis, Chatham and Shelburne,
Egremont and Halifax, Grenville and Burke sought a general
and comprehensive plan of Empire. Behind them were their

3

Riot and Resistance: 1764–1774

THE PREVAILING VIEW of the decade from 1764 to 1774 appears to be that there were three main episodes in the development of the American crisis: the Stamp Act of 1765, the Townshend duties of 1767, and the Boston Tea Party of 1773. After each crisis tension relaxed, and it was only British intransigence over the last that caused trouble. This view, like most short cuts to truth, is far too simple. Of the three crises, only the first did in fact produce a nationwide debate in Britain; but throughout the decade successive British administrations puzzled and probed over America, and by their various and often conflicting proposals aggravated American resentments. What was devised in London was neither a large nor a consistent policy, but a mounting series of irritations. And, throughout these years, there was in America an increasing and a widening discussion of constitutional principles. By 1774, when British policy had at last become consistent in its firmness, the two countries had moved dangerously far apart.

The Revenue Act of 1764, the so-called Sugar Act, was mainly a trade act, but it sought also, for the first time, to raise revenue from the colonies. "And whereas it is just and necessary that a revenue be raised in your Majesty's said dominions in America for defraying the expenses of defending, protecting and securing the same. . . ." The money collected was to be kept in a separate account to be "disposed of by Parliament" for the defense of the American colonies. It was expected to total some forty-five thousand pounds. In the colonies the measure was bitterly unpopular. It "occasions much commotion," wrote Franklin from Philadelphia. To try to end smuggling by this device, wrote Jared Ingersoll, was "like burning a Barn to roast an Egg."

Among the many supporting resolutions aimed at raising revenue offered to the House of Commons in 1764 was one declaring that it was proper to levy stamp duties in the colonies. This was postponed for a year to allow Grenville to gather further information from America or to discover alternative methods, but he was empowered to submit a bill along these lines—the target some sixty thousand pounds—if no more acceptable plan came forward. When it did not, on February 7, 1765, fifty-five resolutions were reported to the Commons by the Committee of the Whole House, and approved by 250 votes to 50. The measure passed the Commons at the third reading by 205 votes to 49, the Lords without a division, and became law on March 22, 1765. Three months later, before the news came through of its reception in the colonies, Grenville was out of office.

The Stamp Act, a device used in England since 1694, imposed a stamp duty on newspapers and pamphlets, on many legal documents, and on cards and dice. The taxes were lighter than those levied in Britain; they were to be, said Thomas Whately of the Treasury, who drafted the document, "as little burdensome as possible"; and their imposition in the West Indies raised no difficulty. Together with the sugar revenues they would cover only one quarter of the projected cost of colonial defense. The measures seemed both legal and equitable: some colonies were almost entirely free of taxes and almost entirely free of debt. Moreover, before the imposition they had been fully canvassed. Whately indicated great sensitiveness toward the Americans and sought to tap colonial opinion in advance on the projected Act. The colonial agents were very active, particularly Jackson and Franklin, with various—at times ingenious—proposals. Jackson suggested that the colonists should themselves request the tax, so that there would be no precedent for the imposition of an internal tax without their consent. Franklin still preferred the taxing power to be a matter for a colonial Congress, despite the unfortunate precedent of the Albany meeting; if this failed, he advocated a return to the practice of requisitioning that had prevailed during the war, to which it was precisely Grenville's intention not to return. There was even some discussion of the representation of the colonies at Westminster, although most of them agreed that this was impracticable. These and other proposals Grenville discussed fully with the agents; none of the agents could give any assurance that the colonists would voluntarily supply troops or voluntarily supply the funds to pay them.

There seemed no alternative to the Stamp Act. Indeed, from the promptness with which some distinguished colonial figures (including George Mercer of Virginia or Jared Ingersoll of Connecticut) accepted the posts of stamp distributors—which were confined to Americans—there seemed little sign in London that this was to be a situation of Anglo-American crisis. Franklin, that malleable political animal, reflected the mood of optimism: cynics might even say that the tune he played in London in 1765 was very different from that in Philadelphia a year before, and from the many tunes he was to play under various *noms de plume* in various journals afterward. Writing to his friend John Hughes, whom he put forward as distributor for Pennsylvania, he said:

> A firm Loyalty to the Crown and faithful Adherence to the Government of this Nation, which is the Safety as well as the Honour of the Colonies to be connected with, will always be the Wisest course for you and I [*sic*] to take, whatever may be the Madness of the Populace or their blind Leaders, who can only bring themselves and Country into Trouble, and draw on greater Burdens by Acts of rebellious Tendency.

For once, Franklin misread the omens—and subsequently tried hard to hide the fact, even from himself. What had passed through Parliament with little opposition produced storms and riots, burning of stamps, and intimidation of stamp distributors in the colonies. James Otis of Massachusetts and Daniel Dulany of Maryland had already denied the right of Parliament to impose taxes if the purpose was to raise revenue. Colonial opinion was already suggesting a denial of all taxes imposed without consent; as Professor Morgan has shown, the distinction between external and internal taxes was never quite so sharp as subsequent historians have implied. When the stamps arrived, all vessels in New York harbor lowered their colors—to signify, as the *Boston Evening Post* put it, "Mourning, Lamentation and Woe." On November 1, when the Act went into force, the bells of New Haven tolled, "speaking the word *No-vem-ber* in the most melancholy Tone imaginable." At Portsmouth a copy of the Stamp Act was buried with due pomp, and on the coffin lid was inscribed *"Liberty* aetas 145, *Stamp'd."*

There were uglier portents. They began in Virginia but were most conspicuous in Massachusetts. Under the leadership of Patrick Henry, the Virginia assembly claimed that the people of Virginia had "all the Liberties, Privileges, Franchises and Immunities that at any Time have been held, enjoyed and possessed by the People of Great Britain," and that these powers included the exclusive right to tax. The Henry resolves, and the popular if embroidered accounts in the colonial newspapers of the treasonable things he had said, or threatened to say, were to the Rockingham administration nothing less than an attack on the British Constitution. To Governor Bernard in Massachusetts they were to be an "alarm bell" in New England. The Sons of Liberty attacked officials of the Vice-Admiralty courts, looted Lieutenant-Governor Hutchinson's stately home, and threatened the life and property of all who seemed to favor the enforcement of the law. Stamp distributors in all the colonies were hanged in effigy and forced to resign.

> He who for a Post or Base sordid Pelf
> His Country Betrays, Makes a Rope for himself.
> Of this an Example, Before you we Bring
> In these Infamous Rogues, Who in Effigy Swing.

Nonimportation associations were formed among merchants, and English goods were boycotted. Business came almost entirely to a halt for some months with the general refusal to use the stamps. When it resumed it did so without benefit of stamps, in open violation of the law.

And at the call of Massachusetts a Stamp Act Congress was summoned to meet in City Hall, New York, in October 1765. The newly organized provinces—Quebec, Nova Scotia, and the Floridas—were not represented at this or later assemblies. Neither was Virginia or New Hampshire, North Carolina or Georgia at this congress. The twenty-seven representatives of the remaining nine colonies, however—many of them moderate men —drew up a Declaration of Rights and Grievances. Largely John Dickinson's work, this claimed that the colonists were entitled to all the rights and liberties of subjects born within the mother country; that they could only be taxed "but with their own consent" and by their own representative assemblies; and that the Stamp Act and the extension of the jurisdiction of the Vice-Admiralty courts were both subversive of the rights and liberties of the colonies. The accompanying addresses to Commons and Lords did not go nearly so far as this, and protested undeviating loyalty to Crown and country; they were "subjects of the best of Kings."

In New York, where there was less excitement over stamps, there was much more over the Quartering Act of 1765. The colonies in which these new regiments were to be stationed were required to provide quarters and provisions for them; where local barracks were not adequate, a second Act in 1766 required that taverns and uninhabited houses and barns might be brought into service. Troops could not, however, be billeted in occupied private houses—until the situation of 1774 required even this.

This measure was bitterly unpopular, a variant of an internal tax that also discriminated against those colonies, especially New York, where the majority of troops were likely to be stationed; New York became in fact the British headquarters. It required the holding of two elections, a number of riots—and the threat of suspending the assembly—before New Yorkers agreed to erect barracks at the colony's expense. Pennsylvania, Connecticut, and South Carolina were more obliging.

The Stamp Act and the violence that this enactment occasioned in the colonies produced the first great public debate on the American question in Britain. The second was not to take place until 1782. This first debate was in fact largely a reflection of the Rockingham ministry's political and executive weakness. Replacing Grenville when George III could no longer tolerate him, the Rockingham group had for six months no policy at all. They listened to the complaints of British merchants frightened by the boycott and by the threats to their future trade and past debts, which were put as high as four million pounds sterling. Orders worth some seven hundred thousand pounds were countermanded. There was rising unemployment in Birmingham, Sheffield, and Norwich. Trecothick said that seven eighths of the trade to New England and the Middle Colonies was now stopped. He was supported by the Hanburys, by George Mercer, by John Glassford of Glasgow, by organized protest meetings in Bristol, Glasgow, and Liverpool, and by Franklin's carefully rehearsed performance before the Committee of the Whole House. Franklin stressed, indeed overstressed, the contribution of colonial assemblies during the French and Indian War; he claimed that the colonies had not enough specie to pay the tax; he gave sober warning of the dangers of rebellion and he assured the House that it was only to internal taxes that Americans were objecting —a view that events were not to justify. Yet his role in repeal has probably been exaggerated. There were twenty-two witnesses, of whom all the rest were merchants known to each other and to the chairmen, Rose Fuller and George Cooke. If Franklin was assiduous in preparing the ground, Burke was in touch with the Glasgow merchants and Rockingham himself with Trecothick and the City. The movement for repeal was the work of a lobby of British and West Indian merchants worried about their lost profits.

It is hard to see any shadow of men of principle behind the well-rounded figures of the gambling Glassford, William Reeve the Bristol Quaker, obsessed with antiquities and follies, Masterman the bullion merchant, the Fullers, the rich Hanburys, or bland Ben Franklin. All of them were men of property and peace; they were not contending for justice for America, Franklin apart, and he did not make that his main argument; there was no particular sympathy for the colonies from them; nor were they united except by their temporarily common selfishness. When, in the final stages of his administration, Rockingham amended the Revenue Act of 1764 and lowered the duty on molasses from three pence to one penny a gallon, West Indian and American merchants promptly divided. Not until January 17, 1766, did Rockingham himself come around to the idea not of "amendments and curtailments" of the Stamp Act but of its outright repeal. It was clear by this time that his political future, and the country's, depended entirely on Pitt. The same House that had passed the Act now almost as readily came to repeal it, in March 1766.

Repeal was universally popular in the colonies. It was welcomed by bonfires and public dinners and the erection in New York of statues to Pitt and to the King. The sense of chivalry, like the royal statue, was not to last.

That there was no change of mind in Britain, but rather in fact a hardening of principle, is shown by the retention of the Revenue Act of 1764 and its invigoration by the Act of 1766, and by the passing of the Declaratory Act without a division. This asserted that Parliament had full authority to make laws binding the American colonists "in all cases whatsoever." What concession there was, the government could pretend, was being

made to British trade, not to American opinion. Shelburne noted
that Parliament was more rather than less anti-American in
1766. Those against repeal were hardened in their views by
Pitt's charges that the Americans were justified in their resistance, and by Franklin's denials in the Committee of the Whole
House that Parliament had any right to levy internal taxes at
all—even for colonial defense. The merchants said that repeal
would in fact have gone through sooner if there had been no
American violence. But for a time, at least, the crisis was over
and trade revived.

It is impossible to defend the uneasy and illogical compromise
of 1766. The withdrawal of an act of Parliament but the assertion of Parliament's full right to legislate for the colonies "in all
cases whatsoever" was government by abnegation. Repeal, said
William Knox, would be followed by "addresses of thanks and
measures of rebellion." The government had bowed to a colonial
and commercial storm.

The surrender was culpable on other grounds than this; it carried with it the abandonment of the plans for the western territory. The boundary provisions of the Proclamation of 1763—
not intended to be permanent—now became so. The settlements
that had begun to appear on the Ohio contrary to the Proclamation were to be evacuated, if necessary by force. And, just when
British troops had at last reached the French forts on the Mississippi, and Johnson, Croghan, and Bouquet were bringing peace
to the Ohio Indian country, Barrington, Secretary-at-War, recommended the evacuation of the West and the abolition of forts
and posts. If the colonies became embroiled with Indians in the
future "let them get themselves out of it . . . or let them beg
for military assistance, acknowledge their want of it, and pay its
expense." The defense of the frontier should be left to the
colonists. British troops should be concentrated in Canada, Nova
Scotia, and East Florida and be available, ominously, to curb any
riots or tumults in the seaboard colonies. Grenville's neo-mer-
cantilism of 1764-65 had now been replaced by an avowed "Little

Englandism." And the question of 1764, how best to raise a
revenue for the defense of an Empire, had become involved by
1766 in more fundamental—and normally unanswerable—questions of right and principle.

The Chatham administration (1766–68) was conspicuous for
the elevation of its leader to the Lords and his absence (because
of illness) from its debates. He left to Grafton, his loyal but em-
barrassed deputy, a heavy responsibility—a ministry devoid of
unity, and particularly devoid of unity on America. He be-
queathed to him the even heavier tasks of raising revenue and of
settling the American question. Here Chatham was ambiguous:
"measures for the proper subordination of America must be
taken" was later explained as not implying violence "unless
absolutely necessary." By 1767 there were many new American
issues: New York merchants were petitioning once more against
the Revenue Act of 1764; they were requesting the establishment of a vast number of free ports; the New York Assembly
steadily refused to comply with the Quartering Act or to provision British troops. Opinion in Britain was hardening: even
the Rockingham Whigs and Beckford were losing patience;
even Chatham, it was thought, was all for stern measures. In
Chatham's absence it was Townshend, the Chancellor of the
Exchequer, who determined American policy—Townshend,
whose meretricious brilliance has been forever indicted by
Horace Walpole's judgment: "He had almost every great talent
. . . if he had had but common truth, common sincerity, common
honesty, common modesty, common steadiness, common courage
and common sense."

Grafton was compelled in 1767, by a proposal carried against
his wishes, to reduce the land tax in Britain in order to relieve
the burden on the country gentlemen, the major economic interest in the country and in the House of Commons. To cover the
loss of revenue involved, Townshend—who had earlier distinguished himself by assertions of full parliamentary authority
over the colonies, by refusing to accept Chatham's own distinc-

tion between internal and external taxes and by voting both for the Stamp Act and for its repeal—undertook to obtain an American revenue. He introduced new duties on colonial imports of glass, lead, paints, paper, and tea. As external duties at the ports, these were not open to the charges brought against the Stamp Act. From their proceeds, however, Townshend proposed not only to meet the cost of defense but also the salaries of royal officials and thus reduce the control exercised over them by colonial assemblies.

Moreover, the machinery of trade enforcement was improved: colonial justices were authorized to issue writs of assistance, permitting a right of search of homes and stores by customs officers; Vice-Admiralty courts were established at Halifax, Boston, Philadelphia, and Charleston; and an American Board of Customs Commissioners, directly responsible to Britain, was established in Boston and armed with a galaxy of revenue cutters and sloops, searchers, and spies. And the governor of New York, which had refused to comply with the Quartering Act, should be restrained from approving of any measure of the assembly until it showed itself more obedient to the will of Parliament.

Even by the standards that had obtained before 1763, these measures were perfectly legal. By those standards also they were disturbingly efficient. Between 1768 and 1774 some thirty thousand pounds sterling were collected annually, at a cost of thirteen thousand pounds per year for the service. They were consequently vehemently opposed. The Massachusetts General Court issued a *Circular Letter* (the work of Samuel Adams, James Otis, and Joseph Hawley) appealing to other assemblies and claiming that only they could tax the colonists. Governor Bernard branded this as seditious—as did Hillsborough—and ordered it withdrawn; the General Court refused to withdraw it by a vote of 92 to 17, and many a meeting under many a Liberty Tree thereafter was punctuated by the ritual cries of "Forty-five"—a salute to Wilkes' issue No. 45 of *The North Briton* and to liberty—and "Ninety-two." The seventeen on the wrong side became the butts of attacks by the Sons of Liberty, and seven of them lost their seats at the next election. The *Circular Letter* was endorsed by seven other colonies.

Rioting, endemic in eighteenth-century society, now became recurrent. Liberty Poles were torn down as soon as erected, rarely without bloodshed. Customs agents were attacked in Boston, New York, and Providence. When, in June 1768, customs officers attempted to seize Hancock's sloop *Liberty* with a load of Madeira aboard, they were driven to take refuge in Castle William, on an island in Boston harbor, to escape mob violence. They put out appeals for help to Gage and to Admiral Hood. When the Boston garrison was increased by two regiments of infantry (the 14th and 29th) the personnel found themselves, if officers, socially boycotted or, if privates, physically assaulted. The Boston Town Meeting declared that the regiments could remain in the colony only by authority of the assembly. When John Hancock deeded his new concert hall to the town, he stipulated that no British revenue, army, or navy officer should be admitted to it. According to Governor Hutchinson, the situation when the troops landed was very close to revolution.

In 1769 the ministry put before Parliament a report on its difficulties in Boston, and both houses resolved that "wicked and designing men" were responsible, that they should be visited with "condign punishment," and, if treason were proved, that they should be brought home for trial. The culmination was the Battle of Golden Hill in New York (January 1770), in which soldiers clashed with citizens and blood was spilled by both sides around a Liberty Pole, but not fatally, and the snowballing in March 1770 that ended in the Boston Massacre. On this occasion five Bostonians, one of them a Negro, Crispus Attucks, were killed in a clash with British troops. Even the military, however well disciplined, were ceasing to be instruments of order. Under strict injunctions not to fire and confined to camp in Boston— or after 1770 secluded in Castle William—they were more often the victims than the masters of local situations. And their mere presence was a permanent local irritant.

These episodes were not as significant, even so, as the mounting debate now raging in America. Echoing Massachusetts, sympathetic resolutions were introduced in the Virginia House of Burgesses. John Dickinson, in his *Letters from a Farmer in Pennsylvania* (a reprint from a series of articles in the *Pennsylvania Chronicle*), attacked the Townshend duties on the grounds that, although they were external duties, they were unconstitutional because their purpose was not to regulate trade but to collect a revenue. Defense of Canada, Nova Scotia, and the Floridas was of no benefit to the colonies but only to Britain. Dickinson made reference, moderate though he was, to the ambiguous phrases of an earlier revolution, to the "rights of man" and the "law of nature," and argued that Heaven itself "hath made us free." Recourse again was had to nonimportation, first in Boston and then—not without difficulty in Philadelphia —at other seaports. There was less support in the South than in the North. New York merchants protested that other towns were more active in resolving what they ought to do than in doing what they had resolved. But the Virginia Burgesses, after Botetourt dissolved the assembly, reconvened in the Raleigh Tavern and framed a nonimportation agreement of their own, in May 1769. New England's trade with Britain was cut by half and New York's by seven eighths. This time there was little echoing excitement in Britain, either in commerce or in the House of Commons, since there was a growing market for British goods on the Continent.

In America itself many merchants became alarmed at the violent features of the movement, frightened of the power of the mob and its radical leadership; others were quite ready to continue to trade and to prosper—if they could—at the expense of their more dedicated countrymen. The boycott was now a political instead of an economic weapon, the work of the town meeting rather than the counting house. Trade remained a powerful curb on "liberty"; profits did not yet coincide with patriotism.

In any event Grafton was already putting out hints of a repeal of the duties. It was clearly unwise for Britain to tax her own goods when they were sold abroad. And when Lord North took office, in 1770, the government concluded that the Townshend policy was unprofitable and—on the day of the Boston Massacre, as it happened—withdrew all the duties except that on tea. North promised that there would be no new taxes. The Quartering Act was quickly allowed to expire. Again face had to be saved, and the tea duty was retained—by a margin of a single vote in the Cabinet—"as a mark of the supremacy of Parliament, and an efficient declaration of their right to govern the colonies." New York City abandoned nonimportation after a house-to-house inquiry, and other ports gradually followed. Virginia was the last to give way, in July 1771.

There were disturbing parallels here to the events of 1765–66. Under pressure, the government had once more completely reversed its policy; the attempt to raise a colonial revenue by direct taxation was abandoned. Having done so, it had yet again piously declared that it retained full and complete authority over the colonies. The colonies for their part avoided payment of the tea duty whenever possible, and only their propagandists worried over resounding declarations of imperial supremacy. Laws made in London were devoid of sanction and of permanence. No sooner had one minister devised a policy than he left its implementation to another, rarely of similar mind to himself. Fate assisted the malevolence of faction; Townshend, after devising his own subtle solution, died in 1767; Grenville died in November 1770; and Whately, one of the authors of the Stamp Act, in May 1772. The frequent changes prevented any chance of a consistent approach to this, or any other, problem of state.

They particularly handicapped a policy for the West. Shelburne was never a trusted member of the Chatham or Grafton administrations, especially after the master had gone. Secretary of State for the Southern Department from 1766 to 1768, he held

on to the office for a few months after the third secretaryship
was created. A Chathamite in the fullest sense, he believed in
British sovereignty but denied that it included the right to tax.
He thought optimistically that revenues might be raised from
quitrents on past and future land grants and by requisitions on
the provinces freely granted by their own assemblies. Unlike
most of his contemporaries in Britain, he saw the future of the
West. By 1776 he believed it to be quite impossible to prevent
westward expansion: there had been no such intention in his
earlier proposals and it was only the emergency created by
Pontiac that led Hillsborough, his successor then at the Board of
Trade, to suggest that all settlement must cease at the crest of
the Appalachians. The colonies, Shelburne thought, should regulate Indian affairs; the costly and difficult Indian establishment
could then be dismantled. New colonies should be established,
one based on Detroit, one on the Ohio, another in the Illinois
country. A new western boundary would be needed.

Shelburne's plan had many merits: it substituted for Grenville's highly centralized system a decentralized empire; it accepted the fact of colonial expansion and assumed that it would
for a long time delay colonial manufacturing to Britain's advantage; it gave the colonies in many important matters control
of their own affairs; not least, it won the support of Franklin
and all interested in the various schemes for western land development. In some ways it foreshadowed the Ordinances of
1787. In some ways, too, if less explicitly, it foreshadowed the
notions of devolution of the present British Commonwealth.

When Hillsborough took over the newly created Colonial
Department in 1768, however, all such plans for western development were dropped. The only aspects of Shelburne's plan that
were applied were those favoring economy. The control of trade
was passed back to the individual colony; garrisons were reduced; but no new settlements were to be made, to the chagrin
of Franklin and Washington. The Indian boundary was to be
fixed by the military and the Indian Superintendents; title to

Indian lands was to be purchased for the imperial government; settlement was to be directed by the Crown. It is true that Hillsborough listened with some sympathy to Franklin's case for the "suffering traders," the victims of the Pontiac war, and that this took shape as the Wharton or Vandalia project; it involved a tract large enough to constitute a new colony, incorporating some earlier land claimants like the Ohio Company of Virginia. On Gage's advice, Hillsborough then decided against such rashness; he ordered the commander-in-chief to pull his troops back and to abandon the forts in the Illinois country, even Pittsburgh. When the Privy Council, under the blandishments of Franklin and Samuel Wharton, in turn overruled him and supported the project, Hillsborough resigned (August 1772). Dartmouth, his successor, supported it and returned to Shelburne's idea of quit-rents as a source of funds for western development. Legal difficulties still delayed the Vandalia project, and they had not been overcome by 1776.

In the absence of regulation from home, the western boundaries were defined by *force majeure*. At the Treaty of Fort Stanwix, 1768—a conclave of some two thousand Iroquois presided over by Sir William Johnson—the boundary in the north was drawn through central New York and Pennsylvania. The Iroquois, claiming to be able to dispose of Shawnee and Delaware land as well as their own, surrendered territory east of the Allegheny and Ohio rivers. In 1768 the Cherokees surrendered territory east of the valley of the Kanawha and in 1770 added further territory east of the Kentucky River, much of it at Shawnee expense.

But these boundaries themselves had already been crossed. The "long hunters" led by Daniel Boone moved into the dark and bloody ground of Kentucky, and the stories grew of its wealth of blue grass and hardwood and of its vast quantities of game. The settlement on the Watauga, made without title in 1769, was organized in 1772 by John Sevier and James Robertson into a formal government, the Watauga Association, which made its own treaty with the Cherokees. Dunmore made many grants to veterans of frontier wars, and in 1774 was himself leading the Virginians in a war with the Shawnees. After Andrew Lewis' victory at Point Pleasant, the Shawnee chief Cornstalk surrendered all title to lands south and east of the Ohio. The Ohio Valley was, in fact, occupied by settlers from Virginia, whatever the "policy" devised in London. The Indian chief Ackowanothio of the Delawares, speaking in 1758 of a "parcel of covetous gentlemen of Virginia called the Ohio Company," had said all too prophetically that they were "as numerous as musketoes and gnats in the woods . . . where one of these people settled, like Pidgeons, a thousand more would settle. . . ."

On the surface, the prospect in 1770–72 was pleasing. For the colonies, trade revived after a long postwar depression; in many colonies the Boston Massacre went unregarded; smuggling continued, although on a more discreet scale; in New England fishing and shipbuilding prospered; there was a widening rift between merchants and radicals. The radical group lost control in Massachusetts in 1770, and both Hancock and John Adams broke with Sam. As prosperity waxed, the ardor for high principle waned. The British soldiers involved in the Boston Massacre were defended by John Adams, given a conspicuously fair trial, and acquitted. Settlers were pushing west despite the conflicting views of Whitehall and Westminster. Parliament, for its lugubrious part, had at least established the principle of taxation, albeit on a puny scale. There it would have been well if it could have stayed.

Nevertheless the years 1770–72 saw their own crises. When Rhode Islanders boarded the revenue cutter *Gaspée,* aground off Pawtucket south of Providence, overpowered her crew, wounded her commander, and burned the ship, the law officers could not agree on appropriate action; the commission of investigation was given immense—and to the colonists frightening—powers but proved utterly unable to discover any conspirators. Yet there were eight boatloads of them; they were led by men of social distinction in the colony—including its leading merchant, John Brown; and they had acted quite openly. Civil disobedience could hardly go further. To counter it, the culprits would—if they could have been found—have been brought to England for trial. Also to counter it, Governor Hutchinson of Massachusetts announced that henceforward he and the judges of the Superior Court would receive their salary direct from the Crown. It was to meet this threat that Sam Adams put out a call at a Boston town meeting for the creation of a standing committee of correspondence. For it he prepared a list of infringements and violations of rights which was an impressive summary of the colonial viewpoint. Other committees were promptly organized, ready to concert action if there should be need. "It is natural to suppose," wrote Franklin to Thomas Cushing, "that if the oppressions continue, a congress may grow out of that correspondence." The oppressions continued.

It was the *Tea Deum* of the Sons of Liberty in Boston, defending smuggler Hancock's illicit gains as well as the constitutional principle of the wickedness of the three-pence-per-pound tax on tea, that brought in the third and the decisive stage. By 1773, tea and coffee were popular beverages in the colonies; they used much of the East India Company's tea, as well as a great deal smuggled in from the Dutch West Indies. To relieve the East India Company, then in financial difficulties but with a surplus of seventeen million pounds of tea in England, the North government gave it remission of duties on all tea sent to America; it was also to be allowed to sell direct to chosen and privileged retailers in the colonies. This measure did a number of helpful things for the Company: with its taxes in Britain refunded and with American importers and middlemen ousted, it could now sell in the colonies tea bearing the three-pence-per-pound duty that was still cheaper than smuggled tea. In the process it would destroy the smuggling rings and the prosperity of the tea importers. And it hoped to demonstrate that, if the tea were cheap enough, the colonists would be ready to pay the duty levied on it. In doing so they would implicitly admit the right of Parliament to tax, and "barter liberty for luxury."

This move was opposed everywhere. The Philadelphia, Charleston, and New York consignees were—like stamp distributors earlier—induced to resign their commissions. The Boston consignees, who included Benjamin Faneuil and two sons and a nephew of Governor Hutchinson, were less amenable. The committees of correspondence organized effective resistance. Neither British warships nor troops were able to enforce the law. The tea that reached Charleston was stored quietly in warehouses and was not offered for sale until the revolutionary government in 1776 auctioned it to raise funds; the supplies that reached New York and Philadelphia were returned to Britain. Both ship and cargo in Annapolis were burned. At Boston, against the advice of both his council and assembly, Governor Hutchinson insisted that the tea must be landed. A mass meeting, estimated at two thousand or more people and chaired by Sam Adams, discussed its own course of action; it adjourned with curious promptness and some of its members, disguised as Mohawk Indians, reconvened as a boarding party and on December 16, 1773, threw the 342 tea chests into Boston harbor. A similar fate befell a private consignment landed secretly in New York in April 1774.

Defied for a third time, the home government now determined on a policy of firmness. Parliament since 1769 had been considering an inquiry into Massachusetts. The rendezvous of the Navy had already been moved from Halifax to Boston. In the spring of 1774, to be effective in the summer, the "Intolerable" or Coercive Acts were passed. The port of Boston was closed until the tea should be paid for. The Quartering Act was re-enacted for all thirteen colonies and included occupied dwellings. The Administration of Justice Act provided for the removal for trial to Britain, or to other colonies, of royal officials accused of capital offenses in Massachusetts, despite the fair trial given the "offenders" in the Boston Massacre. The Massachusetts Govern-

ment Act substituted for a civil a new military governor, General
Gage, with an appointed council and appointed sheriffs and
justices. The town meeting, cradle of New England democracy
but now the center of sedition, was to meet only by permission of
the governor and after he had approved its agenda. The colony's
government was transferred to Salem.

Merchants, antimonopolists, radicals, pamphleteers, northern
and—less avidly—southern patriots could now coalesce, with an
exhilarating sense of suffering under tyranny. In all revolutionary
situations there comes a climax where the pieces form a discernible pattern, where the events—thus far apparently unrelated
—suddenly acquire their own momentum. In America, it was
provided by the Boston Tea Party and the British decision at
this point to be firm—a decision made (as always) reluctantly
and (as almost always) too late. Boston, "obstinate, undutiful
and ungovernable from the very beginning," must be brought
to heel. The "punitive acts" of 1774 were passed in a mood in
Britain of near-unanimity.

Of these measures the Quebec Act was thought to be part. It
had actually been designed before the news of the Boston Tea
Party reached London. To the colonists, however, it was particularly alarming because it settled the northwest land question
with a vengeance by transferring to the province of Quebec the
lands—and the fur trade—between the Ohio and the Mississippi
in which Virginia, Pennsylvania, Connecticut, and Massachusetts
had interests, and gave to it (even more ominously as Boston
saw it) French civil law and the Roman Catholic religion. The
regime provided was centralized, in keeping with the customs
of the province; there was to be no trial by jury, and all but
purely local taxation was reserved to the British Parliament.
Chatham and Burke, Fox and Barré attacked it vehemently, and
their bitterness confirmed colonial suspicions. Although an
honest and tolerant measure, drafts of which had been prepared
as far back as 1763, it was singularly ill-timed and appeared completely out of line with American constitutional development.

The colonists were now ready to sniff the approach not only of tyranny but of popery and prelacy in every tainted political breeze. There were fears, in Chatham's phrase, of "popery and arbitrary power"; fears too of a "popish army" being called in to reinforce Gage in Boston, and of French and Indian raiders reappearing in the frontier towns. Petitioning was no longer adequate, wrote Joseph Reed from the first Continental Congress to Lord Dartmouth. "The people are generally ripe for the execution of any plan the Congress advises, should it be war itself." "The die is cast," said the King. "The colonists must either triumph or submit."

Despite George III's statement, the die was not cast in 1774. Compromise was still possible in the two years of storm and crisis ahead. But the decade since 1764 had been profoundly important, less for these events than for the hardening of opinion in both countries. For during these ten years of argument and hesitancy, and behind these episodes, two sides had emerged in the Anglo-American debate. They were not identified with the two countries: on the American side of the ocean a large number of most diverse people and groups stood loyally by Britain; and on the British side America had its supporters in the followers of Pitt and Shelburne, Burke and Fox, Wilkes and the City, radicals and dissenters, merchants and former agents, and those many junior officials or ex-governors like Thomas Pownall or John Temple whose loyalties were to be permanently divided and who did not in the end know which country to call home. In them through the years 1774–78 lay the one dwindling chance of conciliation. From them came in 1782 the intermediaries who finally made peace. But for the majority, on both sides of the Atlantic, a position of some rigidity had by 1774 been reached. And it is important to recall how narrow by that year the room for maneuver had become.

After a succession of short-lived ministries, the King had at last obtained in Lord North a skillful parliamentary lieutenant whose maintenance of power was at first a source of surprise to everyone, including himself, but by 1774 was a source of profound relief to the King. For the first time since his accession it was possible for George to carry through a consistent policy, and by 1774 he was convinced that the colonists should be firmly disciplined. The issue was indeed no longer that of making a modest contribution to their own defense. The amounts contended for had always been small, and the amounts actually collected, by a most complex hierarchy of officials, tiny. What mattered by 1774 was that a challenge had been made to authority. The time had come for the ideas of the Declaratory Act to be made explicit.

There were many who had from the beginning felt this way, and who in a crisis put first their allegiance to the King's government. Among their number were all the King's Friends—some of whom, like Knox and Jenkinson, were the drafters of legislation and were not ill-informed. They included the Scots MPs, now among the King's best friends. They included the country gentlemen prompt to cry havoc. They included many a liberal ex-colonial officer, like Wentworth or Wright. Earlier hesitations in London had been treated as signs of weakness. Britain had erred from "over-levity and want of foresight," as Mansfield said in the Lords. The time had come for strength. This view was a natural reaction to events in Boston. When it came to the test, all but a minority in Britain agreed with Dr. Johnson: "In sovereignty there are no gradations." And there could be equally only a minority in America ready to accept this view, if it were to be enforced. As Franklin had written in 1769, "if continuing the Claim pleases you, continue it as long as you please, provided you never attempt to execute it. We shall consider it in the same light with the Claim of the Spanish Monarch to the Title of King of Jerusalem."

The political manipulation imposed on the King by earlier factional politics and by the constant changes in the composition of ministries had now ceased. This factionalism had been a major source of weakness, but it had at times at least allowed intervals of negotiation, in which a Franklin or a Trecothick could please and persuade. Such intervals disappeared after 1770. By the accidents of politics, moreover, the two groups most hostile to the Americans were in the ministry—the Bedfords from 1767, the Grenvilles immediately after the death of their leader in November 1770—while the two most sympathetic to the colonies were powerless in opposition—the Rockinghams from 1766; the Chathamites, some from 1768, all from January 1770.

The economic pressures ceased also. Merchants, hitherto sensitive to bans on their imports, were cushioned against the events of 1774 and 1775 by good harvests and by the increase in their exports to northern Europe, to Spain, Italy, and the East Indies. If the American market was not to be totally lost, Britain must be firm. The trading class in Britain was never much interested in the question of constitutionality, and at times they had stood in the way of liberal proposals. They forced Townshend to drop his suggestion of 1767 that colonial ships be allowed to sail directly from Spain and Portugal with cargoes of ore, wine, and fruit for the colonies; whatever happened, there must be no concessions at their expense. In any case, their organizers of victory had gone: Trecothick ceased to sit in the House after the 1774 election; Franklin, their mentor in 1766, was by 1775 in Philadelphia. Their West Indian colleagues—untroubled by riots and rebellion—ceased to make common cause with those engaged in the American trade. The merchants, then, were no longer a force making for compromise, and war contracts soon compensated for what losses there were. As William Lee wrote from London (March 10, 1775):

> the Ministry knew well enough the merchants, except 2 or 3 of us, were not at all serious, hence it is, that our petitions are almost all . . . little else than milk and water. The Glasgow merchants played the same game but with less trouble, they sent a strong petition to the H. of C. in favour of America, but at the same time

gave Lord North to understand by their Member Lord F. Campbell that they did not mean any opposition, but to gain credit in
America, and thereby more easily collect their debts.

Equally, radicalism had ceased to be a useful ally. Many liberals had esteemed Wilkes not as man but as victim. By 1774
the radical societies had become objects of suspicion, largely because of the aid and sustenance they gave to French volunteers
bound for America and the appeals they received from the revolutionary provincial congresses. Horne Tooke's Society for Constitutional Information in 1775 granted a hundred pounds to
"our American fellow-subjects, murdered by the King's troops
at Lexington and Concord." Before the end of the year, Tooke
was arrested. The same fate overtook the American friend of
Chatham and former Sheriff of London, Stephen Sayre. Such
activities and such charges discredited all friends of American
liberty.

Throughout these years, also, one impressive figure consistently
urged firmness: Thomas Gage. The young colleague of Washington on Braddock's expedition in 1755 served as military governor of Montreal from 1760 to 1763; becoming deputy to
Amherst, he succeeded him as Commander-in-Chief in North
America in 1764, with his headquarters in New York. Whatever
might be the problems of paying for defense, Gage ran the military machine with a minimum of friction in these years. He
was responsible for more than fifty stations and garrisons from
Newfoundland to Florida, from Bermuda to the Mississippi, for
communications between them, for relations with the Indians,
and, until they had civil governors, for the supervision of the
new territories in the Floridas and Quebec. He was involved
therefore in all the trade and diplomatic issues raised by the
western boundary question. He was patient, tactful, and capable,
important not merely because of his office but because he came
to be consulted repeatedly by the home government.

Gage in fact was the one permanent colonial adviser serving

in America in these troubled years, and his advice did much to
confirm the changing ministries in their hardening opinions of
the colonists. He criticized colonial governors and assemblies for
failing to control their own traders with the Indians and for
making no contribution to the cost of Indian administration;
and the government by 1768 had washed its hands of the Indian
trade. He met innumerable difficulties in deciding on the sites
of forts in the Indian country and from the small number of
men at his disposal available to garrison them; he had therefore
small faith in them. Experience of the Pontiac conspiracy confirmed these doubts. He thought that the West could be controlled by troops on the perimeter, guarding the points of entry
north, south, and center. These should be supplied from a central
reserve of manpower in New York. These considerations greatly
influenced Hillsborough in 1770 in his decision to withdraw
troops from the West. Faithful to his mandate to prevent un-
authorized expansion westward, he was angered by the endless
chicanery of the provincial assemblies which refused to accept the
ban on westward migration. He saw no value at all in colonies
in the Illinois country—they were bound to promote manufactures.

If his dispatches confirmed the government in its sense of
frustration in the West, they did little to promote a favorable
view of the seaboard colonies. Quartering he found a repeated
matter of difficulty; so was profiteering. He recommended that
the Quartering Act be extended to permit the billeting of soldiers
on butchers and bakers and all who profited by the troops, as
was the practice in Scotland. It was under his pleading that in
the end quartering on private houses was permitted. Colonial
assemblies, in his view, were slow to help in returning deserters
to camps, and were too prone to encourage attacks on his troops.
While Gage was scrupulous in using the military only after he
had been expressly authorized to do so, and kept his men firmly
in check, his dispatches suggest a state of endless bickering between assemblies and military.

And his private opinions were clearly unsympathetic. He noted the "language of Billingsgate," "the seeds of anarchy and licentiousness . . . thick sown through the colonies," the power of lawyers, the difficulty of controlling town mobs. Writing to Barrington as early as January 1767, he said:

> The Colonists are taking great strides towards Independency; it concerns Great Britain by a speedy and spirited Conduct to shew them that these provinces are British Colonies dependent on her, and that they are not independent states.

He never found occasion to modify this view. In 1770, again to Barrington, he wrote:

> My private opinion is that America is a mere bully, from one end to the other, and the Bostonians by far the greatest bulleys, and I think you will find them so upon tryal.

At an audience with the King in March 1773, he thought the colonists, "lyons whilst we are lambs," would be "very meek" if Britain took "the resolute part"; four regiments would be enough to keep unruly Boston in order. It was largely because of his evidence that the administration of justice was added to the Boston Port bill.

If by August 1774 he was less confident about the docility of Boston, he dismissed the South. They talk very high, "but they can do nothing; their numerous slaves in the bowells of their country, and the Indians at their backs will always keep them quiet." To Barrington he pleaded:

> If you will resist and not yield, that resistance should be effective at the beginning. If you think ten thousand men sufficient, send twenty, if one million [pounds] is thought enough, give two, you will save both blood and treasure in the end. A large force will terrify, and engage many to join you; a middling one will encourage resistance, and gain no friends.

By February 1775 he was insisting that "the troops must march into the country." His views were confirmed by Sir Guy Carle-

ton, the commander in Canada, who insisted on the reliability
of French Canada, the importance of Quebec and New York
and of a line of forts between them. They were endorsed by
Haldimand, by Johnson—"Humanity should Yield to good
Policy"—and by Croghan, Johnson's deputy.

Sentiments akin to these were becoming general. They abound
in the dispatches of colonial governors. The Bernard-Barrington
correspondence or the C.O.5 file in the Public Record Office in
London is a rich store of harsh—and highly readable—comments
by the governor of Massachusetts. Demagogues in America were
"determined to bring all real power into the hands of the people." As early as 1768 Bernard thought all government in Massachusetts "at an end," the mob dominant. The only hope was to
increase the powers of the governor—and to institute a colonial
nobility, "appointed by the King, for Life, and made independent." Recalled home and made a baronet, by 1773 he was a
close adviser of North. He had long pressed for the removal of
the executive power in Massachusetts "from the democratic part
of government." With the revelation by Franklin of the Hutch-
inson-Oliver letters, colonists assumed—with much truth—that
all governors were writing in similar terms and hardening the
hearts of the ministries.

Many a junior official was equally scornful. Henry Hulton of
the Customs Board, writing from Boston during the siege of
1775, grieved that

> gentlemen, brave British soldiers, should fall by the hands of such
> despicable wretches as compose the banditti of the country, amongst
> whom there is not one that has the least pretension to be called a
> gentleman. They are a most rude, depraved, degenerate race, and
> it is a mortification to us that they speak English and can trace
> themselves from that stock.

But even the more sympathetic ministers could be quoted to the
same purpose. When the New York Assembly refused to pass
the Quartering Act, it was the liberal Shelburne who favored

billeting troops in private houses and who pressed for the removal of the governor, Sir Henry Moore, and his replacement
by a man "of a Military Character" with authority "to act with
Force or Gentleness as circumstances might make necessary."

In the party negotiations of 1767-68 consequent on Chatham's
illness, even the Old Whigs were ready to consider taking office
with the Bedford group on a policy of asserting or maintaining
—they argued over the terminology—"the rights of Great Britain
over her colonies." Both sides began to use words of similar
high-sounding principle, words on which it was impossible to
compromise. As late as 1770, Chatham declared that the Americans "must be subordinate. In all laws relating to trade and navigation, this is the mother country, they are children; they must
obey and we prescribe."

And the Tea Party produced an almost unanimous chorus:
"The popular current," wrote Burke, "both within doors and
without, at present sets sharply against America." Their conduct
could not be justified, said Rockingham; the destruction of the
tea was "certainly criminal," said Chatham. Charles Van, a
wealthy Monmouthshire squire who sat for Brecon Borough
1772-78, speaking on the committee stage of the Boston Port bill,
urged that the town should be demolished, *"Delenda est Car-
thago. . . .* Make it a mark that shall never be restored." William Lee, Sheriff of London, writing in June 1774 and not
risking his name to his letter, noted that there was little opposition "without doors" to the government's measures, and went on:

> You have not a friend, nor indeed is their [*sic*] one friend even to
> the liberties of this Country, in the whole administration. Lord
> D—tm—h, notwithstanding his fawning & deceitful expressions
> to the Americans, is in the Cabinet as determin'd & violent an
> enemy to you as any in this Country. . . . The great misfortune to
> this Country as well as America is, that the Rockingham &
> Chatham people have no confidence in, or connection with each
> other, & till they firmly unite there will be no chance of the present
> ministry being shaken, or any other that may be appointed, even if

they were all coblers or shoeblacks, for indeed the leaders of the present set are all Scotch adventurers, & a worse set cannot be picked out of the whole Kingdom.

"When the supreme power abdicates," Mansfield had pontificated in 1766, "the Government is dissolved."

Yet it was Dartmouth, in the summer of 1774, who spoke for an almost united opinion when he wrote privately to Joseph Reed in Pennsylvania. He said that "the supreme legislature of the whole British Empire has laid a duty (no matter for the present whether it has or has not the right so to do, it is sufficient that we conceive it has). . . . The question then is whether these laws are to be submitted to? If the people of America say no, they say in effect they will no longer be a part of the British Empire."

If any doubts remained in London, they were dispelled by the election of 1774, in which North had an ample majority, giving him less need for caution in government, and in which the American question had played little part except in Middlesex and Westminster, the "free" constituencies. If Burke was returned for Bristol on a mildly pro-American platform, even he thought in 1774 that "American and foreign affairs will not come to any crisis." And Gage reported wearily that mobs were now hunting and harrying his councilors as before they had bedeviled stamp agents and customs officials. He wanted reinforcements, preferably mercenaries from Germany. "These provinces must be first totally subdued before they will obey." Failing severe measures, the Coercive Acts should be suspended. When the trusted lieutenant on the spot himself seemed to have such doubts as these, the time seemed to have come for firmness. It was in Britain, not America, that the die was cast: it was there that vacillation had in the end given way to obstinacy.

A similar process was at work on the American side through these years. The victim—not the initiator—of policy, exercising

no direct influence on Westminster or Whitehall, it is possible
to read the colonial story in as episodic a fashion as the British,
as a story of occasional protests and riots. But by 1774 government had become all but powerless in most colonies. There were
many in America, of course, who were loyal to the links with
"home," liberals among them. As late as 1775 Franklin thought
that if Parliament dropped its claim to the right to tax, trouble
could still be averted; Jefferson still accepted as his goal "dependence on Great Britain, properly limited"; very few as yet criticized George III, and declarations of loyalty to him were still
customary. But by 1774 there had emerged in America a coherent
body of opinion making for separation.

There was now not merely recurrent rioting; there were also
organizations to further it. The Sons of Liberty, appearing first
in New York and then in Connecticut, Massachusetts, and Virginia, had become active in all the colonies. By their petitions
and propaganda, by their hanging of officials in effigy, by their
arrangement of funerals for the victims—few though they were
—of tyranny, they kept alive that sense of grievance that is indispensable to revolution. These organizations "cultivated the sensa-
tions of freedom," wrote John Adams in his diary August 14,
1769. Their meetings "tinge the minds of the people; they im-
pregnate them with the sentiments of liberty; they render the
people fond of their leaders in the cause and averse and bitter
against all opposers."

Those who came to love liberty in America loved it and supported it for many different reasons: the Cabots and Hancocks
because of the interference with their smuggling profits; lawyers
for reasons of conviction, for love of controversy, and for noto-
riety; the propertied because of the wickedness of taxes, whether
legal or illegal; the propertyless as an occasion for boisterous fun,
in a century when most fun was boisterous, with a spice of real
risk when redcoats were involved. All such supported, even if
they did not always join, the Sons of Liberty. The most dangerous aspect of the activity of these and similar pararevolutionary

groups—the Mohawk River Indians, the Philadelphia Patriotic
Society, the Sons of Neptune, the gangs led by Ebenezer Mackintosh in Boston or by Isaac Sears in New York—was the contempt they induced for the law and for the governors, the
officials, and the troops who tried, often half-heartedly, to enforce it. The customs commissioners reported from Boston as
early as 1768:

> We shall find it totally impracticable to enforce the Execution of
> the Revenue Laws until the Hand of Government is strengthened.
> At present not a ship of war in the Province, nor a company of
> soldiers nearer than New York, which is two hundred and fifty
> Miles distant from this Place.

It mattered little whether the method of flouting the law was by
burning ships or destroying cargo or, in more gentlemanly
Virginia, by reconvening in the Raleigh Tavern to discuss illegal
action.

Rioting was problem enough in the eighteenth century. It was
more ominous when, as more than one customs report indicated,
there seemed to be discipline behind the riotous behavior, when
it was clear that there were leaders and led. More ominous still
was the rioting against troops. There was both fear of and contempt for the "lobster-backs," a readiness to pick a fight with
them individually or in small groups, a hatred of their presence,
particularly when they were quartered in private homes. It was
strongly felt in Boston and New York. Relations between regular
troops and a native population are always potentially explosive—
as Ben Butler discovered in New Orleans in 1862. There were
in the colonies enough troops to provoke unrest and periodic
violence; there were not enough to ensure order. This was the
first prerequisite for revolution.

By 1774 there was not only an instrument available; there was
also a body of doctrine. It had been expressed by a succession of
writers—by Otis and by Daniel Dulany, by John Dickinson in

Pennsylvania, by Patrick Henry and George Mason with their Resolves in Virginia, by Richard Bland in his *Inquiry into the Rights of the British Colonies,* and by Sam Adams and Ben Franklin as professionals and under a variety of names in these years. Protesting at first against an internal tax, the colonists had come in the end to a total denial of Parliament's right to tax them without their own consent. This the lawyers in both countries saw clearly as an issue from the beginning. Henry took one view. Mansfield took the opposite—"I seek for the liberty and constitution of this Kingdom no farther back than the Revolution [of 1688]: There I take my stand. And in the reign of King William an act was passed avowing the power of this legislature over the colonies."

The importance of the radical protest in this decade was that it altered the grounds of the debate. The justice of Grenville's original proposals had quickly got lost in a bigger question of justice: the Parliament seen in Britain in 1763 as hallowed by the events of 1688 was seen in the colonies not only as vacillating but as itself tyrannical. James Otis had already charged it with being so over writs of assistance in 1761. The Wilkes case in Britain gave support to this view; so did Franklin's reports and those of other agents; so, by 1774, did Burke's speeches: Old England was corrupt as well as incompetent. Again, this was—certainly until 1774 and perhaps until 1776—an attitude of negation rather than of assertion. The colonists were not prompt to "intellectualize" their discontents. They campaigned against particular evils, normally pledging devout, affectionate, and at times obsequious loyalty to the imperial tie. There was little appeal as yet to natural rights. So far it was simply Parliament's authority that was being challenged, by James Wilson in his *Considerations on the Nature and Extent of the Legislative Authority of the British Parliament,* by Jefferson in his *Summary View,* and by John Adams in his *Novanglus* letters. By 1774 a dangerous consensus was being reached: the leading colonial writers were now close to a dominion theory; accepting the fact of Empire, they sought to be masters in their own house.

What was important about the colonial argument from 1764 to 1774 was not its content so much as its increasingly national character. Franklin had hinted at this in 1766. By 1774 it was clear that the leaders of colonial resistance were coming from highly varied groups: planters like Richard Henry Lee and Jefferson; frontier lawyers like Henry, town lawyers like John Adams in Boston and John Morin Scott in New York; merchants like Christopher Gadsden in South Carolina, Alexander McDougall in New York, Hancock in Boston. This growing unity was helped by improving roads, by the movement of tutors and parsons through the colonies, by the gradual diffusion of ideas. Governor Bull of South Carolina blamed the Stamp Act troubles there largely on the news of what had happened in New England. The printing press, the periodic urban slumps, the concentration of royal officials in the towns: these gave the lead to Boston, Philadelphia, and Charleston, seats though they were of wealth and privilege far more than of equality. Almost all the newspaper editors were "patriots"; Rivington in New York was the conspicuous exception. Dickinson's *Letters* were promptly published in the *Virginia Gazette* and in other journals outside Pennsylvania. The support given to the Massachusetts House when it issued its circular letter in 1768 was both speedy and unanimous.

Alongside the Sons of Liberty and the pamphlets and gazettes and courants there appeared after 1772 the various standing committees of correspondence. Locally they had come into being in November 1772 as part of Sam Adams' handiwork; within three months Governor Hutchinson reported that there were more than eighty in Massachusetts. In Virginia in March 1773 Dabney Carr, Jefferson's brother-in-law, persuaded the Virginia Assembly to appoint a similar committee; it was essentially an illegal standing committee of the Assembly and brought business to its un-

official headquarters, Hays' Tavern, across the street from the
Williamsburg capitol. It was indeed from Hays' Tavern that the
call for the First Continental Congress went out in 1774. By
February 1774 every colony except Pennsylvania and North
Carolina had its committees of correspondence, "the foulest,
subtlest and most venomous serpent ever issued from the egg of
sedition," as Daniel Leonard called them. They kept in touch
with each other, colony by colony; they acted as a combined
headquarters staff and self-elected politburo in each colony, a
committee on rules which could make its own. And behind
them were the more legal agencies, not least the Boston Town
Meeting, a joint platform-cum-caucus of Sam Adams from
which he could "instruct" the Massachusetts Assembly, and the
proud but liberal lead of the Virginia House of Burgesses. All
these made very smooth the transfer of power from London to
the colonial capitals.

In form, there was still loyalty to the King, but not to the
Establishment. Neither the Congregational nor the Presbyterian
churches emphasized the links with Britain. The Episcopal
Church was under heavy fire. Unpopular in the South because
it was tax-supported, it was seen in New England as Laudian
and hierarchical. "Ascending by various gradations from the dirt
to the skies," wrote Jonathan Mayhew of it in 1763, officered by
"the mitred, lordly successors of the fishermen of Galilee," it
was ready to compass sea and land "to make us proselytes."
There was a pervasive fear of an American episcopate, of what
John Adams described as "those tyrants in religion, bishops,"
"the sight of lawn sleeves more terrible than ten thousand Mohawks." And, even before the Quebec Act, much more after it,
there was unease about Roman Catholicism. "What we have
above everything else to fear is Popery," said Sam Adams.

And by 1774 no hope at all was placed in the ministry. While
individual members of Parliament were listened to, what impressed in their speeches was what confirmed colonial fears. No

trust had been put in Hillsborough or in Dartmouth. Of the
first, Franklin wrote in 1771 in a private letter to Thomas Cushing:

> The character of the American Secretary is proud, supercilious,
> extremely conceited (moderate as they are) of his political Knowl-
> edge and Abilities, fond of everyone that can stoop to flatter him,
> and inimical to all that dare tell him disagreeable Truths. This
> Man's Mandates have been treated with Disrespect in America,
> his Letters have been critis'd, his Measures censur'd and despis'd;
> which has produced in him a kind of settled Malice against the
> Colonies, particularly Ours, that would break out with greater
> violence, if cooler Heads did not set some bounds to it.

As for his successor, Dartmouth, "Apparently meaning no ill,
he will never do any good," was American-born Arthur Lee's
comment on him.

Colonial governors, too, were now thought of with small
respect; there was too full a knowledge of the methods and the
nepotism by which they were selected—"Whenever we find ourselves encumbered with a needy Court-Dangler, whom on account of Connections we must not kick downstairs, we kick him
up into an American government." William Franklin's appointment to New Jersey in 1762 was regarded with mingled awe and
contempt—"a burlesque on all government," said John Watts of
New York. There were few among them exceptionally distinguished, hardly any who were disinterested, and one or two who
were incompetent. Their tasks, however, were daunting and
most of them fought manfully against the tide. Governor Hutchinson, although in colonial eyes a haughty figure, surrounded,
like many a governor, by a rapacious clan of in-laws, emerges
from his own *History* as a man of intelligence, balance, and
courage. Botetourt, Junius' "cringing sword-bearing courtier,"
won Virginia's respect; Tryon, ruthless in North Carolina in the
eyes of the "Regulators," handled New York with some skill;
John Wentworth in New Hampshire and Sir James Wright in

Georgia acted with vigor in their own crises. But by 1774 they were seen as patently the agents of parliamentary tyranny. And the Hutchinson correspondence was taken to damn the whole species.

A body of constitutional doctrine; agencies for riot and rebellion; a number of leaders: was this then a "national" movement, was it yet an American revolution? The answer in 1774 is clearly *no*. In the colonial scene sectionalism was still more striking than unity. The first Congress, a coming together of ambassadors, was marked by an anxious process of mutual exploration—of each other and of each other's sections. It had, said John Rutledge, "no coercive or legislative authority." It was a machine for allowing the colonies to "resent in one body," as a Virginian put it—still negative, not positive. Moreover, while the leaders in 1774 were coming to be united against Britain, there was no program either of social or political reform, and no sign of agreement on doctrine.

The previous ten years had seen many examples of colonial division. In Pennsylvania in 1764 the march on Philadelphia of the Paxton boys from the frontier indicated how wide was the gulf between Quaker Philadelphia and the Indian-haunted and Scotch-Irish-settled frontier. Here the unequal system of representation, which favored the eastern counties, was held to be "an infringement of our natural privileges of freedom and equality," for which the seaboard rather than Britain was responsible. Not until 1776, in the Pennsylvania constitution, were these grievances redressed. Similarly, the Regulators in the Carolinas protested against inadequate political representation and against the absence of courts, clergy, and churches. Defeated at the Alamance in 1771, and their grievances disregarded, they failed during the Revolution to support a cause that had shown them no sympathy, and they were, in their violent but ill-disciplined way, on the Loyalist side. There were many areas along the Alleghenies or along the Congeree and Wateree that were loyal to Britain in 1776—from Quaker pacifism or German quietism, from fear of the Indians or from lack of sympathy with the Tidewater. If the dispute was over representation, they were not represented anyway; if over taxes, they paid few; if over tea, this was not a frontier beverage.

Thus far the movement against Britain was not primarily a social protest. In New York John Morin Scott showed no sympathy for the poor tenant farmers. Sam Adams was slow to trust the farmers of Massachusetts. Indeed in Massachusetts it was Boston, not the frontier, that led the movement for independence. "River gods" across the Connecticut River, like Israel Williams and John Worthington, were on the whole Loyalist until compelled to change their minds.

And in 1770–72 and more sharply in 1774, despite the appearance of unity, there was in Boston itself and in the other ports a cleavage between merchants and radicals. The merchants were unwilling to stop all trade with Britain as the town meetings were once more requesting. They were strongly opposed to the Intolerable Acts, but they were now almost as much in fear of the mob. They offered to pay for the tea destroyed—a loss estimated at ten thousand pounds—if only the ports were reopened. John Andrews saw ahead not only war with Britain but civil war as well. They tried, quite unsuccessfully, to capture the Town Meeting and to destroy the committee of correspondence. And their doubts and hesitations were reflected in Philadelphia when the first Continental Congress met. To some of them at least, the Congress was to be a device not only for thwarting Britain but for averting social revolution.

4

Rebellion: 1774–1776

THE FIRST Continental Congress met in Carpenter's Hall Philadelphia, on September 5, 1774. John Adams, Sam's sobei cousin from Quincy, Massachusetts, was greatly stirred by it "There is in the Congress," he noted in that painstaking diary of his,

> a collection of the greatest men upon this Continent in point of abilities, virtues and fortunes. The magnanimity and public spirit which I see here make me blush for the sordid, venal herd which I have seen in my own Province. . . .

Fifty-five delegates attended this Congress, from all thirteen colonies except Georgia: a remarkable conclave. Its most important practical achievement was the formation of the Continental Association to bring pressure on British merchants: non-importation of British goods was to begin on December 1, 1774, nonexportation of colonial products on September 10, 1775. In the interval, it was hoped, Britain might come to terms. Even this mild threat was not won without compromise: the loss of their British markets was altogether more daring for the South than the North, and South Carolina threatened secession unless its exports of rice to Europe were permitted. Britain's current prosperity made these measures of little avail and, coming from an illegal and federal agency, they were far from popular. They hurt

the colonies—British exports to New York fell from £437,937 in
1774 to £1228 in 1775, to Maryland and Virginia from £528,738
in 1774 to £1921 in 1775—but by stimulating local production
and pride in frugality they gave zest in the end to the common
cause.

Yet this was hardly intended, for the Congress was almost
equally divided between radicals and moderates—"one-third
Tories, another Whigs, and the rest Mongrels," said Adams. And
this division in opinion was to be as significant as anything else.
The most prominent figures in debate were Richard Henry Lee
and Patrick Henry of Virginia and the still more outspoken
radicals of Massachusetts; but there were many moderates.
Among them was John Dickinson, moving now more cautiously
than in 1768 because he was more aware than most of the com-
bustible elements—

> The first act of violence on the part of administration in America,
> or the attempt to reinforce General Gage this winter or next year
> will put the whole continent in arms, from Nova Scotia to
> Georgia . . . a determined and unanimous resolution animates
> this continent.

But he stood by his counsel of 1768: action should be taken
"*peaceably—prudently—firmly—jointly.*" Or, as he put it to Cushing in December 1774, "Procrastination is preservation." What
was to be guarded against was "an Excess of virtuous Zeal." Behind Dickinson was Edmund Pendleton of Virginia, who, although a poor boy by birth, had become a prominent planter-
lawyer, voicing the fears of his class of nonimportation and
alarmed at the tone of the debates; to him and his like threats of
violence were distasteful and unwise. Was there not danger in
endless talk of "rights"? These views were shared by John Jay
and James Duane of New York and by Joseph Galloway of
Pennsylvania, whose statesmanlike *Plan of a proposed Union between Great Britain and the Colonies,* providing for an American
legislature or "Grand Council" within the Empire, barely failed

to win agreement. The radicals insisted on erasing all record of
the plan from the journals of Congress. These differences of
emphasis were to leave their mark.

The Congress then was at first neither belligerent nor republican. It "cheerfully" accepted parliamentary regulation of external
trade; it denied parliamentary taxation without colonial consent.
"We ask only for peace, liberty and security. We wish no diminu-
tion of royal prerogatives, we demand no new rights." But in
fact its Declaration of Rights and Grievances did demand "the
rights of Englishmen," the repeal of the Intolerable Acts, and
the dismissal of the King's "designing and dangerous" ministers;
and the Suffolk Resolves, already accepted by a convention in
Suffolk County, Massachusetts, denied all obligation to obey recent Acts of Parliament, described George III as a sovereign
"agreeable to compact," and threatened armed resistance. Given
British intransigence, this was now a revolutionary position to
take, in a body itself revolutionary. Galloway, after the defeat of
his plan, charged the radicals with aiming at revolution, delud-
ing the people "by every fiction, falsehood and fraud." They
were "Congregational and Presbyterian republicans, or men of
bankrupt fortunes, overwhelmed in debt to the British merchants." Gage felt the same: all moderate opinion, he said, was
horrified; but it was also pusillanimous.

Newspapers from 1774 onward openly discussed independence.
So did James Wilson in his *Considerations on the Authority of
Parliament* and John Adams in his *Novanglus* papers. Jefferson's *Summary View* described the King as the "Chief Magistrate" of the Empire and denied the legislative supremacy of
Parliament. An appeal from Congress went out through the
committees of correspondence, which were to transform themselves into committees of safety and to be elected in every town
and county—vigilance societies to defend American rights and
to denounce, browbeat, and "persuade" the hesitant. The mood
now quickened. Provincial congresses—extra-legal but almost
identical with the legal assemblies in composition—came into be-

ing. Generals were appointed. Militia forces were organized. The minutemen undertook to equip themselves "with an effective fire-arm, bayonet, pouch, knapsack and round of cartridges ready made" and "to convene for exercise in the art military, at least twice every week." Independent companies began to drill. The Massachusetts provincial congress established an army and appealed to the rest of New England for quotas of troops "for the general defence." And, as a contemporary put it, "sedition flowed copiously from the pulpits." Colonial governors wrote anxiously for instructions to the Earl of Dartmouth, Secretary for the Colonies, and began, not always discreetly, to store arms. On returning from the first Continental Congress, Washington found himself offered the command of seven of the county militia companies in Virginia. He now put on the buff and blue of Fairfax, to make of it the symbol of liberty on two continents.

When the new Parliament met in November 1774, after the election, there was a similar mood of near-unanimity. There was broad endorsement of the King's position: "The New England governments are in a state of rebellion, blows must decide." It was thought that Boston was the center of discord and that Massachusetts could be isolated from the other colonies. Gage was now without any such illusions; he sought a large army—and not for Massachusetts alone. Colonial governors were instructed in January 1775 to prevent the election of delegates to the second Continental Congress. When Burke delivered his speech on conciliation, he was defeated by 270 votes to 78. In February Parliament declared that a rebellion existed in Massachusetts and urged the King "to enforce due obedience to the laws and authority of the supreme legislature"; in March came the New England Restraining Act, limiting the commerce of New England to Britain and the British West Indies; in April a similar measure was applied to New Jersey, Pennsylvania, and the South. This was treated in the colonies as a crude device to divide and rule by giving preferential treatment to New York.

Along with these was a resolution for reconciliation, promising that Parliament would cease to tax any colony that agreed to provide money for defense and civil government. But this and the many conciliatory petitions of British merchants were little heeded. "It is no time to parley with a robber about your purse," orated the *Virginia Gazette,* "when he has a pistol at your breast.' By August 1775 in the eyes of Parliament the colonies were in "open and avowed rebellion."

The last act of the first Continental Congress had been to summon the second Continental Congress, which met in May 1775. The majority of delegates—now sixty-five, and Georgia sent five in September—were still against independence. John Dickinson's "Olive Branch" petition from "your faithful colonists" was adopted—to be scorned in London; in the eyes of radicals as cantankerous as John Adams it was the work of "a certain Great Fortune and piddling genius," giving "a silly Cast to our whole Doings." The time for petitioning was past. "Powder and artillery are the most efficacious, sure and infallible conciliatory measures we can adopt."

In the colonies there was now a clear recognition of the need for defense—although it was still defense against a "parliamentary" army. And, as the Congress was assembling, the news came through that confirmed this need for defense—on April 19, at Lexington, the first clash had come when Gage tried to seize "rebel" stores and tried to arrest Samuel Adams and Hancock; and when Patrick Henry arrived in Philadelphia he brought the tale of Governor Dunmore's seizure of powder from the Horn in Williamsburg on April 27. Two weeks later, Ticonderoga and Crown Point were captured by a mixed band of volunteers under the colorful and quarrelsome leaders Ethan Allen and Benedict Arnold. With curious facility for a non-military people unfamiliar with the organization of war, the delegates in Congress agreed to aid Massachusetts by raising an army and choosing a commander. "A powerful Army on the side of America," said Joseph Warren of Massachusetts, was "the only means left to stem the rapid progress of a tyrannical ministry."

On June 16, 1775, George Washington, "six-feet two and straight as an Indian," accepted with his customary protestations the commission of Commander-in-Chief. He wrote to Martha at Mount Vernon assuring her that he would be home by Christmas. There is no evidence that he felt himself the leader of a revolution. Yet such he was, for on the next day came the first battle of the war—Bunker Hill. The British casualties here were 1150 out of 2500 men engaged—the price paid for what a participant called an "absurd and destructive confidence." The Americans lost 400 out of some 1500 engaged.

Accompanying these steps, Congress issued, on July 6, 1775, its Declaration of Causes of Taking Up Arms. Although it rejected independence, it asserted that Americans would rather die than be enslaved. The war thus began at least a year before the Declaration of Independence, with the shots fired at Concord Bridge and Bunker Hill, with this Declaration and with Washington's appointment. It began as a defense of the colonies against "the tyranny of irritated ministers," in order to bring them to terms; it was to be short, only a demonstration of force. But here again events were now not so easily controllable. What might have been designed as a further pressure on London was taken in London as confirmation of revolution. "Government can never recover itself but by using determined Measures," wrote Gage to Dartmouth. "I have no hopes at present of any Accommodation, the Congress Appear to have too much power, and too little Inclination . . . and it Appeared very plainly that taxation was not the point, but a total Independency."

In 1775, independence was still in fact unsought by almost all the colonists. It was now not a question of hope of conciliation—which was all but abandoned—so much as a fear of the alternatives. It was all but universally agreed that Britain was in the wrong. But if she continued to do nothing, where would the momentum of events, including by this time the ascendancy of the mob and its leaders, carry the colonies? The struggle was ceasing to be, to use Carl Becker's famous phrase, a question of home rule and becoming a question of who should rule at home. The fears of merchants and colonial *aristos* were now explicit. Conservatives like the De Lanceys in New York sought to swamp the radicals in the Committee of Fifty-One. It soon became a Committee of Sixty, with mob support, and by May 1775 a radical Committee of One Hundred. In his very shrewd letter to John Penn in May 1774, Gouverneur Morris of New York was cynical but disturbed; the movement was the work of "the Jack Cades of the day, the leaders in all the riots, the bell-wethers of the flock." "A great metamorphosis" was taking place, the work of "the god of Ambition and the goddess of Faction." He saw a sharp distinction between a powerful group of "tribunes" and a powerless group of "patricians." If the dispute with Britain continued, "we shall be under the worst of all possible dominions; we shall be under the domination of a riotous mob." It was in the interest of all men to seek for re-union with Britain. And at the least it was essential that if there were to be mobs, they should be provided with leaders from those with a stake in society.

These sentiments led some conservatives, like Galloway, to loyalism; they led others, like Dickinson, to seek to delay revolutionary action in Congress. A number of planters and merchants went along with independence, but in fear rather than conviction, hoping somewhat gloomily to curb or to restrain it. In April 1776 Carter Braxton of Virginia saw clearly all the clashes of colony with colony; if independence were asserted, he thought that "the continent would be torn in pieces by intestine wars and convulsions." Dickinson predicted in thirty years' time a separate commonwealth to the north of Hudson's River. Two of the leading proponents of the colonial case at the beginning of the colonial debate—the two most concerned to distinguish between internal and external taxes—had ceased by 1776 to lead the cause: Dulany became a Tory; Dickinson, though he stayed a patriot, was highly cautious. In October 1775 James Allen of Philadelphia joined a battalion to defend the city against Britain, but in a mood of distrust: "a man is suspected who does not. . . . I believe discreet people mixing with them may keep them in order." In March, with "the Mobility triumphant," he thought "The madness of the multitude is but one degree better than submission to the Tea Act."

In the same month, John Adams, whose diary suggests a nervous and naïve enjoyment of the danger and excitement of these months, wrote to Horatio Gates, now Washington's Adjutant-General and Chief of Staff, that from fighting half a war they were now about to wage three quarters of a war. But even this "is not Independency, you know, nothing like it. . . . Independency is a Hobgoblin of so frightful Mien that it would throw a delicate person into Fits to look it in the Face." New York and Philadelphia in particular were reluctant converts to the idea of separation.

Yet the fact of independence was becoming abundantly clear. The newspapers—and they were almost all revolutionary by this time—were supporting it. Every day and every post, said John Adams, independence rolled in on Congress like a torrent. Unless Congress acted swiftly, Hawley wrote to Sam Adams, a "Great Mobb" would march on Philadelphia, purge Congress, and set up a dictator. Britain had declared the colonists rebels and proclaimed a blockade. She was now seeking to destroy coastal towns—Norfolk, Charleston, Falmouth. She was avow-edly seeking foreign troops—German, as the colonists knew, and Russian, as they heard it rumored. Dunmore's recklessness in threatening a Negro insurrection in the South led to a curfew for slaves, patrolling of towns, and panic on Tidewater estates. In May Congress instructed the colonies to suppress British author-ity and to establish governments elected by the people. By May North Carolina, Massachusetts, and Virginia instructed their delegates to Congress to vote for separation from Britain. On

June 24, 1776, Congress passed the Allegiance and Treason Resolves, branding the King an enemy. On June 7, under instructions from the Virginia Assembly, Richard Henry Lee had introduced his resolution that "these United Colonies are, and of right ought to be, free and independent States." John Adams seconded.

There was still no unanimity; delegates from the Middle Colonies and from South Carolina were under instructions to oppose such a motion, and John Dickinson and James Wilson of Pennsylvania were loud in their opposition. Their case was not of ends but of means. They accepted by June that there could no longer be any form of unity with Britain, but they doubted, as conservatives always are apt to do, whether the time was ripe. The speech made in opposition to independence by Dickinson is as moving a statement, and as severe an indictment of Britain, as the ultimate Declaration itself.

Because of the opposition and the instructions against independence of Pennsylvania, New Jersey, South Carolina, and New York a final vote was postponed for three weeks. Congress, on July second (John Dickinson and Robert Morris absenting themselves), approved the resolution and on the fourth adopted Jefferson's draft of the Declaration of Independence, though it was not until July 15 that New York came into line. As always, the moment of truth was a moment of deep anxiety, of doubt and hesitation; yet this was the great divide. In making it so, Congress accepted a quite new theory of which there had been very little heard before 1776; it was no longer Parliament that was the tyrant, but the King.

The goals now were separation—and republicanism. In justifying its decision to become independent, Congress no longer claimed "the rights of Englishmen" but "natural rights." The American people, it said, had voluntarily associated themselves with Britain thus far, and had voluntarily acknowledged the same King. By his arbitrary acts this King had now forfeited their allegiance, and these acts were specified "to a candid

World." There were twenty-seven charges, almost all of them charges of political tyranny. Behind the Jeffersonian grace of the second sentence of the Declaration ("We hold these truths to be self-evident. . . .") twenty-seven empirical arguments for separation were listed. If they had ceased to ask for "the rights of Englishmen," the American people were never more English than in the slow, reluctant stages by which they reached, and the steady, factual indictment by which they justified, their independence.

On July 3, the day before Congress adopted the Declaration, Sir William Howe seized Staten Island, and led his men ashore from the largest armada thus far assembled in North American waters.

Independence was then a decision taken reluctantly, in the face of British intransigence, and with many in America and in Congress doubtful of its wisdom—Loyalists in all colonies, the in-groups around colonial governors, the back-settlers in the Carolinas, and New York and Philadelphia merchants. Among them were men as noble and as gifted as any of the revolutionaries. Neither side was particularly rich in wisdom—or in heroes. But between 1774 and 1776 a number of distinct forces had thrust them toward this decision.

The first of these was the Continental Congress itself and its own dominant minority: Sam and John Adams, John Hancock, Franklin, Patrick Henry, Richard Henry Lee, Thomas Jefferson—the men Gouverneur Morris called tribunes, although some of them were also patricians. By February 1776 they were appealing to the colonists for "instructions" supporting independence. In May they urged that new colonial governments should be chosen, deriving their sanction from the people.

In all crises in history, demagogues and revolutionaries are constantly engaged in a process of agonizing self-justification. As John Adams' diary reveals, in convincing others they seek also to keep their own convictions alive. They are apt to be men whose careers have been marked either by failure—Hancock's business was in difficulties, Sam Adams had had a succession of disasters—or by a love of popular applause, as with Patrick Henry and John Adams. Their talk in Congress was of a show of spirit —"the reason of every madman," declared Rutledge of South Carolina. There was talk too of foreign aid and of the shape of the new federal government. There was rumor of the British use of German troops and indignation at the threatened invasion into New York from Canada. But indignation was also giving way to a mood of creative excitement; in John Adams a mood of glee, in John Dickinson of gloom, and in Sam Adams of gloating. To use a later and an unfortunate phrase, this could be called a group of willful men; John Adams, with an eye on his cousin, in 1770 had called them "designing men."

One of them at least—Sam Adams—had from 1768 willed a revolution. Impractical and unsuccessful in his own career, slovenly and unkempt in manner, he was nevertheless the first of the revolutionaries as organizer of gangs, correspondent in newspapers, representative of the city of Boston in the General Court. He was patient and in some ways otherworldly—but like many another idealist he could be also fanatical, contentious, unscrupulous, and gifted in expedients. Joseph Galloway, reflecting on events in London in 1780, described him as one who was not distinguished by brilliant abilities but "equal to most men in popular intrigue and the management of a faction. He eats little, drinks little, sleeps little, thinks much, and is most decisive and indefatigable in the pursuit of his objects. It was this man, who by his superior application managed at once the faction in Congress at Philadelphia, and the factions in New England." He was not to be the dominant figure in national politics that he was in the Caucus Club, "The Bunch of Grapes," or "The Green Dragon" in Boston, and there were others almost as skillful in propaganda. But if revolutions are ever the handiwork of individuals, the American Revolution can be credited to Samuel Adams; he was America's first *apparatchik*. Gage was right to seek to capture him at Lexington. Adams, for his part, was right to rejoice in escaping, "O what a glorious morning is this!"

But there were forces outside Congress. If most of them were ill-organized, there were by 1776 two formidable pressures: an army and a near-united press. Although Washington's numbers were well below his expectations when he took command at Cambridge in July 1775, it was a continental army that gathered around Boston, swollen not least by the volunteer riflemen who came pouring in from Pennsylvania, Maryland, and Virginia. They were less disciplined than the farmers of New England, and less discreet than congressional committees; they started skirmishing on their own. Although Washington deferred to Congress, the existence of an army gave him a personal sanction and drew the militants and the professionals to his side. "By referring the matter from argument to arms, a new era for politicks is struck; a new method of thinking hath arisen," said Tom Paine. In his interchanges with Gage over prisoners, Washington, the least revolutionary-minded of American leaders, found himself voicing a theory of popular sovereignty far beyond his own intentions even five months before.

By his situation, and by his own temperament, Washington found it hard to confine himself to defense; he equipped privateers to attack Britain at sea, he sponsored an invasion of Canada, and by seizing Dorchester Heights in March 1776 he compelled the British to withdraw from Boston. In August 1775 he was proclaimed a rebel. From October 1775—so he said later (August 1776)—he had favored independence. Even if this is so, he favored it reluctantly and largely as a result of the military rather than the political situation. But the instrument of coercion was now itself a force making for independence. The Continental Line was as potent a cause of the Revolution as mercantilist grievances, constitutional theory, or the arguments of the Continental Congress.

Propaganda reinforced the debates in Philadelphia and the army of farmers and frontiersmen gathering around Boston.

What declarations came from London were now seized on as fuel for the flames. In December 1775, the American Prohibitory Act had ended the trade of the colonies with Britain, made their goods subject to capture and in effect outlawed them. This was "the piratical or plundering Act." To John Adams it represented independence by the act of Britain's Parliament. He and his cousin used it skillfully. He had long taken pride in "a curious employment, cooking up paragraphs, articles, occurrences etc., working the political engine!"

It was estimated in 1765 that there were twenty-one colonial newspapers. By 1775 there were at least thirty-seven. They were far more organs of opinion than records of news; they were heavily concentrated in New England; and as each year passed they became more heavily patriot. The stamp duty and the Townshend duties on paper, in striking at the press, had antagonized the articulate classes and confirmed them in their liberal and radical leanings. The press too concentrated on constitutional issues because they were common to all the colonies. Its language even before January 1776 was apt to be personal, incendiary, and strident. This was not an objective press; comment was indubitably free, but no facts were ever quite sacred; and liberty of speech, it believed, belonged only to those who used the speech of liberty. It drove Tory editors out: John Mein left Boston in 1769, New York was too hot for Jemmy Rivington by 1775. By September 1775 scattered attacks on the King had begun in the press. In January 1776, with the publication of Tom Paine's brilliant pamphlet *Common Sense,* of which a hundred thousand copies were circulating by the spring, came the theory that was implicit in all these developments. The King, who sixteen months before had been described as the "loving father" of his people, was now "the royal brute." "The blood of the slain, the weeping voice of nature cries, 'Tis Time to Part.'" The ties of a century and a half were dissolved in a tidal wave of anti-monarchical feeling.

In this situation Parliament was not only ineffective and obstinate; now its very remoteness was crippling. "When Jove is distant, lightning is not to be feared," Chief Justice Oliver had said. There were not troops enough to curb Massachusetts, still less to curb a continent. "No Troops, no Money, no Orders or Instructions and a Wild Multitude gathering fast, what can any Man do in such a situation?" cried Sir James Wright in Georgia to Lord Dartmouth. "Not so much as a ship of war of any kind . . . these things, My Lord, are really *too much*." William Franklin echoed the despair—"We live only upon Sufferance, nor is it in our Power to mend our Situation." The home government had failed: failed to enforce its policy when agreed upon, failed to protect its officials—stamp distributors, customs collectors, tea consignees—from attack, failed to redress genuine grievances, failed to provide civil peace, failed, when it was ready to invoke the use of force, to make force available. When blows did come to decide, it was still more damned by the hiring of foreign troops—the treaties with German states were printed in the American press in January 1776—and by the absence not of Loyalist sentiment, of which there was much, but of any center around which it could rally: a coherent cause, a journal to voice it, or a leader to direct it. The Board of Associated Loyalists was no answer to the Continental Line; its president, ex-Governor Franklin, no answer to Washington; Daniel Leonard as dialectician no equal of Franklin or Adams. The emigration of the United Empire Loyalists and the story of the later settlement of New Brunswick showed that there were potential leaders here. They were inadequately mobilized in 1776 and thereafter.

What then caused the American Revolution?

By 1776 trade was not the main issue: the question had gone beyond the control of merchants. Trade grievances are mentioned only once in the Declaration of Independence.

It was not caused by taxes—which the colonists could well afford to pay and most of which were, in any case, abandoned— but by the unwillingness of a number of colonial leaders to ac-

cept the principle of taxation by Parliament for any purpose
about which they were not consulted, and by the train of events
that followed from it.

It was not caused by their lack of representation in that Parliament; very few of them seriously wanted this (Otis was one
who did, and so were Bollan and Maseres and Pownall in London) if only because it would permit taxation all too readily.
The Stamp Act Congress expressly denied that the colonists
wanted to be represented at Westminster. The suggestion was
treated facetiously by Soame Jenyns; it would be cheaper, he
said, to pay their army than their orators. And as every British
politician knew, every subject was taxed but fewer than one in
twenty was represented. There could be little sympathy at home
for this grievance, since so many at home were equally aggrieved.
An imperial Parliament representative of all the colonies has
never been a highly regarded device, either to placate America in
the 1770s or to placate Malta in the 1950s.

Nor could a solution be found in discussion of a federal system, close though some colonial pamphleteers came to suggesting a "commonwealth" pattern—Otis and Galloway among
them—and often as American historians have discussed this proposal. Hardly a voice was raised in sympathy with this view in
London. Nor could it be. Pitt and Camden conceded the right
to tax; they did not and could not concede the question of
British sovereignty. Pitt the liberal was also Pitt the Empire-
builder. Even in his proposals for reconciliation in 1775, he insisted on colonial subordination to the British Parliament and on
Parliament's unquestioned right to maintain British troops in
North America. The liberal British parliamentarians could indeed make the concession least of all: liberalism was for them
bound up with the sovereignty of King-in-Parliament. And that
sovereignty of King-in-Parliament was unitary, not federal. It
was they, far more than George III, who could not envisage a
King reigning but not ruling and who in particular could neither
envisage nor trust a King ruling in America beyond the hardly

won restraints of Westminster. It was Rockingham, a Whig, who passed the Declaratory Act; Townshend was Chancellor to no other than Chatham. Nor could a governor like Hutchinson see it; it was impossible, he thought, for two independent legislatures to exist in one and the same state. So long as he was a real force in government, the King could not be the symbol of a wider commonwealth. It is now clear to us that there is no solution to the problem of imperial control short of complete self-government. But we are accustomed to sovereigns who reign but do not rule. This was not yet so in the 1770s. Moreover, the American Revolution was the first break of the sort; federalism was unfamiliar; philosophies of state were monolithic. To attribute the disaster of 1776 to the lack of a Lord Durham is to misread the temper and the history of the times.

Again, the Revolution was not primarily caused by Britain's western policy. Here as elsewhere she was vacillating and contradictory; but here as elsewhere her policy had rarely been enforced. Dunmore did not think it could be. "I have learnt from experience," he wrote to Dartmouth, "that the established authority of any government in America and the policy at home are both insufficient to restrain the Americans, and they do and will remove as their avidity and restlessness incite them. They acquire no attachment to place, but wandering about seems engrafted in their nature." At least thirty thousand settlers moved west in the five years after 1763, despite the Proclamation Line. Only once—at Redstone in 1766—did Gage destroy a settlement made across the Line. In successive Treaties—Fort Stanwix with the Iroquois and Hard Labor and Lochaber with the Cherokees—the line was pushed back. In 1767 Washington told William Crawford, his agent on the Youghiogheny, that he had never seen the Proclamation of 1763 as anything but "a temporary expedient to quiet the minds of the Indians" and encouraged him to continue his land deals with "silent management." The actual settlers were hardly at all affected by British enactments. But there was resentment—in the Tidewater, not the Piedmont; in

Philadelphia and in Williamsburg more than in the Alleghenies. In the years from 1766 to 1774 Wharton Baynton Morgan and Company, along with the Ohio Company of Virginia, eagerly awaited news of the approval of the Vandalia project, itself the size of a country, and meanwhile, in anticipation, were buying up land from the Indians. The news never came through, but the Indians lost their lands. In 1774 it was a colonial governor, Dunmore, who was fighting the Shawnees in the Kanawha country, in flat disagreement with instructions from home—indeed, claiming that he did not even know of the Proclamation of 1763.

There was, however, much irritation because of British vacillation, some resentment in Pennsylvania, some dislike of bureaucratic interference and the cancellation of land patents. The price of government land was raised in 1774. Quitrents on land sold were doubled. All new grants of land were to be surveyed first; the small purchaser was to be protected against the speculator. But there was little general excitement on this topic, and few entrepreneurs in the West were seriously impeded from acquiring land. If Morgan was a revolutionary, Wharton stayed Loyalist. Of the Quebec Act, the religious provisions were as alarming to Tidewater Virginia as the new boundary. It was the arbitrary government of Quebec as much as its enlarged boundaries that called forth Jefferson's criticism in the Declaration of Independence.

Further, the American Revolution was not the result of a national movement in the colonies, skillful though the propagandists were, prompt though the colonial extra-legal conventions were to act, all but unanimous as were the newspaper editors. For there was as yet no nation. The debates of the second Continental Congress are as full of the danger of division and secession as of the appeal of independence.

A revolution is due primarily not to "causes" but to the failure of a government to govern. This was abundantly so in 1776. The American Revolution was the product of executive weakness, not tyranny; of parliamentary, not royal, vacillation; and of chronic irresolution before pressure groups, both at home and in the colonies. It was the product also of mounting and mutual anger and bitterness; a situation had been permitted to develop from which there was no escape except by force.

That this situation had arisen was due to the actions of men, or their failure to act. There were not many of them, and they were often the reverse of heroic. Smuggling merchants like Cabot, Brown, and Hancock became embittered. Demagogues like Patrick Henry and Samuel Adams sought—not always successfully—fame and power. In the two key states, Virginia and Massachusetts, politics was as faction-ridden as in Britain; the Randolph–Robinson interest in the one and the Caucus Club in the other ran political affairs and were as concerned with place and patronage—in Virginia—and as unprincipled in opposition—in Massachusetts—as any Henry Fox or Duke of Newcastle.

Men of principle who were genuinely concerned over issues—like Galloway, Dickinson, and Dulany—found that they had unleashed a force they were not always capable of controlling. Few of them were among the men who finally led the revolution to victory; hardly one became a front-rank executive later. Given British intransigence after 1774, however, it was these men of ideas and ideals who came to give direction and to provide momentum to the colonial movement in the two decisive years 1774–1776. Under the direction of two masters in propaganda, Sam Adams and Tom Paine, a unified mood of political and social protest was building up. Each stage transformed it still further, each issue now widened the gap still more. But the movement and the momentum were not in the climate and the geography, the racial admixtures, the political differences, the distance that divided the Old World and the New. These were the raw mate rial of discord, but they were played on by interested men. There was no inevitability here, no predestination. Revolutions, like other human phenomena, are caused by decisions taken—or not taken—by individuals. By 1775 the decisions had been taken in London. By 1776 they were also taken in the colonies, and by only a few men in both cases. The American leaders can be called heroes; they were also, and no less, traitors to their King. "If it succeeds, none need call it treason."

That it did succeed in the end was hardly at all their doing. The tiger they unleashed was ridden to victory by steadier and saner men, neither ideologues nor idealists—not always even liberals. And the conservatives, Washington and Hamilton, John Adams and John Jay, who achieved this victory were themselves helped by the continuing intransigence, the faction-ridden counsels, the continuing executive weakness of London. The "situation" that had arisen had ceased to be resolvable except by war. *Silent leges inter arma.*

5

Revolution: Winning the War
1776–1783

ABOUT THE WAR, as about its causes, there has grown in the textbooks a rich mythology. According to this, it was gravely mishandled in London by corrupt ministers—by a cowardly Germain, who succeeded Dartmouth in 1775 as Secretary for the Colonies, a dissolute Sandwich at the Admiralty, and an inefficient Barrington as Secretary-at-War. From London they dictated plans and imposed strategy on their commanders in the field, in complete ignorance of American conditions. In particular their confusions wrecked the Saratoga campaign. The commanders on the spot were in any case complacent and casual men, products of a system in which nepotism and wealth were the sole methods of promotion. There was overmuch reliance on mercenaries and on Loyalists. Without these errors of commission, the vast British military machine would have ground the colonists into submission. In the light of their failures, however, it became possible for the small and ragged armies of colonials, held together only by a devotion to liberty and assisted after 1778 by France, to win through to victory. In fact, not one of these beliefs has any validity.

Historians are at the mercy of their sources; the sources of information on the American War of Independence are lavish but unbalanced. There are very many more American journals and letters than British; they are mainly from officers; they are reinforced by the spate of pamphlet literature justifying the war and by the flood of material after 1783 that glorified it. Naturally they stress the Spirit of '76. Of the slighter British material there is more from senior officers than from junior or non-commissioned officers, and most of it has only become available recently. Clinton remained a dim figure until Professor Willcox published his *Narrative* in 1954; it was not until Robert Bass attempted his study of Tarleton (*The Green Dragoon*) that the Tarleton papers were found—they had been missing since 1833; the 107 volumes of the Carleton papers were graciously presented to Her Majesty the Queen in 1957 by Colonial Williamsburg and are now in the London Public Record Office, as yet largely unexplored.

British commanders in the eighteenth century were almost as addicted to print as those in the twentieth, and in their agonizing reappraisals after defeat they devoted themselves to self-exculpation. Howe published his defense in a *Narrative* in 1780; Cornwallis in 1783 replied to the charges Clinton had made against him in 1781; Burgoyne criticized Gage as soon as he reached America. There were and are available also many letters and accounts by politicians; the effect has been to concentrate attention on the political failure of London, the jealousies between civilians and soldiers, or the military errors and conflicts of the general officers. Hence the belief that the war was planned—and lost—in London, when in fact both Howe and Clinton complained precisely of the little direction and attention they had from London. Too little is known of how the British junior officer and the (largely illiterate) other ranks fared and fought—Sergeant Lamb of the Royal Welch Fusiliers is an almost unique figure; only recently with Dr. Uhlandorf's edition of the Baurmeister manuscripts have we a clear picture of one of the Hessian units; the Loyalists remain in history as in life an enigma. As a result, while the events of the war are clear enough

and show all too well how the British lost and how the Americans won, the reasons for the failure and in some measure the
reasons for the success remain elusive.

Certainly, Britain appeared in 1776 to have immense advantages. She had infinitely greater resources than the thirteen colonies; in manpower she outnumbered them at least four to one,
and in ships of war a hundred to one. Even after the entry of
France into the war in 1778, Washington noted that "the maritime resources of Britain are more substantial and real than those
of France and Spain united . . . in modern wars the longest
purse must chiefly determine the event." Control of the seas
gave Britain the chance to concentrate at points of her own
choosing. When Howe, who had replaced Gage in command,
evacuated Boston, Washington could not be sure that he was
bound for Halifax. When he sailed south in 1777, Washington
thought his destination Wilmington, then Charleston, and moving in step with him was "compel'd to wander about the country
like the Arabs in search of corn." Britain patently was richer and
had a better credit, she could afford to hire foreign troops, she
had a professional army and navy, and her younger officers had
overweening confidence. Lord Rawdon (the later Marquess of
Hastings), writing from Boston in January 1776, did not believe
that the Americans could survive the year if the British were
given "the necessary means of carrying on the war with vigour."
But Bute's son, Major Charles Stuart, serving with the 37th
Regiment, foresaw, as did Burgoyne, a "most bloody civil war."

The early victories of British troops in the field suggest that
there was little wrong with their fighting spirit, and that no
sharp distinction can be drawn between American and British
other ranks. There was perhaps a greater "ardor" for battle
among some Americans, but there was less discipline; Morgan's
riflemen may have had a spirit and marksmanship of their own,
but even this was eroded at Valley Forge; even Morgan—and
Schuyler, Sullivan, and Hamilton—resigned before the war was
clearly won. It is difficult to criticize the British soldier. Clearly

his morale suffered from Howe's caution, from the lack of activity, and, as time passed, from the mounting sense of failure, but at Bunker Hill, in New York and Philadelphia the redcoat moved and carried out orders with a drill-yard precision. That he was, as in Wellington's day, "the scum of the earth, recruited for pay," drawn from jails (three whole regiments in 1776 consisted of reprieved criminals) and press-ganged out of taverns, does not seem to have weakened his quality.

Despite appearances, Britain had not enough troops. The numbers in the Army had been allowed to run down after 1761. It was only in August 1775 that the establishment was increased from thirty-three thousand to fifty-five thousand men—and they had still to be found. The Navy in peacetime had only one fifth the numbers it needed in war. "A man who went to sea for pleasure," wrote a contemporary, "would be likely to go to hell for a pastime." When war came, foreigners were recruited for both services by every device, legitimate or otherwise. The recruiting campaign of 1778, which made all "idle and able-bodied" men between seventeen and forty-five liable for service—in 1779 it became sixteen to fifty—was ineffective; the majority of British volunteers were in fact Irish or Scots. But they too have never been noticeably distinguished by a lack of fighting spirit. The war was not lost by the British other ranks. Nor, hard though it was to recruit them, were their numbers in the end particularly small. Howe had some thirty-four thousand men when he finally landed them at New York. There were still thirty-four thousand available in 1781. For an eighteenth-century colonial war these figures were high—higher and better disciplined than ever before, and far superior to the numbers opposed to them. They were still not enough to conquer a continent.

But from the beginning it was clear that there were worried and divided counsels among the senior British officers. These were far more in evidence in America than in London; and there was far more anxiety than complacency. Some distinguished officers—like Amherst, the leading general of the day, and Lord

Cavendish—refused to serve in America. Howe himself hesitated. So did Admiral Keppel, a follower of Rockingham, until the war became a war with France. The Earl of Effingham resigned his commission. "This is an unpopular war," Colonel Mackenzie noted, "and men of ability do not chuse to risk their reputation by taking an active part in it."

Gage had from the outset urged the immediate need for numbers and for decision. He had not got them. Neither had Admiral Graves, who had twenty-seven vessels, of which only three were ships of the line. As a result they were inactive. Alone among the experts, Gage had always urged that the American goal was independence and that the colonials were not the despicable rabble they were too often held to be. He urged the use of foreign troops and of Negroes if necessary, but his advice was not heeded. Nor were his tactics culpable. He made only two tactical errors, the abandonment of Charlestown Neck and the failure to fortify Dorchester Heights. The various route marches into the countryside, though they alarmed the people of Massachusetts, were designed to relieve the boredom of his near-besieged troops and perhaps to allow the march on Concord to be carried through more smoothly than in fact it was. The costly frontal assault on Breed's and Bunker's hills was designed as a display of British strength, carried out in all too orthodox a fashion. It reflected a sense of superiority that was to bedevil the next, as it had bedeviled the last, eight years.

In September 1775 Gage was replaced by William Howe, who had arrived as one of a strange triumvirate—

> Behold the *Cerberus* the Atlantic plough,
> Her precious cargo, Burgoyne, Clinton, Howe.
> Bow, wow, wow!

Within three months Charles Stuart was hoping that more worthy generals would be sent from home, for these were "a pack of the most ordinary men . . . who give themselves trouble

about the merest trifles whilst things of consequence go unregarded." But Howe, ultracautious though he was, was slow
to a purpose. He had taken command only on the assurance
from the King, to whom he was related, that he could carry an
olive branch as well as a sword. Drawing on the repute won by
his brother at Ticonderoga, he believed that he might bring the
colonies to terms after a decisive defeat in battle. He had in fact
the same sort of faith that Washington had, the belief that the
threat of war would bring the enemy to a negotiated peace.
Howe and Clinton, moreover—almost as much as Washington—
sought to avoid battle wherever possible and trusted, in good
European fashion, to a war of posts and maneuver. But the situation was very different for Britain: time and terrain were on
Washington's side. What Howe meant by negotiation was in
fact American surrender.

This procrastination weakened the morale of the British
officers and men, who in the early days were spoiling for a fight
and expected easy and quick success, not least as it became clear
that tactically Howe was Washington's superior, as he showed
at Brooklyn and at Brandywine. Although the Americans knew
the country, Howe did also, for he had commanded light infantry under Wolfe; against him, they were repeatedly and easily
outflanked and outmaneuvered. But after each tactical triumph
Howe delayed, hoping for negotiation to follow. This hope was
furthered by the curious relations of Charles Lee and Gates—
both formerly British regulars—with their former comrades.
After his capture in the Jerseys in 1776 Lee was as ready to advise
the British on how to defeat Washington as formerly he had
been to do the reverse. He certainly gave Howe a vivid picture of
a Philadelphia that only awaited his coming to demonstrate its
loyalism.

By 1778 this policy of "ca' canny" was unsuccessful and unpopular. Colonel Frederick Mackenzie recorded in his diary in
September that "the mistaken levity of Government has pro-
longed the war." The same officer had argued at New York two

years before that if Howe had treated the garrison at Fort Washington with severity "it would have struck such a panic through the continent as would have prevented the Congress from ever being able to raise another Army." At the beginning of the war, Carleton had acted with similar misguided magnanimity. He allowed the forces retreating from Quebec to escape, for "the way to mercy is not yet shut." This quasiregal role, less that of soldiers than of commissioners ready to pardon offenders, was a source of military weakness. It permitted the American forces to survive when they could have been destroyed; they began to acquire, said Charles Stuart, "the notion of victory." It discouraged loyalism from rearing its head, as it well might have done in New York and Pennsylvania. It failed to impress neutral opinion as anything but incompetence; and the King rightly thought the policy futile from the first—"When once those rebels have felt a smart blow, they will submit." The smart blow never came. And tempers mounted. By 1778 Mackenzie wanted Philadelphia burned to the ground; by 1781 he thought a policy of deliberate harshness was needed. It was certainly an error in tactics to permit generals to be diplomats and to allow them to decide which role to play, and when. In the words of Sir John Fortescue, war cannot be waged on the principles of peace.

Understandable though his motives might be, Howe's caution and the concern for his troops, which allowed no repetition of Bunker Hill, destroyed the morale of his men. Like McClellan eighty years later, he was a popular figure among them, but not a driver. And in 1777 he gravely misjudged the situation. Advised to give support to Burgoyne in his drive south from Quebec, he misread the signs; he thought he could take Philadelphia, which he believed to be Loyalist at heart, while Burgoyne was moving south, and thus his success at Brandywine and Germantown and his high festivities in Philadelphia were offset by Saratoga, the first major disaster to British arms since Braddock's defeat at Duquesne in 1755 and diplomatically a decisive stage in the war. The fault here was Howe's far more than

Germain's; he prepared three distinct and different plans for 1777, and, given the distance and the divided command among Carleton, Burgoyne, and himself, there could be no direction from London. It was General Howe, not Germain or the Admiral, who chose the Chesapeake instead of the Delaware: he gained twenty miles but lost a precious month in which the fortunes of war turned against Britain.

To dejection and despair, disgrace had now to be added; the British army in America never recovered from this lack of confidence in its leaders, from the general disgust at mismanagement, and from the sense that the war was coming to be a story of inactivity offset only by disaster. Desertion and discontent increased; there were a number of suicides; security and intelligence were poor. As Trenton and Bunker Hill showed, the effort to appear overwhelmingly superior became indistinguishable from carelessness in the one engagement and wastefulness in the other. Captain James Murray, serving with the 57th Regiment in the Jerseys and Philadelphia, sought only to get away from "a barbarous business and in a barbarous country." And in this "disgraceful situation" it was natural and indeed correct to put the blame on the commander, for on a military commander is visited responsibility alike for success and failure. Howe was suspected of more than laziness and caution. As a junior colleague, Major Wemyss, put it with a junior colleague's discretion, he was "addicted to private conviviality." As an enemy versifier put it,

> Awake, awake, Sir Billy, There's forage on the plain,
> Ah! leave your little filly, And open the Campaign.
> Heed not a woman's prattle, Which tickles in the ear,
> But give the word for battle, And grasp the warlike spear.

There was some substance in the charge. When Captain Hammond went aboard his flagship for the crucial discussion on the Chesapeake–Delaware question, he found him still abed— whether alone or not he does not say—at ten in the morning.

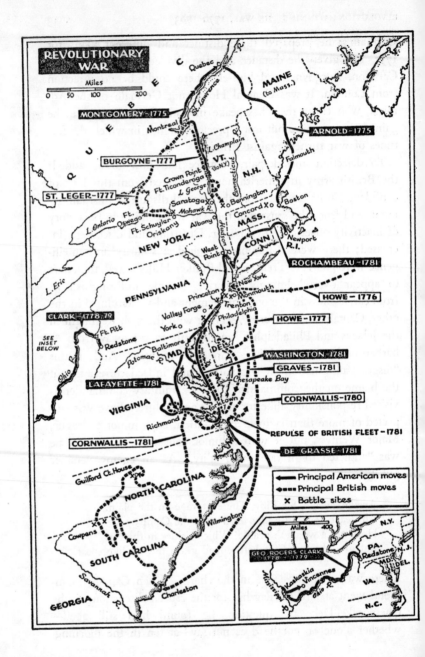

One cynical view of him at home was that he should be raised to the peerage as Baron "Delay Warr."

The best verdict on Howe is that of Colonel Allan Maclean He thought him

> a very honest man, and . . . a very disinterested one. Brave he certainly is and would make a very good executive officer under another's command, but he is not by any means equal to a C. in C. . . . He has moreover got none but very silly fellows about him—a great parcel of old women—most of them improper for American service. . . . Men of real genius cannot long agree with Howe; he is too dull to encourage great military merit—our great men at home seem to be as little anxious about encouraging true military abilities as our Commanders here. . . . Had we a man of real capacity as the head of the Army, the rebellion would have been at an end.

The extent to which Howe allowed diplomacy and politics to affect his role as commander, and how well he knew the working of a politician's mind, is attested in his own account in his *Narrative* of his views on Saratoga:

> I shall not be thought to speak absurdly if I say that had I adopted the plan of going up Hudson's River, it would have been alleged that I had wasted the campaign with a considerable army under my command, merely to ensure the progress of the northern army, which could have taken care of itself, provided I had made a diversion in its favour, by drawing off to the Southward the main army under General Washington. Would not my enemies have gone further, and insinuated, that alarmed at the rapid success which the honourable General had a right to expect when Ticonderoga fell, I had enviously grasped a share of that merit which would otherwise have been all his own? and let me add, would not Ministers have told you, as they truly might, that I had acted without any orders or instructions from them, that General Burgoyne was directed to force his own way to Albany, and that they had put under his command troops sufficient to effect this march? Would they not have referred you to the original and settled plan of that expedition . . . to prove that no assistance from me was suggested? and would they not readily have impressed this house

with the conclusion that if any doubt could have arisen in their minds of the success of such a well digested plan, they should from the beginning have made me a party to it, and have given me explicit instructions to act accordingly?

Howe's successors were as unfortunate and as hesitant as himself. Clinton was equally dilatory, alternating between timidity and overconfidence. Prompt to give advice to others, he was slow to take it himself; Charles Stuart thought him unfit to command even a troop of horse. His vacillations contributed to Burgoyne's surrender at Saratoga; aware of Burgoyne's position and of Howe's plans, he sent Vaughan to Kingston but retired with his own force from Fort Montgomery to New York. His hesitation equally contributed to Cornwallis' surrender at Yorktown. "In his later campaigns," says Professor Willcox, "he became so addicted to the bread of carefulness that he lost what taste he had ever had for audacity. . . . He was utterly self-centered, but the center was out of focus; he never attained the integrated, ruthless egoism that often makes a general great."

Burgoyne by contrast did not know the meaning of diffidence, and no one could question his courage or his generosity. Of all these figures, Gentleman Johnny is in fact the easiest to criticize but the hardest to know. Himself playwright, parliamentarian, man about town; vain, romantic, and in all he did the *cabotin,* he has not been helped by his biographers, and he has been permanently damned by the *Memoirs* of the Baroness von Riedesel, wife of the commander of the Brunswick troops with him. Her picture of the dwindling, straggling, hungry but still-disciplined army and of its commander is brilliant and hostile. His nights were spent singing and drinking "and amusing himself with the wife of a commissary, who was his mistress, and who as well as he, loved champagne." His difficulties and limitations are well recorded by her. His major error was no doubt the size of his baggage train; but for his own reputation the error was to include in it the good baroness—and some two thousand other women. Burgoyne's other main affliction was the rhodomontade of his style; Horace Walpole calls him General Hurlothrombo and General Swagger. When he put pen to paper, which even for a general he did frequently, he rarely did himself justice. He was treated with marked injustice by Germain and the Court on his return, and denied the court-martial he requested.

Cornwallis was decisive enough, but could be both reckless— as in the invasion of North Carolina and then of Virginia against orders—and ruthless. He was at fault in not attacking Lafayette before Yorktown and in deciding not to withdraw into South Carolina. Only Carleton showed both dignity and skill. He kept Canada loyal during the invasion of 1775–76; he came to command in America far too late; although his manner was reserved and cold, he alone of the British commanders condemned the plundering raids of Indians, Tories, and regulars.

Of the British tactical commanders, there were two, however, who were both clever and positive, now deeply buried though they are in the seventh circle of execration in America: Arnold and Tarleton. Benedict Arnold's advice, had it been heeded, might have led to the French army being defeated before it was reinforced or entrenched. In 1781 he was as vigorous in Virginia fighting for Britain as he had been in 1776 and 1777 fighting against her. Banastre Tarleton's reputation has suffered from his later adventures. Whatever his relationship with Mary (Perdita) Robinson, who helped him write his book on the war as well as his parliamentary speeches, and whom, true to his lights, he deserted, Tarleton showed an energy and capacity all too rare among British commanders. To Rochambeau, however, as to all Americans, he was "a butcher and a barbarian."

There is little evidence that these men were complacent, though much to suggest that most of them were worried, hesitant, and indecisive. There is equally little evidence that any of them were the puppets of a wicked Colonial Secretary, prompt though they were to blame him, or anybody else, once they needed a scapegoat. Before he took office Germain appreciated, as he told Suffolk, that "the distance from the seat of government necessarily leaves much to the discretion and resources of the General." He gave wide latitude to all his commanders, particularly to Howe, whose experience in light infantry he esteemed highly. Howe had for two years complete discretionary power to act as he thought fit. He had no instructions to help Burgoyne in the Saratoga expedition, but he did not require them; most of his subordinate commanders, however, thought that he ought to have gone to his aid. His plans for Philadelphia had already been made, and it seemed quite possible that he would be able to come in at the kill. Before he left New York in July 1777, Howe was informed by Burgoyne that his army was before Ticonderoga and in good spirits. There seemed no cause for alarm even in early September. And until the news of the disaster reached London, the expectation was of a great and glorious victory. When Howe's conduct was examined by the Committee of Inquiry, it was clear that Germain had carefully refrained from giving any fettering instructions. Nor was Saratoga "planned" in London. The notion of a campaign to isolate New England from the other colonies was common talk in these years and fully foreseen by Washington; it had taken shape in a request from Carleton in 1775. It was developed by Burgoyne in London in his "Thoughts for Conducting the War from the side of Canada," and because of Germain's dislike of Carleton it was left to Burgoyne to carry out.

In any war politicians are easier sport than generals. With his reputation already tarnished as a result of Minden, Germain was all too vulnerable to attack, and the Whigs took full advantage. The criticism of North and of Germain was endless. As North said himself, "on military matters I speak ignorantly, and therefore without effect." Germain can be faulted only for failure and for being oversanguine; he was arrogant and unpopular but not inefficient. The failure, as so often, was less in the Colonial Office —or the War Office—than in the field. All the general officers insisted on having "latitude" and "discretion"; only Carleton used them with any success.

There was, however, a lamentable failure of coordination in London; the lack of prime minister and of energy in government was all too evident. "I never have interfered in any of their Departments," said North of his colleagues; what he said in self-defense can be seen now as one of the causes of the disaster. Even sea transport was handled by three different boards: the Board of Ordnance for artillery and engineers, the Navy Board for cavalry, infantry, clothing, and hospital stores, the Treasury for provisions. What was needed—as was provided in 1757 and in 1940—was more, not less, direction and energy from the center, and greater wisdom—or luck?—in the selection of generals. The Revolution was caused by political failures in London, seized on by colonial leaders. The war was lost by the lack of energy at the center and among military commanders on the spot. Of these, Howe's failure was cardinal, for it was in the early months, particularly when Washington was driven across the Jerseys, that the dwindling American army could have been destroyed. By 1778 British morale was low, and France came into the war.

Equally, much of the criticism that has been leveled at Lord Sandwich for Britain's unpreparedness at sea has been misplaced. Here again the man's public name has been attacked because of his private reputation. His profligate ways and his activities at Medmenham were notorious; the madness of his wife and the spendthrift habits of his son that may have driven him to this curious refuge were not. His immorality was attacked by very competent judges, his ex-friends Wilkes and Charles Churchill— "Too infamous to have a friend. Too bad for bad men to commend." But these things are irrelevant to his role as First Lord of the Admiralty. For here Sandwich was industrious, talented, and dedicated. He had good administrators under him, such as Lord Mulgrave. And his work was praised by one not ostentatious in giving tributes, Horace Walpole. It was North from 1772 to 1774 who pushed through, against Sandwich's vehement opposition, the decommissioning of ships and the cuts in the number of naval recruits, a policy of economy and would-be conciliation that left Britain sadly crippled in 1775. The bills came in later too; in the years from 1775 to 1783 seventy-six ships were lost by accidents that were the result of inadequate fittings and poor materials. A bare two months before France entered the war, Sandwich stressed to North that Britain had only forty-two ships of the line and that a war on two fronts would be impossible to win. Once again, the hesitation here was that of North, not of Sandwich.

And there was, in the decisive first two years, a serious division of opinion in the ministry on the broad strategy of the war. Sandwich and Barrington agreed that France was potentially far more dangerous than the colonists. From this Sandwich concluded that troops should go to America but that the Navy should be kept in home or in European waters. If ships had to go, they must be replaced; this was a costly and therefore an unpopular argument. Barrington, equally logically, argued that it would be very dangerous to denude Britain of her troops; he wanted the troops in Massachusetts in 1775 withdrawn to Canada and the Floridas and a tight naval blockade established. Far earlier than most of his colleagues he recognized the vast problems involved in the conquest of a continent. He was supported by Amherst and by General Harvey, the Adjutant-General, who thought the attempt at the conquest of America by an army "as wild an idea as ever controverted common sense." The colonial governors, on the other hand, held out rosy hopes of Loyalist risings if only British troops showed the flag.

From this division of purpose much followed. Generals such as Burgoyne blamed admirals such as Graves. Barrington's gloom—all too prescient—grew with the years, and its very prescience made him unpopular and ineffective with his colleagues; he was not in any case a member of the Cabinet. Sandwich responded like a weathercock to every report of aid to the colonies from

France, but to his pleas to keep pace with France in ships the King and North replied by pleading either economy or the unwisdom of antagonizing France. Germain became a bitter critic and in the end, an open enemy of Sandwich because of the serious lack of naval force in American waters; gradually other issues arose to worsen relations between them, among them the selection of naval commanders and the use of privateers. Until Rodney appeared in West Indian waters hardly a single naval commander was decisive or even talented. Rodney, visiting North America in 1780, noted the general "slackness." And there were too few ships and too few men in them. The pre-1775 pattern persisted: not of tyranny, efficiency, and autocracy, but of vacillation and divided counsels at the center and timidity on the spot.

Whatever these handicaps, there were in any event overwhelming, and perhaps insuperable, obstacles in the way of British success. In this Barrington, like Gage before him, was quite correct. The country to be subdued was continental in scale, thickly wooded, hot and insect-ridden, with many rivers and few bridges, with many ravines and few adequate roads. The South was dotted with creeks and swamps, and its coast with sandbars. As Major-General Grey told the House of Commons, "That part of America where I have been is the strangest country I ever was in; it is everywhere hilly, and covered with wood, intersected by ravines, creeks and marshy grounds, and in every quarter of a mile is a post fitted for ambuscades. Little or no knowledge could be obtained by reconnoitring, every hundred yards might be disputed." Howe thought that almost every movement of war in North America "was an act of enterprize, clogged with innumerable difficulties." The soldiers with Burgoyne gave a more accurate view of his difficulties than Baroness Riedesel; the country was "peculiarly unfavourable" for military operations, said Lieutenant Anburey. Of the country round Ticonderoga, Ensign Hughes wrote that "the mountains were so steep we

were obliged to pull ourselves up, and let ourselves down, by
the branches of trees."

These conditions dictated a revolution in tactics and particularly in the use of light infantry. This was fully appreciated by
Germain—"the manner of opposing an enemy that avoids facing
you in the open field is totally different from what young officers
learn from the common discipline of the army." It could only be
learned by experience, and in fact it was learned very slowly. A
number of grenadier companies were formed into a Battalion of
Grenadiers, and a number of light companies into the 1st
Battalion Light Infantry at Halifax in 1776, but many more were
needed. The traditional formations were hard to dissolve.

All the British commanders were clearly happier in close-order
battles, however expensive in lives, in maneuvering men in the
open, or in sieges, had there been enough towns to take, than in
the guerrilla warfare and the use of cover and of wooded country
to which Americans were accustomed. "Our European discipline
is of little avail in the woods," wrote Anburey. Cavalry was of
very small use. "Never had the British Army so ungenerous an
enemy to oppose; they send their riflemen five or six at a time
who conceal themselves behind trees etc., till an opportunity presents itself of taking a shot at our advance sentries, which done
they immediately retreat. What an unfair method," wrote William Carter, "of carrying on a war!" Sergeant Lamb noted at
Saratoga how serious was the lack of men to oppose the American rifle corps. It was this in part that led to the use of Indians,
and to the improvising of light infantry units—sometimes at the
expense of the rest of the regiment, as at Cowpens. The tactics
were determined by the terrain, not by the rulebook of the open
battles of Europe. Wars here could not be won by concerted
volleys, though some battles might. Daniel Morgan's riflemen
with their deadly marksmanship were the most successful units
to appear; it was not until later on in the war that a similar corps
of riflemen was organized in the British Army. Only Simcoe of

the Queen's Rangers, Robert Rogers, and Patrick Ferguson saw this need for new formations and for new tactics.

The Pennsylvania Dutch craftsmen and the sharpshooters from Virginia, Pennsylvania, and Kentucky produced a more effective instrument than Brown Bess. Shirts and leggings were equally a more suitable uniform than the red coat and stock, the gaiters and cocked hat born of the parade ground and of a more ceremonious warfare—"all peace parade and St. James's Park," as Burgoyne once described it. Each of Burgoyne's soldiers carried a knapsack, a blanket, a haversack, a canteen for water, a hatchet, a musket, and sixty rounds of ammunition—the whole weighing some sixty pounds. His most effective weapon was the bayonet, but he was given few opportunities to use it. Riedesel's Brunswick dragoons wore jackboots, leather breeches, and stiff gauntlets and carried a broadsword that weighed twelve pounds, a heavy carbine, and a quantity of flour for baking bread. "Their very hats and swords," says Stedman, the contemporary British historian, "weighed very nearly as much as the whole equipment of one of our soldiers."

The British won very many of the pitched battles of the war. After ten years' service in America (1773-83) the Royal Welch Fusiliers had been defeated only once—at Yorktown itself. Where these battles were ordered affairs the British won easily, on copybook lines: Bunker Hill, Brooklyn Heights, Brandywine, Camden, Guilford Court House. But they were expensive victories: 68 were killed and 180 wounded at Lexington; two fifths of the force at Bunker Hill and one third of the force engaged at Guilford were lost. And the surrenders were disastrous. At Saratoga five thousand men and at Yorktown seven thousand stacked their arms. But, despite the cost, there were not enough battles to end the war; the enemy disappeared, the conquest of territory and towns—New York, Philadelphia, Charleston— brought no advantage. Washington could speak of withdrawing intact if necessary across the Alleghenies. In the end, unless the British numbers were unlimited, the supplies constant, the lines of communication unbroken, it was the land—with its vast forests, its wide creeks, and its untenable mountains—that would win. For the scale of the operation, neither the numbers nor the supplies were sufficient; although, used decisively, they could have been overwhelming in the first two years. By 1776 Howe was requesting fifteen thousand reinforcements; he got less than one fifth of what he asked. By 1781 Britain had still only thirty-four thousand men in North America, and these were widely dispersed and tied to their ships and supplies like dogs on leashes. What was particularly striking was the loss of Germans—largely by desertion—and the failure to recruit Loyalists in the expected numbers. Only nine hundred Loyalists joined Howe in Philadelphia—"after the most indefatigable exertions during eight months," as he put it. By 1778, as he recognized, the rebellion, which twelve months before was "really a contemptuous Pygmy," was now a giant, "more dreadful to the minds of man, than *Polyphemus* of old."

After Saratoga, Amherst considered that victory in America would demand an army of forty thousand, and since this was impossible recommended a naval war only. Once France was in the war, Clinton was ordered to send five thousand men to the West Indies and three thousand to St. Augustine and West Florida; Philadelphia would have to be evacuated and the Carlisle Commission would seek peace; if this failed, New York would in turn be evacuated. Some at least of the rebellious provinces were to be abandoned. By 1778, the real enemy was France, and there was now less hope than ever of reinforcements, of major victories in battle, or of winning over doubting Thomases. By the Franco-American treaty of February 1778, what had started as a colonial rebellion had become an international conflict.

The conquest of a continent posed acute problems of supply and communication. In the winter of 1775-76, of forty transports from home only eight reached Boston, and after 1778 the supply lines were still more hazardous. Since the continent was in arms, supplies had to be ferried from home; they had to wait for convoys; more than a third extra had to be ordered to offset losses to privateers or looting by corrupt contractors. This uncertainty and delay interfered with all campaigns. Gage complained in 1775 that his difficulty in moving out of Boston was not the enemy but "no rivers for the transportation of supplys and hand carriages are not to be procured." Howe complained at greater length to General Harvey in the same year—"No Survey of the adjacent country, no proper boats for landing troops—not a sufficient number of Horses for the Artillery, nor for Regimental baggage. No Forage. . . . No Waggons. . . . Very few or no Spies. We are therefore Entirely Ignorant of what they are about in the Neighbourhood." Howe repeated the complaint in 1776, Burgoyne in 1777. "Our long stay at Skenesborough to make a bad road scarcely passable, fit for carts etc. and in procuring a sufficient quantity of carriages etc. . . . was a primary cause of the miscarriage of Burgoyne's expedition," said Ensign Hughes. The British could never safely move far from the sea or from their river supply lines. They were never able to hold any important inland areas for long. Howe made his movement to Philadelphia by sea, and it was painfully slow. Cornwallis was forced to retreat in North Carolina when he failed to get supplies up the Cape Fear River. When Cornwallis' army attempted to discard its baggage in North Carolina, it was reduced to an equally desperate state: the lack of rum was found particularly distressing.

And through all the campaigns local people moved, now as friends, now as enemies, learning all that was planned, carrying rifles in their hands but with General Howe's certificate of loyalty, for insurance' sake, in their pockets. The sharpest reflection on the weakness of loyalism is the inadequacy of British security and intelligence—in Boston, at Sullivan's Island, and in the Hudson Valley. And whenever the colonial forces showed any prospect of victory, local militia were prompt to join them, as the growth of Gates' numbers and the guerrilla activities of

Marion, Sumter, and Pickens in the wake of Cornwallis reveal.

The British need for supplies and support nevertheless made the aid of Loyalists vital. At New York and Philadelphia they eased the burden greatly. But they responded only slightly elsewhere. John Adams' famous assessment that one third of the Americans were Loyalist, one third patriot, and one third neutral appears an overdecisive judgment on the ways of men. And there is some doubt whether he meant this to apply to the American Revolution or to American attitudes to the French Revolution. The great majority in each colony were trimmers who went with the tide; and certainly far less than one third of the colonists were ready to declare themselves Loyalist until it was clearly wise to do so. By 1781, outside New York many more than one third were patriots; anyone still neutral by that time was likely to be mistaken for a Loyalist. Equally, however, the expectation that many Loyalists awaited the British led to a dispersal of forces, especially by 1780 in the South. It was, said Mackenzie, "a capital error." The British appeared, Loyalists were called on, and then the British marched away, leaving their friends to the mercy of revolutionary committees. It was an error that was cultivated by Loyalists in exile, who inflated the numbers—no doubt in all innocence. Perhaps as many as thirty thousand Loyalists fought with the British, and some eighty thousand went into exile. But all figures for them are debatable.* In New York, in the Tory Rangers and the Royal Greens and in the South in Tarleton's Legion and Rawdon's Volunteers, they fought with bitterness and indeed with savagery; they had much to lose. But their numbers were never so great as was expected; they were untrained and they were sadly ill organized; and where they were present, as in the Mohawk, Wyoming, or

* Professor Van Tyne in his *Loyalists in the American Revolution* (1902) said fifty thousand took up arms for Britain, a very high estimate. Sabine, writing a generation earlier, put it at twenty-five thousand. Germain constantly exaggerated their number, probably equally in innocence. On September 1, 1781, Sir Henry Clinton's figure is only fifty-four hundred Loyalists in service (RHMC, Stopford-Sackville MSS II, 211–212).

Cherry valleys or at King's Mountain and Hanging Rock, the conflict had indeed the ruthlessness associated with a brothers' war.

To this chronicle of misfortune, one further point has to be added: the use of Hessians and Indians. The employment of mercenaries, though habitual by Britain and other powers in the eighteenth century, was unwise in the colonies. This was less because it angered the colonists, who had used the 60th or Royal American Regiment, itself recruited from foreigners, for policing their own frontiers than because it was militarily so guileless. With their haversacks and long-skirted coats, their long swords and their canteens, the Germans were, as at Saratoga, even less prepared for the terrain than were the British. They were surprisingly casual—as at Trenton—about security. Haldimand, who as himself a Swiss professional might be thought to be reasonably objective about them, wrote from Canada in May 1778 that the German troops with him were quite unfitted for an American war and deserted in shoals. Anburey repeated the charges. The Hessians and Brunswickers appear to have been more cruel than the British, and they were bitterly unpopular. Ambrose Serle, Lord Howe's secretary, thought their employment inflamed Americans "more than two or three British Armies . . . the dread, which the rebels have of these Hessians, is inconceivable: they almost run away at their name. Indeed, they spare nobody, but glean all away like an Army of Locusts." They deserted heavily among their own folk in Pennsylvania. Of the thirty thousand (who cost Britain four million seven hundred thousand pounds) some twelve thousand were killed or stayed in America.

The employment of Indians, which was even more alarming in American eyes, was of greater psychological than military value. Chatham, forgetful of his own practices in an earlier war, attacked that of "mixing the scalping-knife and the tomahawk with the sword and the firelock." The Indians were erratic allies and sadly averse to discipline. They were used mainly on the

frontiers, where the war was often savage. For this reason John
Stuart tried to keep Creeks and Cherokees neutral in the South.
Joseph Brant of the Mohawks was a noble Loyalist leader but his
braves were barbarous allies, as the Wyoming and Cherry Valley
massacres revealed. Indians were used also of course by the
Americans, but on a much smaller scale.

The British Army, then, lost the war by a dreary series of errors
of judgment and of tactics. It lost it far more to the terrain than
to the enemy, and it had lost it perhaps as early as 1778.

It was this fundamental matter of geography and geopolitics
that Washington seemed to sense from the first: the continent
in all its diversity, its untamed forests and broad rivers, was on
his side. And from his own journeys in the West he knew more
of its character than did most of his contemporaries. As he told
Congress at the beginning, the war should be a war "of posts,"
of defense in fortified camps, of position and maneuver. He was
not by nature a Fabius: witness his frustration at not being able
to launch an attack on Boston; his explosions of temper at Kip's
Bay in New York, where he was beating his men with his cane
in his anger at their retreat; his crossing the Delaware and raid-
ing Princeton; or his attitude to Lee at Monmouth. The defensive strategy was quite alien to him, but was imposed on him
by the continent and by circumstances. To keep an army in
being, to avoid battle in open country, and to survive was in
the end to conquer. As Greene put it in 1781: "Don't you think
that we bear beating very well, and that . . . the more we are
beat, the better we grow?"

Washington's difficulties are familiar enough. Yet his achievement in any telling remains one of the great sagas of modern
history. Unlike any of the British triumvirate, he had from the
beginning sole responsibility and was at first overwhelmed by
the conditions that he found at Cambridge. There was no military establishment, and there were no reliable statistics. There
were probably no more than two hundred gunsmiths in the

colonies. His men were ill equipped and badly disciplined; enlisting often only for three months, they sometimes deserted in two. At least half of the militia enrolled during the Revolution deserted, estimates Allen Bowman; and perhaps one third of the Continental Line.* Officers were casual and negligent; senior officers jealous over seniority, juniors chosen mainly by election and lacking authority and knowledge. Charles Lee's description is all too revealing:

> We found everything exactly the reverse of what had been represented. We were assured at Philadelphia that the army was stocked with engineers. We found not one. We were assured that we should find an expert train of artillery. They have not a single gunner and so on. So far from being prejudiced in favour of their own officers, they are extremely diffident in 'em and seem much pleased that we are arrived. . . . The men are really very fine fellows, and had they fair play would be made an invincible army.

All Wellington's scorn for his troops can be traced in the early remarks of Washington, Lee, and Montgomery. Montgomery called his New Yorkers "the sweepings of the streets."

Washington's generals were of extremely varied quality. Ward did not stay long; Putnam, the beloved old fire-eater of Connecticut, was loyal and energetic but undistinguished by talents; Sullivan had the usual ill luck of his Irish race; Montgomery, the ablest of the early senior officers, was killed at Quebec. As Washington was prompt to recognize, Arnold in all his egoism was the best of the natives and had a distinguished record in Canada and in the Hudson Valley. In the end, Arnold sold his cause for ten thousand pounds. Of Washington's early native associates, only the stiff-legged Greene and the stentor-voiced Knox grew in military experience and in skill as the war proceeded and came to enjoy more and more of his trust. Knox, the big, jovial bookseller-turned-gunner, showed that it was possible to learn war even from artillery manuals; he was to show

* Allen Bowman, *The Morale of the American Revolutionary Army* (1943), p. 70.

later that political administration is not learned quite so easily. And Greene, good soldier though he was, was ready to engage in wartime speculation. "Few," said Washington of Arnold, "have virtue to withstand the highest bidder." Or as he put it on another occasion, reflecting on his officers' origins as much as on their quality, "Take none but gentlemen."

Not the least of Washington's services was his at first unwelcome emphasis on rank and distinctions, on discipline and conspicuous uniforms and gorgets for his officers. All the foreign "experts" expressed their scorn at the lack of discipline, the short terms of service of militia, and the confusion of ranks. De Kalb noted that the army teemed with colonels. "The very numerous assistant-quartermasters are for the most part men of no military education whatever, in many cases ordinary hucksters, but always colonels. The same rank is held by the contractors-general and their agents. It is safe to accost every man as a colonel who talks to one with familiarity. . . ." But, whether gentlemen or not, some able generals emerged—Daniel Morgan, whose appearance on his march with Arnold across the Maine-Canada divide "gave the idea history has left us of Belisarius," John Glover and his marines, Wayne and Stirling, George Rogers Clark and "Light-horse Harry" Lee.

What is more surprising is how little real help the professionals and the foreigners were to Washington. Gates and Charles Lee, both ex-British regulars and both of whom had been his guests at Mount Vernon, were in varying degrees as much traitors to Washington as they were to their King. Gates, if not an organizer of a cabal against him, was ready to intrigue with Congress; not until Camden was his incapacity revealed. Fate overtook Lee's reputation more suddenly. Court-martialed for cowardice and insubordination after Monmouth, he died in poverty in 1782, his mind unbalanced.

By 1778 Washington was coming to be surrounded by foreign experts. Some, like Conway, an Irishman serving France, were intriguers against him. De Kalb came to America originally to persuade Congress to replace Washington by his patron, the Comte de Broglie; he fell at Camden fighting as an American patriot. One of the earliest French emissaries, du Coudray, insisted on being given command of the artillery, superseding Knox; he was by happy chance drowned in the Schuylkill, although some did not think his removal accidental. When Conway was promoted, more than twenty "natives" had to be passed over.

This is not to minimize the value of some of these experts. Von Steuben, whatever his rank or title in Europe and however inadequate his English, was an invaluable disciplinarian at Valley Forge, bringing not only drill but vigor and humor to the thinning and hungry ranks. Louis Duportail, the engineer, was a source of strength in the crisis after Camden. Rochambeau was in 1781 the co-organizer of the march on Yorktown, solid and trustworthy. But there were so many of them, and they had all been promised such inflated rank, that Washington found it hard to suffer them gladly. The shining exception was the enthusiastic and innocent Lafayette, who made up in zeal and in his social standing in France what he lacked in military skill. But Lafayette's affection was small compensation for the frustrations and complications and his role, then and since, has perhaps given an exaggerated importance to the French "volunteers." There is no clear evidence that, Rochambeau and Von Steuben apart, any one of them made a decisive contribution to victory. If a single British general has to be selected as the most culpable, it is Howe; but there are other candidates. If a single American general has to be selected as responsible for victory, there can be no denying that it is Washington. There are no other candidates.

Nor did his contribution lie only in a sense of country, a sense of strategy, and a sense of timing. Washington was a bolder figure in tactics than any of his British opponents. He lacked Howe's capacity for maneuver on the field—indeed he had had no experience on this scale at all; he chose some bad sites, as in the Brooklyn and New York campaigns; De Kalb was scornful over the choice of Valley Forge for the winter of 1777 and thought Washington "the bravest and truest of men" but too easily led; by some he was thought indecisive (Lee, Gates, Congressman James Lovell) and by others a dangerous authoritarian receiving "superstitious veneration" (John Adams); at Brandywine he revealed inadequate knowledge of the ground and failed to use his cavalry; he was overaddicted to councils of war; he lacked the flair that Lee showed all too erratically; he lacked Arnold's dash and vigor in action; he never defeated the main British army in the open. Yet, though tactically an amateur, he made distinct contributions to the art of war: the use of light infantry and skirmishers; the employment of riflemen, not least Morgan's Virginians; the readiness to attempt difficult operations and often to move at night—as at Trenton and Princeton; the refusal to recognize a "closed season" for battle, to the horror of those who played at war by a European code of rules; the vast combined operation of Yorktown. He won in the end by choosing the right moment to strike.

The Revolutionary War was notable for some remarkable military disasters. In the war as a whole there were fourteen actions in which the defeated force was either captured entire or destroyed, and in nine of these the better-supplied, better-disciplined British Army was the victim—Moore's Creek, Trenton, Bennington, Saratoga, Vincennes, Stony Point, King's Mountain, Cowpens, Yorktown. Three of these, Trenton, Saratoga, and Yorktown were psychological or military turning points, and two of them were won by Washington. In these nine engagements the British losses exceeded twenty thousand, losses that were decisive in a war waged on this scale.

Even more important, however, than Washington's tactical achievement was the psychological. He took command of what he called "a mixed multitude of People . . . under very little discipline, order or Government." His army was short of everything. Problems of supply and clothing were not overcome until 1782, even with French aid; even then there was never enough clothing for the men to be deloused; pay was always short, the winters always long. Of his first force, the majority had enlisted only until the end of the year; by December, the Connecticut and other militia were disappearing—and taking their muskets with them. While he was besieging Boston he was in fact re-enlisting men for a completely new army. The problems of desertion and of discipline, of thieving and of drunkenness, of recruitment, food, and smallpox stayed with him. It was three years before a system of drill was established and before some measure of steadiness and exactness under fire was imposed on his men.

Washington's strength in 1775-76 was his complete lack of illusion. He knew the "dirty mercenary spirit" of his men—he had some harsh and unpolitic things to say of Yankees in the early days—and he dealt with it less by exhortations to duty or to democracy than by rigorous discipline. For democracy in any event he had little sympathy. He lived from week to week and from hand to mouth; "living," he called it, "by expedients." But by discipline and lashes, by money—sometimes from Congress, sometimes from France, sometimes his own—and by promises of money he kept an army in being. If he never made it the drilled machine of Howe's or Knyphausen's, and if mutiny was often just below, and sometimes in the Pennsylvania Line in 1781 just above, the surface, he gave his small and ragged army a character of its own.

As British morale declined, colonial morale grew. British contempt disappeared by 1778. Colonel Harcourt noted of the Americans in March 1777 that although they lacked precision when they moved as units, they had the qualities of good troops —cunning and industry, activity and enterprise. They were by nature familiar with spade and with rifle, "very ready at earthworks and palisading" as Burgoyne admitted, working, in

Paine's words, "like a family of beavers." As Dorchester, Saratoga, and Yorktown showed, when protected by earthworks or trees, their fire was deadly and discriminating; Daniel Morgan instructed his men, often posted in the treetops, to pick off the British officers. "Look for the epaulets!" he ordered at Cowpens. And the victory of Morgan at Cowpens showed how a militia force could be handled. Their own nature, and the country's, made "every private man in action his own general," as Burgoyne put it.

Washington was scornful of his militia; "the long faces," he called them. "They come in, you cannot tell how; go, you cannot tell when; and act, you cannot tell where; consume your provisions, exhaust your stores and leave you at last at the critical moment." But it was from such haphazard material, from country storekeepers and clerks, from pine-woods squirrel-hunters with buckskin shirts and long Kentucky rifles, from rough and unkempt mechanics and farmers with sun-cracked hands that Washington built a people's army. The Army was his creation. He led it for eight years during which he won only two major engagements; yet he won the war, defeated an enemy twice his size, secured the independence of his country—and built a nation.

Indeed, his deference to the civil power was among his greatest qualities. No small part of the confidence with which, with small exception, Congress treated him throughout the war was due to his own respect for that feeble and much-maligned body which constituted nonetheless the only federal government there was.

By 1779 he was being described in Pennsylvania as *der landes Vater*. Valley Forge was blamed on Congressional intrigue and indifference to the Army. From 1777 to 1780 by keeping an Army in being, as in 1775 by taking the command, he made and kept the cause alive. "The Atlas of America, and the god of the army: his authority is gentle and paternal," wrote the Chevalier de Fleury in 1779. To survive was in the end to conquer: it was true not only of the Army and of the country but of reputations too.

American success owed far more to Washington's achievement in creating and maintaining an army than to the entry of France into the war. France had of course been aiding the colonists tacitly with money, and on a small scale with volunteers, from the beginning; not from love of America, and certainly not from love of democracy (a suspect cause in Bourbon eyes) but as part of a long-cherished plan of the Duc de Choiseul and of Vergennes for revenge on Britain. France greatly assisted the Americans with subsidies and supplies (some eight million dollars in all) but she did this before and after 1778. This was in fact a much-debated policy in Paris; Louis XVI disliked the risk of war that secret aid implied, Turgot disliked Vergennes' extravagance. Vergennes' motives were more commercial than territorial. When France deemed it safe to declare war—after Saratoga—she intervened as a sea power. Her objectives were West Indian sugar islands rather than American independence, and she gave that cause in fact small assistance. D'Estaing gave no effective help in 1778, and apart from an unsuccessful appearance off Savannah in 1779, no French fleet operated in American waters for the next three years. The Rhode Island operations of 1778 and the Savannah operations of 1779 were bungled. In 1781 itself, de Grasse had to be persuaded by Rochambeau and Washington, at a famous parley on his flagship *Ville de Paris,* to stay long enough in Chesapeake waters to allow the siege of Yorktown. He stayed long enough to be disastrous for Britain, but it was touch and go.

France put some nine thousand troops into America, of whom three thousand were landed from de Grasse's ships in 1781. The important contribution was Rochambeau's force of five thousand which arrived in 1780, well disciplined, well dressed, and psychologically of great importance. But the American war could still have been won without the formal intervention of French troops. And few French observers believed that an independent United States would last long; the Bourbons had no wish to invest in revolution.

For Britain, however, the entry of France was decisive. This was the long-awaited and much-feared step foreseen by Barrington and Amherst, Sandwich and Chatham. The first result was an attempt at concessions to America. North's Conciliatory Propositions of February 1778 made a number of surrenders, especially of the right to tax. The colonists would raise their own revenues, maintain their own army, and, if they chose, keep the Continental Congress in being as a subordinate branch of the imperial Parliament. The Coercive Acts were withdrawn and a commission, nominally headed by the Earl of Carlisle but directed in fact by William Eden, was sent to Philadelphia empowered to offer anything short of independence. The hope was held out of a return to the status quo of 1763. Britain sought, that is, to retain only the power to regulate external trade. Franklin contrived to let Vergennes know that the Americans were receiving peace overtures, and this in turn drove France to sign the alliance. The arrival of the commission was in any event mistimed, for by April 1778 Clinton was abandoning Philadelphia and the American treaty with France was already signed. The commission was not aware until its arrival that Philadelphia was to be evacuated. Congress refused to negotiate except on a basis of independence and a withdrawal of British forces.

The entry of France produced a national war effort in Britain, however, that the war against the colonies had not quite aroused, high though feelings had risen by 1778. It totally transformed British strategy. Until 1778 Britain could blockade American ports and attack the coast where she chose. The colonies had put tiny fleets to sea under Esek Hopkins, but they could not go beyond commerce-raiding. Privateering was more important; more than two thousand privateers were commissioned during the war. They made many a fortune, but in doing so they attracted men out of the Army, and they brought little help to the American cause as a whole.

With France and Spain, Holland, and the League of Armed Neutrality at war with her by 1780, the British grip on the Atlantic and on the American coast was imperiled. More than this, America became a military side show. Invasion of Britain became a real threat; in 1779 a Franco-Spanish armada was dispersed only by a gale in the Channel. John Paul Jones, part freebooter, part hero, but in any guise material for legend, raided his own familiar Solway, threatened Leith, and fought his greatest battle off Flamborough Head within sight of the Yorkshire coast. Gibraltar was besieged, India threatened, and West Indian islands lost. The troops to defend the Caribbean, as in the St. Lucia expedition, were taken from the main American theater of war. If Britain were invaded, said Barrington, there was no general in the country fit to direct the army.

Not for the first time America was to profit from European discord and from Britain's agonizing dilemma. Benjamin Franklin's greatest achievement was not so much to make France an active ally as to widen the struggle into a world war, in such a way that at its height the original belligerent could quietly make peace without consulting its ally. As he saw, the war France fought was never quite the same war as America's, and, never unduly concerned over protocol, he was content to withdraw when he could. For Britain the European conflict became primary and it was, except at sea, equally disastrous. It seemed as though she had ceased to be the privileged child of fate she had been in the earlier eighteenth century. But fate, as Bertrand de Jouvenel has reminded us, is merely "the shape taken by history when men fail to act." The British government failed in political invention and good will between 1763 and 1775. She failed disastrously in action from 1775 to 1782.

If anything can be said in exculpation, it is that by the grace with which she accepted the imperial disaster Britain did something to atone for her earlier failures. This was to be in character. It was made possible only by North's resignation in March, when Shelburne became first Secretary of State and, on Rockingham's death, Prime Minister. At first he opposed the idea of independence, but not for long. With the merchant Richard Oswald as his emissary in Paris, negotiations were opened with Franklin and Jay in April 1782 and concluded by November. They were helped not only by the friendship of Oswald and David Hartley for Franklin, but by the all-too-tight alliance of France and Spain.

Vergennes had no wish to see the rise of a powerful republic in North America, and Spain wished it still less. He hoped to create in the area between the Alleghenies and the Mississippi a mixed dominion to be shared among Britain, Spain, and the Indians. Spain sought to recapture her former territory in the Floridas and to set up a buffer on the Mississippi; she had close relations with the Creek and Choctaw Indians; it was not until the failure of the Conspiracy of 1797 and as a consequence of Napoleon's dominance that she finally abandoned her hopes of pulling into her own orbit the Kentucky and Tennessee country.

Franklin's discourtesy in drawing up a separate peace—an act as farsighted as it was unprincipled—was unpopular, for a time, in Congress. His instructions after all bade him rely implicitly on the wisdom of Vergennes; his own flair, reinforced by Adams' Puritanism and Jay's Huguenot blood, taught him to trust his own superior wisdom. And in the thick air of spying and counterspying in Paris, where secret negotiations were pursued all too openly, it was hardly possible for Vergennes to be unaware of what was happening. Indeed the lack of charity of the American commissioners not only seemed to prove the risks that were run in having republicans as allies; it had the more useful advantage of excusing Vergennes from his embarrassing obligation to secure Gibraltar for Spain.

By the terms of the Treaty of Paris, Britain recognized the

independence of the United States and accepted her western boundary as the Mississippi River. The navigation of the river was to be open to both British and Americans. The boundaries to the north and south were ill defined and were to be matter thereafter for long and acrimonious debate. By the terms of the treaty there was to be no opposition by Congress to the collection of debts, and the states would be urged to restore property to Loyalists. If Congress honored her part of the bargain, the states can hardly be said to have done the same. Canniness triumphed in Paris and in the colonies; the new United States won by diplomacy far more than they were entitled to by force of arms. By 1783 British sea power had regained something of its prestige, with Rodney's victory off the Saintes, and had averted direct invasion; and her diplomacy had by 1783 contrived to split asunder the dangerous allies of 1778. Spain did regain the Floridas, but not Gibraltar. France won some West Indian islands and the satisfaction of an all-too-modest revanche on Britain. The cost of her revanche was high, and six years later the bills came in.

6

Revolution: the Home Front
1776–1787

A NEW NATION had thus proclaimed itself, under the impact of a history of repeated injuries and usurpations, real or imagined, and had won its freedom. Protests against Britain before 1775, like the war itself, had produced passionate appeals to nationalism. At the Stamp Act Congress of 1765, Christopher Gadsden had declared "There ought to be no New England man; no New Yorker, known on the continent, but all of us Americans." Nine years later, Patrick Henry orated "The distinctions between Virginians, Pennsylvanians, New Yorkers and New Englanders are no more. I am not a Virginian, but an American. . . . All distinctions are thrown down. All America is thrown into one mass." "When the honest man of Boston who has broke no law, has his property wrested from him, the hunter on the Allegany must take the alarm," said the freemen of Botetourt County, Virginia, in October 1775. "Unite or die," pleaded Franklin.

The thirteen colonies, however, were very precariously united against Britain. They were, as Professor Van Tyne observed, thirteen independent states "temporarily acting together in the business of acquiring their individual independence." The struggle against Britain by the Continental Army was accompanied

by a struggle for power, for influence, and for land between each
state and section—a struggle, that is, over who should rule at
home. Alongside the rebellion against Britain there were several
conflicts less obvious but quite as significant: Tidewater *versus*
frontier, planter *versus* merchant, and everywhere, in greater
or smaller degree, Loyalist *versus* patriot. Some of these tensions
took explosive form. The revolution was not the smooth, ordered,
gradual transition that American nationalists or British liberals
have, for different reasons, made it. There are in American history so many examples of tension, violence, and war that it is
hard to maintain the great American myth that they are an
unbelligerent people.

There were many border and sectional problems that threatened conflict. There was the twenty-year-old dispute over Fort
Pitt between Pennsylvania and Virginia. Connecticut had claims
on the Wyoming Valley along the Susquehanna and was attempting to settle it with armed men. New York and New
Hampshire were wrangling over the possession of the Green
Mountains. The seizure of Ticonderoga and the rivalry of Allen
and Arnold were part of a local as well as of an international
war. There was suspicion, still a reality in Maryland until 1781,
over the sea-to-sea claims of the Old Dominion. Many besides
Otis, Galloway, and Braxton believed that only British power
prevented the outbreak of a number of civil wars between the
colonies.

More alarming were the social tensions inside each section, of
which there had already been significant indications in the years
between 1763 and 1776. They were found particularly in Pennsylvania, New York, and the Carolinas; Virginia, Maryland,
and Georgia had a happier record. In 1763 the Scotch-Irish on
the Pennsylvania frontier, alarmed by the Pontiac rising, murdered twenty friendly Conestoga Indians near Lancaster. Frontier justices and juries proved indifferent to Governor Penn's
proclamations ordering the culprits to be tried. Out of this grew
an ugly frontier challenge, and the march on Philadelphia in

1764 of six hundred Paxton Boys, named after one of their townships, seeking a voice in the Assembly. Sixteen thousand voters in the three eastern counties had twice as many members in the Assembly as the fifteen thousand voters in the five western counties. The Paxton Boys were placated by Franklin; their leader, Lazarus Stewart, moved out into the farther frontier of the Wyoming Valley, where he was killed in 1778. They made a common front with the mechanics and their popular leader in Philadelphia in the Revolution, and most of their demands found expression in the Pennsylvania Constitution of 1776.

In 1776 the New York Assembly took a more sympathetic view of the Quartering Act than it had a year before. It requested the help of royal troops when it faced a series of riots over land tenantry and high rents in Westchester and Duchess counties. John Morin Scott and Robert Livingston handed down severe sentences on the "Levelers," out of the conviction, as a cynic put it, that "no one is entitled to Riot but themselves."

From 1764 to 1771 there was persistent trouble in North Carolina. The settlers in the back country, many of them recent immigrants from the North via the Great Valley of Virginia, were fighting over land claims in Mecklenburg County in 1765. By 1767 they were campaigning against the corruption of treasurers and sheriffs in the frontier counties and against the exorbitant fees of lawyers. In 1768 they organized "The Regulation," a vigilance society in intention, and were curbed only by Governor Tryon's calling out the militia and promising reforms. In 1769 they captured control of the Assembly, but Tryon dissolved it because of its attitude to Britain; no reforms were forthcoming. In 1771 he led a colonial militia against them, defeated them at the Battle of the Alamance, and executed some of them. Again, there was a frontier evacuation, this time into Tennessee, and a legacy of bitterness.

For this struggle, which was as much against the Assembly as against the governor and not at all against Britain, conditioned the state's attitude toward the Revolution. When their enemies of

1771 became revolutionaries in 1776, and when Governor Martin showed a sympathy for them that Tryon had not, many of the Regulators remained Loyalist. They fought for Britain at Moore's Creek Bridge and continued an ugly but tiring civil war on her behalf and their own for five more years. But if most Regulators were lawless, not all were Loyalist. Governor Martin thought their military value small and disappointing, and Washington was scornful of their quality.

The South Carolina interior was similarly disturbed, due again to the lack there of law courts, of magistrates, and—embarrassingly—of clergy, and to the sense of being the victims of Tidewater and of Episcopalian domination. The gracious planter-merchant aristocracy of Charleston was Januslike, liberal and Whig as it looked across the Atlantic, hard-faced and Tory as it looked west across the pine barrens. It did in the end make some provision for circuit courts, and these helped avert the civil war that affected North Carolina.

Behind these examples there were forces in the West that were to be at work throughout the revolutionary period and were to erupt again in Shays' Rebellion in Massachusetts in 1786, and in the Whiskey Rebellion of 1794. Courts of law were too few and justice remote, unpredictable, and expensive; the one court of law in South Carolina was seated, in Woodmason's words, "not central but in a nook by the seaside." In Pennsylvania there was fear of Indians, and in the Carolinas still more fear of other whites. "We live not as under a British government . . . but as if we were in Hungary, or Germany, and in a state of war, continually exposed to the incursions of hussars and pandours. . . ." Prophetic demands were being voiced: for a paper currency; for more adequate roads; for the replacement of a poll tax by a tax levied in accordance with capacity to pay, and to pay in kind; for election by ballot; for a curbing of the speculators, who had acquired their vast and empty estates through their influence "back East"; and for a fairer representation of the West in eastern assemblies, the common cry from the Mohawk to the Smokies.

If Woodmason's diatribes against "vexatious pettifoggers or litigious miscreants, Rogues and Whores," have been thought fevered by later historians, there can be no querying the less eloquent but more moving petition of the 260 inhabitants of Anson County, North Carolina (October 1769), ending with the request

> that Doctr Benjamin Franklin or some other known patriot be appointed Agent, to represent the unhappy state of this Province to his Majesty, and to solicit the several boards in England.

They did not once mention the Proclamation Line or the wickedness of Britain; they wanted justice, good order, religious freedom, and democracy; their enemies were mercenary attorneys and little bureaucrats in the Tidewater, doing the harm here that Britain's agents were doing at the ports. This was the country for which Patrick Henry spoke; and it was in Waxhaws that Andrew Jackson spent his formative years. South of Virginia, the frontier tended to loyalism throughout the Revolution. In Pennsylvania, in New England, and not least in Vermont, it was avidly patriot.

There were almost everywhere basic differences between Piedmont and Tidewater. They were separated by distance, and in the Carolinas by barrens and by empty land. One was a country of small farms, few slaves, and fewer aristocrats, and with a marked mixture of races—Scotch-Irish, German, Welsh, and English—and of religions—Presbyterians, Baptists, and various pietist groups. The other was characterized by small towns or plantations, with slaves in considerable numbers in the South, and with a church and a society that reflected in its tone and uniformity a new colonial establishment. If there were not thirteen revolutions, there were certainly at least two distinct societies in America in 1776. They were at times at war not only with

Britain but with each other, and to keep them in gear was a major political achievement.

On March 23, 1776, John Adams wrote to Gates:

> all of our misfortunes arise from a single source—the reluctance of the southern colonies to republican government. The success of this war depends on a skilful steerage of the political vessel. The difficulty lies in forming constitutions for particular colonies and a continental constitution for the whole. Each colony should establish its own government, and then a league should be formed between them all. This can be done only on popular principles and maxims which are so abhorrent to the inclinations of the barons of the south and the proprietary interests in the middle colonies as well as to that avarice of land which has made upon this continent so many votaries to Mammon that I sometimes dread the consequences. However, patience, fortitude and perseverance with the help of time will get us over these obstructions.

The middle way and the skillful steerage were evident in the political and social reforms of the war years. Despite the fears of the aristos, while there was some violence there was no anarchy, except perhaps in North Carolina, where it was hardly a novelty. There was no widespread destruction. No royal governor lost his life, not even Dunmore, who most deserved to.

Congress declared in May 1776 that all royal government was to be suppressed and that new state governments should be set up. This was smoothly done. Each state produced a constitution —sometimes, as in Connecticut and Rhode Island, by altering existing charters. Except in Massachusetts, they were all drafted within a few months. They were normally drawn up by the provincial congresses, but Pennsylvania summoned (and needed) a special convention. Massachusetts submitted her draft to a referendum of the voters, and many features of the undemocratic result—the work of John Adams—long survived. All were soundly based on colonial experience and in this sense were evolutionary, not revolutionary. All were written documents and the work of lawyers; all contained declarations of rights; all em

phasized separation of powers and the primacy of the elected
legislature, elected by those people with some—although now a
smaller—stake in the community (from the payment of a small
poll tax in New Hampshire, North Carolina, and Pennsylvania
to Virginia's requirements of twenty-five acres of settled or
fifty acres of unsettled land).

In Georgia and in the Carolinas, in Massachusetts and New
Jersey, only Protestants could hold office. There were normally
property qualifications imposed on members of legislatures or
state officials. In Massachusetts the governor had to own one
thousand pounds' worth of freehold property; in South Carolina
he was worth ten times that amount. The legislature usually
elected the governor, who held office for only one year and who
lost his veto power in practically all states. In Pennsylvania,
where the franchise was unusually wide and all taxpayers had
the suffrage, and in Georgia's first constitution, there was only
one House; elsewhere there were two, the second, sometimes
chosen by an electoral college, designed to act as a check on the
"mobility" that James Allen and John Adams and many other
revolutionaries feared. The western areas in Pennsylvania and
the states south of the Potomac were given increased representation; they gained some seats but not usually their fair share,
least of all in South Carolina. Only in Pennsylvania, North
Carolina, and Georgia could the new constitutions be said to be
really democratic documents. Pennsylvania's was so democratic,
with a denial of veto to the executive, a referendum, and a council of "censors," that it survived only for fourteen years.

Nor was the social revolution much more pronounced than the
political. There was the striking disappearance of the Loyalists,
and there was confiscation of crown and proprietary lands by
decision of Congress in 1777. The estates of Sir John Wentworth
in New Hampshire, of Sir William Pepperrell in Maine, of Sir
John Johnson in the Mohawk Valley, of the Phillipses in New
York, Lord Fairfax in Virginia, Henry McCulloch in North
Carolina, and Sir James Wright in Georgia were taken over.

But when Loyalist land was sold the motive was punitive or fiscal rather than egalitarian: Tories must pay for the war. Except in New York, where there was unusual breakup of the fifty-nine confiscated estates, the land was usually sold as a unit to wealthy men or to speculators; practically all the state governors were interested in real estate. Revolutionary leaders like the Livingstons and the Van Rensselaers added to their holdings. So did Washington, not only the first, but also one of the wealthiest, of all the Presidents. The prices and terms of sale were in fact much less favorable to "little men" than the British had been; but in the end, some land did percolate down to smaller holders and carried voting rights with it as it came.

The right to acquire and possess property without restriction was indeed as important a civil right as free speech, and to most people in the eighteenth century it meant more. Property was largely real estate and was widely dispersed; it was esteemed in America as the reward of effort and success rather than of inheritance. The disappearance of its feudal aspects was strength rather than weakness. Quitrents were abolished in every state between 1775 and 1789; they prevented the easy acquisition of land, and they were resented as remnants of feudalism. Entail and primogeniture disappeared also from New York and the South: but entail had not been a universal custom, even in the Tidewater; docking had been a common practice and primogeniture had applied only in cases of intestacy. Their removal, egalitarian though it seemed, hardly weakened the plantation economy or the long-tailed families; rather did it indicate a right to do what one liked with one's own in an ever-expanding society in which there was more than enough for all. It seems not to have had the importance that Jefferson foresaw; it would, he thought, open the Republic to "the aristocracy of talent and virtue which nature has wisely provided for the direction of the interests of society"; nor did it have the significance attributed to it by de Tocqueville, who thought it the major factor in the growth of

American democracy. But superficially there was a note of social equality.

Republicanism was naturally associated with the campaign against royalty and loyalism. Titles were unpopular, including *Excellency* and *Honorable*. A number of state constitutions sought to forbid hereditary office-holding and any development of a privileged class. Two forbade the creation of titles of nobility. Jefferson looked forward to the time when the "plebeian interest" would prevail over "the old aristocratical interest." And Royall Tyler, a veteran of the Revolution, rhapsodized in the prolog to his play *The Contrast,* produced in New York in 1787:

> Exult each patriot heart! this night is shewn
> A piece, which we may fairly call our own;
> Where the proud titles of "My Lord!" "Your Grace!"
> To humble Mr and plain Sir give place.

Religious freedom was strengthened, partly by the separation from parent churches, partly by the disestablishment of the Anglican (but not of the Congregational) Church, partly by the spread of rationalism and deism as the philosophical accompaniment to revolution, partly by the growth of militant dissenting sects, and partly by the steady secularization of American life. At the time of the Revolution there were some 3100 churches in the colonies, the majority Congregational, Presbyterian, or Baptist. The number and variety helped the separation of church from state and weakened authoritarian religion. Jefferson thought the Statute of Virginia for Religious Freedom, which he drew up and which became law in 1786, one of his three most important achievements—the others being the writing of the Declaration of Independence and the founding of the University of Virginia. "All men shall be free to profess, and by argument to maintain, their opinion in matters of religion." "Truth is great and will prevail if left to herself." The radicals of the Revolution honored Milton as well as Locke. The Massachusetts constitution of 1780, however, insisted that religion was the foundation of morality and of the state; it required that public funds be used to maintain the churches, and that a man be a Christian before he could hold public office. Deism, curiously, made its biggest inroads in "feudal" Virginia, always a more liberal society in fact than its social system revealed.

There were some trends that can be described without qualification as liberal. The colonial criminal codes were always much less harsh than Britain's—in part because of necessity, since it was easier to provide rules than to provide prisons—and now they were made even more liberal. In the Pennsylvania constitution of 1776, capital punishment was restricted to four offenses. Jefferson's code for Virginia would have limited it to murder and treason; defeated by one vote, it was not enacted until the 1790s. Congress similarly limited capital punishment in the Northwest Territory in 1788. The antislavery movement developed; by the end of the century the majority of states had forbidden the importation of slaves, and all New England, New York, and Pennsylvania had provided for abolition or gradual emancipation. Many southerners thought it an evil and manumitted slaves by deed or will, as did Robert Carter and George Washington. Only South Carolina and Georgia, still in need of slaves, stood out against a complete ban on the institution. It was, overoptimistically, expected that slavery would die a natural death.

Especially in the Jeffersonian circle there was a concern with "causes"; Benjamin Rush had advanced ideas on the treatment of the insane, whom he insisted on describing as the "mentally ill," and he wanted a Peace Department in the federal government; and Anthony Benezet crusaded not only for these but for temperance and for the fair treatment of the Indian as well

Freedom for the person was a real thing. It was, however, tightly confined to one sex. Despite the role of Mercy Otis Warren as poet, historian, and participant in the Revolution and of the active Abigail Adams, women were not held—even by Jefferson—to be the equal of men. If married, they could not hold property or will it. They could not sue in the courts, nor could they easily contrive to be publicly educated. Yet Charles Brockden Brown, America's first professional man of letters, reflected the *Aufklärung* of Europe by publishing in 1797 his *Alcuyn: A Dialogue on the Rights of Women*. One of his female characters complained that "lawmakers thought as little of comprehending us in their code of liberty as if we were pigs or sheep." The first American novel to gain popularity, *Charlotte Temple, a Tale of Truth* (1791), by Susanna Rowson, was a highly sentimental but strong plea for women's rights.

Freedom for the person brought little immediate native blossoming of the fine arts. For the most part, Gilbert Stuart's portraits were stilted, and his confreres were even more derivative than he. Education had suffered during the war. A few schools were established when it ended, but they took shape slowly. Yale for a time was closed; and in 1800 the Harvard faculty consisted of a president, three professors, and four tutors.

Yet there were emerging a new nationalism and a new cosmopolitanism, both in part the result of the presence of French and Hessian troops. Noah Webster's notion of a uniform American speech and Jedediah Morse's geography expressed the first. So did John Trumbull and Benjamin West, Philip Freneau and Timothy Dwight. So too did the Order of the Cincinnati, the society of officer veterans of the Revolution of which Washington and Henry Knox were leaders, and of which the American eagle became the emblem. Even Jefferson took great pride in American flora and fauna. The French language and style became fashionable; the new city on the Potomac was planned by Major Pierre Charles L'Enfant, although with little result in his own lifetime; dueling became a gentlemanly response to insult, with permanent effect on the code of chivalry in the South; neoclassical architecture, already heralded in Jefferson's Monticello, appeared on a small scale; chairs in modern languages and law were established at William and Mary. Even the Iroquois had a French dancing master. The war itself stimulated interest in medicine and dentistry. It stimulated interest too in the theater. Congress voted in 1774 to discourage plays, horseracing, and such diversions, but in fact each side used the stage as propaganda. Wherever the British army moved—such was the leisurely pace of war—it carried acting with it. Philadelphia remembered that fantastic pageant, the *Meschianza,* long after Howe had beat a retreat; and in some of the productions the feminine roles were played, remarkably for the age, by women—women, as one author put it, "such as follow the drum." But in society as on the stage, scandal has always been the twin sister of sophistication.

Liberation brought few signs as yet of America's great practical genius, although Jefferson was experimental in method and catholic in range, his friends were gifted, and Eli Whitney with his cotton gin and Oliver Evans and John Fitch with their steamboat experiments showed specialized skills. Crop rotation and fertilization were introduced under French stimulus. Societies for the promotion of agriculture, industry, and "the useful arts" came into being, most of them short-lived. So did small-scale industrial establishments for the manufacture of cloth and gunpowder and the production of iron. The shipping industry survived the war and was stimulated by it, for privateering could pass as patriotism, but whaling and the West Indian trade that went with it were badly hit. Trade, like taste, began to feel its way, slowly, into new channels—to Dutch ports, to Portugal, and to China; but the export trade in tobacco, rice, and indigo slumped. America was now, for good or ill, without the protection or control of the imperial system.

As yet there was little impetus to manufacturing. Inflation badly hit the Army and all the fixed-income groups. Town workers sought both higher wages and the fixing of prices as a check on profiteers and speculators. Capital was short; so were the skills and the labor. One reason was an unusual one—lack of immigrants; in the years from 1776 to 1800 only some four thousand immigrants per year were entering the United States. This allowed the mold of the country to become fixed; western

land was acquired before the human flood poured in. Yet by
natural increase the population grew rapidly and by 1790 it
was almost four million.

Nevertheless, this was in economic terms an age of unusual
stability behind the political and social tensions. The Republic was
in fact in happy equipoise. Liberal forces were at work but they
were of a traditional and largely an inherited kind. North America had, even in colonial days, enjoyed a far more striking degree
of both freedom and equality than contemporary Europe—without always being ready to appreciate the good fortune. Having
destroyed its aristocracy, its society and its interests were middle-
class. Despite the Old South, they remained stubbornly so. In
almost all the new states, frontier and Tidewater, by 1787 the
men of substance were in control, and the idealists sometimes
proved themselves incompetent executives. Not the least striking
feature of the years of construction from 1776 to 1787 was the
minor role played by the propagandists and pamphleteers of the
decade of agitation. If there was a contest over who should rule
at home, there was no social revolution. It was, in fact, not
needed. "I say again," said John Adams, "that resistance to
innovation and to unlimited claims of Parliament, and not any
new form of government, was the object of the Revolution."

Yet it can be argued that, although the Revolution was begun by
radicals but carried through by moderates, in three respects the
War for Independence was productive of major social and
political change: farmers to some degree and financiers to a
major degree profited from it; Loyalists lost completely by it;
and, at the center, liberty and order were in the end reconciled
in the federal constitutions of 1777 and 1787.

If the merchant class suffered in the war, and if some Tidewater plantations, unable to export their products, never regained
their old prosperity, many small farmers flourished. The number of men in the Army was always small, and agriculture was
little affected by the violence of war, except in the South toward

the end; in New England, military operations almost ceased after 1776. Farmers were helped by the high prices paid for their produce—by both armies—and by the inflation of the currency, which allowed them to pay off their debts. In Rhode Island, debtors pursued creditors in their eagerness to force depreciated currency upon them. The farmer prospered as long as the war lasted. If Benjamin Franklin is to be believed, the farmer continued to be prosperous after the war's end. The crops were good, he wrote in 1787, yet their prices were high; the lands the farmer owned were rising in value; and "in no part . . . are the labouring poor so generally well fed, well clothed, well lodged and well paid as in America."

The currency situation that rejoiced the hearts of debtors improved after 1781 with the increasing amount of foreign trade. The Bank of North America was established in Philadelphia in 1782, and in 1789 similar banks came into being in Boston and New York. Wartime profiteering was transmuted into peacetime land speculation; William Duer and Robert Morris for a time were regarded as financial heroes of the Revolution; their wizardry was short-lived in the strains of peacetime life.

The ties with Britain that were broken by 1783 were social and psychological as well as political. Although the new state constitutions might reflect a British genius for compromise, for seven years Britain was the enemy, and hostility toward her was visited upon the Loyalists. John Adams calculated that one third of the American people were Loyalist at heart; but this was an estimate made in retrospect. Strongest in New York and in the South, they were not found uniformly in any one section or class. They were generally the most prosperous and professional element, though not in the Carolinas. In their ranks were royal officials and substantial merchants, Scots traders around Norfolk, southern frontiersmen, and Anglicans almost everywhere. The Revolution had, after all, the bitterness of a civil war; it separated brother from brother (as with the Randolphs of Virginia, the Morrises of New York and the Starks of Vermont), father from son (as with the Franklins), cousin from cousin (if Nathan Hale was a martyr, Samuel was a Loyalist who was thought to be a party to his cousin's capture), mentor from protégé (Lord Fairfax in the Valley of Virginia and Washington leading a rebel army). Loyalist homes were attacked, their jobs made forfeit, and all legal action was denied them. From 1777 the states began the practice of banishing prominent Loyalists, and everywhere they ran the risk of tar and feathers—the Bostonians paid not only the exciseman in this coinage. A thousand left Boston in 1776 with Howe; Clinton abandoned at least four thousand in Philadelphia in 1778; another thousand left Charleston and a further thousand left New York with the British in 1783. By 1783, perhaps as many as eighty thousand had been banished or had emigrated—to Florida and to Jamaica, to St. John and Halifax.

The size and fate of this Loyalist element has been minimized by American historians.* Their disappearance was immensely important, not only because of the estates they left behind; it marked the disappearance of most of the colonial aristocracy. There was now for a generation room at the top, even though it was not yet for poor men. Today's old families of Boston are for the most part derived from the *nouveaux riches* of the Revolution; Hancock and Cabot, like the Browns of Rhode Island, came up in the smuggling trade or in privateering. Self-made men had long been numerous, of course, in colonial America, but there was a real shift in power in 1783.

A number of Loyalists—like Samuel Curwin or Peter Van Schaack of Kinderhook or Stephen Kemble, brother-in-law of General Gage—returned to America to settle; so, quietly, did the

---

* Note, however, the recent study of R. R. Palmer, *The Age of the Democratic Revolution* (New York, 1959) and his emphasis on the importance of the treatment of the Loyalists. He suggests that there were twenty-four émigrés per thousand of population in the American Revolution, and only five per thousand of population in the French Revolution. "Americans have really forgotten the loyalists" (p. 189). "The sense in which there was no conflict in the American Revolution is the sense in which the loyalists are forgotten" (p. 190).

Tory editor, Jemmie Rivington. There was greater sympathy for their plight in the Carolinas, oddly enough—despite the savagery of the war there—than in New York and Massachusetts. Those who stayed in exile in Britain lived out lonely lives. Those who settled in Canada, where they were granted some three million acres, brought a new vigor and a valuable imperial sentiment to Upper Canada and Nova Scotia. By 1782 the British government was paying seventy thousand pounds in pensions to Loyalist exiles; she paid compensation in the end to those who lost office or property; but decades later she was still being besieged to meet debts outstanding to Glasgow merchants, and unpaid, by the ex-colonists:

> Those vaunted demagogues who nobly rose
> From England's debtors to be England's foes,
> Who could their monarch in their purse forget
> And break allegiance but to cancel debt.

The transition to independence was a great deal easier at the local than at the "national" level. Indeed, many radical leaders in revolting against Britain were revolting against government at any level beyond their own local boundaries. There was no wish to give to Philadelphia a power denied to London. And both locally and at the center that government was best, said Jefferson, which governed least. The nature of the central government has been from the beginning a matter of controversy in the United States. The doubt has in some degree not been resolved even by Appomattox, or by the threats to American security in the twentieth century. It is true that the second Continental Congress had declared the independence of the United States, appointed a commander-in-chief, negotiated with European nations, set up a postal service, and borrowed money. Yet there was no "form" of government, no constitution. Indeed, until independence was avowed there could be no government to replace that of Britain, so Congress was at first clearly a collection of ambassadors rather than an executive agency. For John

Adams the Massachusetts delegation in Congress was "our embassy." For Sam Adams every legislature was "a sovereign and uncontroulable [*sic*] Power within its own limits of Territory." The Articles of Confederation of 1777, the work of John Dickinson, were hammered out with difficulty and submitted to the states. They set up a "superintending power" only, less a national government than a perpetual federal union. It consisted of a unicameral legislature in which each state had a single vote; any important measure needed nine state votes to be effective, and the most important ones required unanimity. An amendment to the Articles needed the unanimous vote of all the states. Congress, although it could declare war and make treaties, borrow money and control currency, could not levy taxes or regulate commerce, raise an army or enforce its own laws. Despite many committees and a semipermanent secretariat, there was neither an executive nor a judiciary. In the midst of a war to check tyranny, Americans were suspicious of government even when it was their own. The war was directed by committees of Congress, of changing and sometimes conflicting members; John Adams, a glutton for work, served on no less than eighty committees. "There is as much intrigue in this State-House as in the Vatican," wrote John Jay, "but as little secrecy as in a boarding-school."

The Articles were not ratified until 1781, since several states (especially Maryland and New Jersey) thought it unfair that those states with sea-to-sea charters (Virginia, Massachusetts, Georgia, Connecticut, and the Carolinas) should obtain all the land between the Alleghenies and the Mississippi or even the Pacific. Maryland was not herself utterly virtuous; some of her citizens, interested in the Illinois-Wabash and Indiana companies, hoped for better terms from Congress than from the other states. None of these land claims was clear. New York's, based on the surrender of their property rights by the Iroquois, perhaps least of all; Virginia's were the largest and strongest and had been reinforced during the war by George Rogers Clark's successes against the Illinois towns in 1778–79. But if maintained, these claims would give vast areas of land, won by a common effort, to particular states, and would allow them to pay off their war veterans and their debts and thus keep their taxes low. When these states agreed to surrender their claims (though before they had all done so), Maryland gave her assent to the Articles. Virginia's surrender was particularly noble, and so far as Jefferson, Madison, and Richard Henry Lee were concerned, was made for genuinely republican reasons. They not only sought a large union; they feared that a very large Virginia could hardly be a democracy at all. It was not until 1802, however, that Georgia, the last of them, agreed to surrender its claims. The United States, when it won its independence in 1783, inherited a great public domain in the West of some hundred million acres as a common possession.

This concession to emergent federalism was a remarkable step for states not thus far notable for their unselfishness. It has been all too little appreciated by historians. Indeed, until recently it has been the fashion to condemn the Articles, under which the country was governed for a decade (1777–87), and to give to these years, after John Fiske, the name of the Critical Period. Fiske, accepting the Federalists' indictment of the Articles, attributed the country's difficulties to the lack of real sovereignty, the lack of power to enforce treaties, the lack of military resources, and the lack of authority to tax. He blamed all these on the Articles. He even attributed the American inaction over British debts and Loyalists to the inadequacy of federal power, ignoring the fact that there was no wish to make any such settlement at either the federal or the state level. Fiske seriously minimized the profound differences between the states.

Merrill Jensen has in recent years offered a salutary corrective to this view. The Articles, he has stressed, were an expression of colonial experience, "a natural outcome of the revolutionary movement within the American colonies," a statement of democratic theory far clearer than that of the individual states. It is

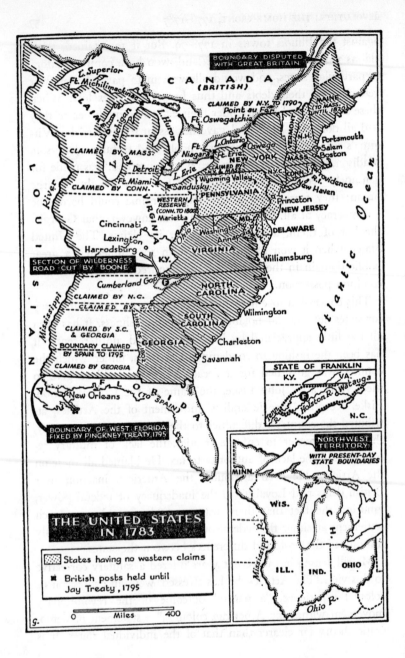

THE UNITED STATES
IN 1783

States having no western claims

British posts held until
Jay Treaty, 1795

0 Miles 400

BOUNDARY DISPUTED
WITH GREAT BRITAIN

CANADA
(BRITISH)

CLAIMED BY N.Y. TO 1790
Point au Fer

MAINE
(TO MASS.
UNTIL 1820)

Ft. Michilimackinac

L. Superior

CLAIM

Ft. Oswegatchie

L. Michigan

L. Huron

VERMONT

N.H.

Portsmouth

Salem

Boston

CLAIMED BY MASS.

Ft.
Niagara

L.Ontario

Oswego

Detroit

Ft. Erie

NEW
YORK

MASS.

CONN.

R.I.

Providence

New Haven

L. Erie

CLAIMED BY
N.Y. & MASS.

CLAIMED BY CONN.

Ft. Miami

Sandusky

Wyoming Valley

PENNSYLVANIA

Princeton

NEW JERSEY

WESTERN
RESERVE
(CONN. TO 1800)

Marietta

Ohio R.

MD.

Washington

Annapolis

DELAWARE

Cincinnati

Lexington

Harrodsburg

VIRGINIA

KY.

VIRGINIA

Williamsburg

SECTION OF WILDERNESS
ROAD CUT BY BOONE

Cumberland Gap

NORTH
CAROLINA

CLAIMED BY N.C.

CLAIMED BY S.C.

Mississippi River

Louisiana River

CLAIMED BY S.C.
& GEORGIA

LINE OF 1802

SOUTH
CAROLINA

Wilmington

BOUNDARY CLAIMED
BY SPAIN TO 1795

GEORGIA

Charleston

CLAIMED BY GEORGIA

Savannah

STATE OF FRANKLIN

KY.

VA.

F

Tenn. R.

Holston R.

Watauga

N.C.

FLORIDA
(TO SPAIN)

New Orleans

BOUNDARY OF WEST FLORIDA
FIXED BY PINCKNEY TREATY, 1795

Atlantic Ocean

NORTHWEST
TERRITORY
WITH PRESENT-DAY
STATE BOUNDARIES

MINN.

WIS.

MICH.

Mississippi R.

ILL.

IND.

OHIO

Ohio R.

G.

true that this meant a powerless executive, the taxing power in local hands, the importance of the legislature. But this was the philosophy of 1776; local self-government was the essence of agrarian democracy. If there was a failure of government in these years, it was due rather to the reluctance of the states to honor requisitions by Congress than to the constitutional limitation of the document. Nor were the Articles responsible for Britain's retaining the fur posts, or for the intrigues of Spain in the Mississippi country. The troubles were diplomatic and economic as well as constitutional. It is inaccurate to attribute to the Articles themselves the acute problems that arose in the period from 1783 to 1787. They were, however, cited by American conservatives as evidence of the need for a change.

Despite the corrective provided by Jensen, and whatever the causes, the problems were serious. There was a severe depression and deflation. The war stimulus to home industry and agriculture ceased. British forces disappeared and farmers everywhere lost a market. Secession from the Empire deprived New England of her West Indian trade, and the South lost its markets and bounties in Britain. When Massachusetts tried to prevent the dumping of British goods, New Hampshire eagerly absorbed them. Foreign nations treated the new Republic with contempt. Britain sent no minister until 1790, and then a junior; she treated John Adams as the first American minister with scant respect; she refused to evacuate the fur posts. France sought extraterritorial rights for her nationals. American shipping was powerless at sea and was driven from the Mediterranean by the Barbary corsairs.

The frontier clashes and tariff disputes of state with state continued. The Green Mountains of Vermont, contested between New York and New Hampshire, were dominated by the colorful and unreliable brothers Allen, and, not yet a state, contemplated union with Canada. Rhode Island, the last of the original thirteen states to join the Union (in 1790), did so only because it was threatened with tariff discrimination by all the rest; its government of farmers was bitterly satirized in *The Anarchiad*. It was indeed in the attempts by Washington, at the Mount Vernon Conference in 1785, to settle disputes of this sort along the Potomac that the discussions began which led to the Constitutional Convention of 1787.

One achievement of the Confederation it would be impossible to question—the settlement of the territories surrendered by the states to Congress in 1781. This Northwest, stretching from the northern edges of the Kentucky country to Canada, was little known, and for this reason was of great appeal to Jefferson in his character as naturalist and scientist—as well as politician. Congress drew up two ordinances (1785 and 1787) for the Northwest. The first provided for a survey of the territory before settlement and the creation of townships on New England lines, to minimize friction with other settlers and with the Indians. Sections were to be reserved for schools and as bounty land for veterans (out of which arose Virginia's Military District and Connecticut's Western Reserve); the rest was to be sold at a dollar an acre, but the minimum sale was to be 640 acres. This gave opportunity not to the little man but, once more, to the land speculator. The law of 1787, based on an earlier plan of Jefferson's, provided for three stages of government for a territory: first, under a governor and judges provided by Congress; next, when it had five thousand free adult males it could elect its own legislature, with the suffrage requiring the ownership of fifty acres of land; when the population reached sixty thousand it could be admitted to statehood on a basis of complete equality with existing states. Out of the whole area not less than three and not more than five states were to be formed: they became Ohio, Indiana, Illinois, Michigan, and Wisconsin. Had Jefferson's draft of 1784 been followed—he had proposed sixteen new states—some of the names would have been more romantic still: he had shown his interest in Old World as well as New World culture by suggesting, in addition to these familiar titles, Metropotamia (the Detroit area), Saratoga (Southern Ohio), Assenisipia (Chicago), Sylvania (Minnesota), and Cherronesus (Michigan).

The Northwest Ordinances are fully as important as the Constitution. They guaranteed freedom of religion, trial by jury, and education to these, and thus to subsequent, new territories; they permanently prohibited slavery in the entire area, north and west, that is, of the Ohio—its first national limitation and one that, by encouraging the entry of the free white settler, gave the area its free character. It took at least one more generation, however, before lower prices and laxer credit laws gave the smallholder his chance. And speculators, meanwhile, like the Reverend Manasseh Cutler and the Ohio Company, had a field day, abetted by corrupt congressmen. Nevertheless, more than any other enactments in the years after 1770, the ordinances extended the principles of the Declaration of Independence and applied them successfully to a vast and virgin land. They set a precedent that was followed by the next thirty-seven states as they came into being. They were noncolonial in spirit; the original thirteen states enjoyed the primacy that came with early settlement, but exercised no imperial control over other states. The ordinances quickened settlement too, although it was not until 1795, at the Treaty of Greenville, that a peace with the Indians was won. However unsatisfactory the Articles might have been, the provisions of 1785 and 1787 were remarkably farsighted and mature.

The Old Southwest presented very different problems. There were three major obstacles to settlement there, but all were being overcome before 1785: they were the Proclamation Line of 1763, ineffective before 1776 and automatically abrogated by the Revolution; the mountain barrier of the Alleghenies itself; and not least the Indians. The Mohawk was held by the Iroquois who, under the influence of the Johnsons, stayed loyal to Britain and whose chief Joseph Brant (Thayendanegea) had fought with his braves alongside St. Leger in 1777. With the support of General Haldimand, the Iroquois were "rewarded" after 1783 with lands in Ontario. The Creeks held the south, and in the years after 1783 they attempted, under a half-breed leader of talent and duplicity, Alexander McGillivray, to play off British, Spanish, and Americans in the Southwest. McGillivray was trader as well as warrior—a member of the firm of Panton and Leslie, which had monopoly rights in the Indian trade in the Floridas. Creeks, Spaniards, ex-Loyalists, and such adventurers as William Augustus Bowles made the Alabama country intractable to govern. It was in any case heavily forested hardwood country, difficult to clear—but its black soil looked tempting.

The central pass through the mountains was the Cumberland Gap on the present Virginia–North Carolina–Tennessee divide. It was at the Cumberland Gap that F. J. Turner, in his famous essay, had his mythical watcher stand in 1793, while, "impelled by an irresistible attraction," passed "the procession of civilization, marching single file—the buffalo following the trail to the salt springs, the Indian, the fur-trader and hunter, the cattle-raiser, the pioneer farmer. . . ."* From the Gap access was easy to the Kentucky blue grass, to the Nashville basin, and to the fertile bottomland of the Cumberland, Great Kanawha, and Tennessee rivers.

The Gap had been discovered in 1750 and a number of settlements had been made near it or beyond. In 1769 a Virginian settlement was begun at Watauga, reinforced in 1771 by Regulators led by James Robertson and John Sevier. In the same year the survey of the Virginia–North Carolina boundary revealed that Watauga was in North Carolina, although the nearest North Carolinian settlement was more than a hundred miles away. The Wataugans had learned independence and valued it; they formed the Watauga Association, based on manhood suffrage

---

* Frederick Jackson Turner, *The Frontier in American History* (1920). Turner's major omission from his list was the land speculator, who, if not in the "procession," was its chief organizer in the East. For a revisionary estimate of Turner see George W. Pierson, "The Frontier and Frontiersmen of Turner's Essays," *Pennsylvania Magazine of History and Biography,* LXIV (October 1940), 449–78, and Professor H. C. Allen, "F. J. Turner and the Frontier in American History" in *British Essays in American History* (ed. Allen and Hill. 1957).

and representative government, which survived until 1776, when they became Washington County, North Carolina. After the Revolution, Sevier led them in forming the "lost" state of Franklin, which provided a government but never won recognition from Congress.

Beyond Watauga, Daniel Boone was active between 1769 and 1775, tracing the Wilderness Road through the Gap to Boonesboro on the Kentucky. To these efforts the Shawnees offered resistance, but they were defeated in Dunmore's War of 1774 by General Andrew Lewis at Point Pleasant, fought near the mouth of the Kanawha. Cornstalk, the Shawnee chief, signed a treaty surrendering all title to lands south and east of the Ohio. Judge Richard Henderson of North Carolina attempted to organize a company for this area like the Ohio and Vandalia companies; by buying up the further titles of the Cherokees, he claimed a feudal mastery over an area stretching from the Gap westward to the junction of the Tennessee and Ohio. He called his domain Transylvania. His hopes of royal support came to a premature end with the Revolution, and the Continental Congress rejected his petition for recognition of his colony because of Virginia's sea-to-sea claims. In 1776 Virginia, acting at the request of the settlers in Harrodsburg, took the area under its all-too-inadequate protection as the county of Kentucky. By 1783 there were perhaps twenty thousand settlers in Kentucky, and a similar number in the Nashville area of Tennessee. Yet numbers increased fast in the Southwest, encouraged by new speculators like William Blount, who persuaded North Carolina in 1783 to open up for sale its Tennessee lands. The first census of 1790 reckoned that the Southwest had almost a quarter of a million settlers.

The problems presented by the West to the new Union were not those of encouraging settlement but of curbing premature government and mediating between many claimants to land and to political authority. Washington's first brush with the Senate was over an Indian treaty. In neither South nor North was it a case of a conservative federal government restraining a democratic frontier. The transmontane frontier was established almost entirely by land speculators—as were the earliest colonies themselves—and until its numbers were considerable it generated opportunism and proprietaries rather than democracy. To propriety it was always less sympathetic.

But the Southwest, with its vast quantities of game, its rich soil, and its long growing season, was developing fast. Kentucky, prospering with the Ohio trade, was admitted to statehood in 1792. Its constitution was the first in the South to provide for suffrage and office-holding without property qualification; although until 1799 the governor and senators were chosen by an electoral college. Tennessee, formed by a merger of the Watauga and Cumberland settlements, became the "Territory South of the River Ohio" in 1790 and a state in 1796. The honor of being the first new state, however, went to Vermont in 1791. If the war unified the country and the new Constitution gave it a federal government, it was the frontier, north and south, that was the greatest nationalizing force of all. If, in Professor Morgan's term, the American nation was the child, not the father, of the Revolution, its other parent was the western frontier.*

* Edmund S. Morgan, *The Birth of the Republic 1763–89* (1956), p. 101. See also Hans Kohn, *American Nationalism* (1957).

7

The Constitution

THE FEDERAL CONVENTION of May 1787 had a somewhat accidental origin. The Mount Vernon Conference of 1785, called to discuss the navigation of the Potomac, had adjourned its meetings to a second conference at Annapolis in 1786, attended by representatives of five states. Two of these representatives, Alexander Hamilton and James Madison, persuaded their colleagues that bound up with commerce were many other questions; the time had come for the creation of a "Constitution of the Federal Government adequate to the exigencies of the Union." A conference was needed of a more fundamental sort. Technically the task of such a conference was to draft amendments to the Articles, but all interested had hopes of devising a completely new document. The body that met in the Philadelphia State House was thus not strictly legal, nor was it very punctual. Rhode Island was not represented. The New Hampshire delegation arrived too late. But in the end fifty-five delegates attended, and thirty-nine of them signed the final draft.

Even allowing for retrospective piety, Jefferson was justified in speaking of them as "an assembly of demi-gods." Thirty-two of them were to become front-rank figures, with among them two Presidents, two Chief Justices, and six future state governors. A number of them had served in the Army; thirty were college graduates. The Philadelphia Convention, by a rare piece of elec-

tive good fortune, contained many of those who were the accepted leaders of their states, and many who sought a stronger
regime. Their achievement is familiar enough, and well chronicled. Yet it was chronicled only with difficulty. The official secretary, William Jackson, was far from efficient. His notes were
not published until 1819, and when they appeared James Madison
of Virginia proceeded, in accordance with them, to alter his own
notes, which had been much more fully kept. These were themselves not issued until 1840, four years after his death, by which
time fiction about the Founders bulked as large as fact. And
Madison's notes, now transformed, were far from reliable. Not
until Max Farrand's *The Records of the Federal Convention*
appeared in 1911 was it possible to see clearly just what had
occurred in Philadelphia.

Among the records not the least vivid are the comments of
one delegate on another, and particularly those of William Pierce
of Georgia on all the rest.

The Virginia delegation was punctual and very strong. Its most
prominent figure was Washington, who had already expressed
the view that the confederation was "shadow without substance,"
"a rope of sand." With a canniness more appropriate to a Yankee
than a Virginian, he hesitated about going lest the Convention
fail. He went, in the end, and since he was in the chair could
keep his own counsel. The delegation included George Mason,
who had drafted the Virginia Declaration of Rights, ambitious
young Governor Edmund Randolph, and lawyer George Wythe,
"remarked," said Pierce, "for his exemplary life." Its directing intelligence, however, was James Madison, "the best informed Man
of any point in debate . . . a Gentleman of great modesty—
with a remarkable sweet temper."*

From New York came Yates, Lansing, and Hamilton—"of
small stature and lean. His manners are tinctured with stiffness,
and sometimes with a degree of vanity that is highly disagree-

* The comments and those that follow are those of William Pierce.

able." From Massachusetts came Rufus King and Elbridge Gerry —"a hesitating and laborious speaker . . . goes extensively into all subjects that he speaks on, without respect to elegance or flower of diction." From Connecticut came shoemaker-politician Roger Sherman—"extremely artful in accomplishing any particular object"—and Oliver Ellsworth.

There was William Paterson from New Jersey ("a Classic, a Lawyer and an Orator"), and from Delaware John Dickinson, the Siéyès-turned-conservative among constitution-makers, to whom Pierce was antipathetic—"With an affected air of Wisdom he labors to produce a trifle,—his language is irregular and incorrect,—his flourishes (for he sometimes attempts them), are like expiring flames, they just shew themselves and go out." Luther Martin and James McHenry were there from Maryland; orator John Rutledge, proud Pierce Butler, and the cousins Pinckney from South Carolina; and, not least, the Pennsylvania delegation, in talent matching Virginia's. It included the "financier of the Revolution," Robert Morris—"he never once spoke on any point"—who ended in a debtors' prison; and the Scots-educated jurist James Wilson—"no great Orator"—who did likewise. There was Gouverneur Morris who "charms, captivates and leads away the senses of all who hear him. . . . But with all these powers he is fickle and inconstant—never pursuing one train of thinking—nor ever regular." A crippled arm and lack of a leg did not prevent Morris from seeing himself as the *beau sabreur* of the American, as he was to seek to be of the French, Revolution; in his zest and wit a d'Artagnan, Percy Blakeney, and Münchausen rolled into one. Accompanied wherever he went by two French valets, he was rightly called "exotic" by Hamilton. And there was his only rival as Münchausen, Dr. Franklin, to Pierce "the greatest phylosopher of the present age . . . the very heavens obey him, and the Clouds yield up their lightning to be imprisoned in his rod. But what claim he has to the politician posterity must determine."

Posterity was to be kinder to all of them—Blount from North

Carolina apart—even than was William Pierce. The majority of them certainly represented the Federalist viewpoint. Those most obviously identified with a radical point of view were absent. Jefferson and Paine were in Europe, as was John Adams. Patrick Henry, though elected, refused to attend. Sam Adams was not elected. There was more than a decade of political difference between 1776 and 1787.

A group, then, of unusually talented men, able to debate in secret and keep secret what they said; a basic agreement on what needed to be done to strengthen the government; and small concern, in contrast with the men of 1774–76, with the "why" of political action. The lawyers, Madison and Hamilton pre-eminently, were now concerned with the mechanics of state-building. To Madison, as a student of constitutions, and to Hamilton, with his taste for executive energy in government, this was a congenial task. The American Constitution was, of course, in Professor Farrand's phrase, "a bundle of compromises"; in the fact that controversy could be resolved by compromise lay its political strength. Again and again recourse was had to statements that sought to reconcile opposing viewpoints, or to a deliberately evasive form of words; thus the two-year term for congressmen was a compromise between one year and three. Yet in essence there was only one compromise. The Great, the Connecticut, or the Sherman Compromise—since it was largely his doing—was fundamental; it determined the shape of the central government: the decision on Federalism.

Arriving early, the Virginians had prepared, or had listened to Madison's elaboration of, a plan whereby there was to be a legislature of two houses, the lower to be elected by the people and the upper to be elected by the lower. Both houses—one directly, the other indirectly—would thus reflect population rather than statehood; this Virginia Plan was, therefore, acceptable to the larger states. There were also to be a single executive and judiciary, both chosen by the legislature. There was bitter feeling on this point, for the disparity of the states in size was striking. Delaware had 60,000 people; Rhode Island 68,000; Virginia, excluding Kentucky, had 750,000, of whom 300,000 were slaves; and Massachusetts, excluding Maine, 380,000, very few of whom were slaves.

New Jersey countered Virginia's Plan with its own, one much closer to the Articles, presented by William Paterson: a legislature of one house, elected by the states regardless of population, and with a plural executive elected by Congress.

The compromise reached after a month's debate gave the states equal representation in the Senate while maintaining the national principle—representation by population—in the House. This was an important result, not merely because it became the basis of the American government but also because it saved the Convention from dissolution. Yet it is possible to argue that, important though it was as a reconciliation of Federal and national principles, it was designed to meet a dilemma—the rivalry of great and small states—that was largely illusory. Maryland, a small state, and Virginia, a large one, shared on the Chesapeake a common economy of tobacco plantations and slave labor. Similarly, Connecticut and Massachusetts were alike in their commercial interests. The rivalry of state against state has never been as important in American history as the clash of sections.

The other compromises were at the time less important but were subsequently to become matters of controversy, largely because they reflected economic and sectional tensions. The first concerned the method whereby slaves were to be counted for both representation and taxation. The northern states wanted slaves excluded from representation, since they were neither citizens nor voters, but included for tax purposes, since they were property. This Yankee subtlety the South could not appreciate. The result was the adoption of the so-called three-fifths compromise whereby a slave was counted as three fifths of a person for both purposes. But this solution was not the result of a compromise in the Convention. It had first been proposed as an amendment to the Articles in 1783 and had been ratified by eleven states before the Convention met. There was here material for future trouble, as there was, also, in the South's fear that Congress might use the commerce power to interfere with the importation of slaves or to levy export duties on her staple products.

That these problems did not arouse the excitement then that they were to do in 1828 or 1861 was due precisely to the legalism and practicality of the delegates. Indeed, the coincidence of the publication of Madison's notes in 1840 with the rise of the slavery question gave an impression that it had been a major issue in 1787. It was not. As John Rutledge put it, "Religion and humanity have nothing to do with the question. Interest alone is the governing principle with nations. . . . If the Northern States consult their interests, they will not oppose the increase of slaves, which will increase the commodities of which they will become the carriers." They did consult their interests and a series of agreements followed: no interference with slave importation until 1808; Congress to be granted the power to regulate foreign and interstate commerce but, to protect the South, all treaties to require for ratification a two-thirds vote of the Senate; Congress to be forbidden to levy export taxes. But none of these matters was very controversial. The most bitter attack on slavery at the Convention came in fact from a Virginian.

On the final problem, the shape and the power of the federal government and its popular base, there was less controversy and less need for compromise, for the Fathers spoke and thought with remarkable unanimity. They declared that the Constitution was the supreme law of the land. The Tenth Amendment, declaring that the powers not expressly delegated to the federal government stayed with the states, has received so much attention that one is apt to minimize that to the Founders the central feature was the creation of this supreme power, as expressed in Article VI, Section 2. The new government should be strong, unlike the Congress of the Articles, and should be clearly sovereign. It was to be national rather than federal. It should act not on the states but on the people. It should legislate for all individuals in all the states. It should be empowered to levy taxes and to coin money; to declare war and make peace; to regulate commerce between the states; it should be able to admit new states on terms of absolute equality with the old; and, not least, have authority to make all laws "which shall be necessary and proper" in order to execute its powers (Art. 1, Sec. 8). The state issue of paper money and legislation impairing the obligation of contracts were prohibited. The new government was something more than "a firm league of friendship" between the states. In many ways it was at once the apogee of the Revolution and its Thermidor.

Accompanying this firmness were expressions of opinion critical of democracy that recalled the debate of 1774–76. Democracy was, said Gerry, the worst of all evils. The people, said Sherman, "should have as little to do as may be about the government." And Hamilton went further than most in devising plans for an executive sitting for life, indirectly elected and with an absolute veto on legislation; for a senate for life also chosen indirectly; and for a three-year assembly. Despite these views there was nevertheless a political caution; Federalism as thus voiced did not go unopposed. Franklin, though he spoke little and was thought by some to be senile, noted that "some of the greatest rogues he was ever acquainted with were the richest rogues." Mason became overtly critical. And so again compromise was reached: a House to be elected directly, the suffrage being governed by the state suffrage; the Senate elected indirectly by the state legislatures; the President elected still more indirectly, by a cumbrously chosen electoral college. The last was the most academic device of all in an otherwise very practical document. It was hit upon in the closing stages of the Convention by a special committee set up to settle a number of questions on which agreement had not been reached. It survives now, emasculated by the growth of political parties, as a curious relic of eighteenth-century political mechanics. The judiciary was to be appointed by the President, subject to senatorial approval but quite beyond popular control.

Yet in all the rich variety of their processes of election, the three branches of government were nicely balanced one against the other. They were to be equal, coordinate, and, so far as could be contrived, harmoniously interlocked. None could for long be seized by either democrats or potential tyrants. The strong government so patiently manufactured was still made as weak and as divided as could safely be managed. The very first Article, like the Articles being "amended," took pains to list at length the powers that the federal government did not have. Least of all did the Fathers attempt, either explicitly or implicitly, to define the government. The omissions again are significant; and wars and near-wars were to be needed to resolve the question whether they were building a nation or a federation, and just what "We the people" implied. But the wars have not completely solved the problem, as the years since 1954 have revealed in the South.

The nation has been built, in 1787 as since, not by federal or judicial enactment but by the common life lived and chosen by its members. This too the Fathers sensed; paper constitutions, they knew, had to be brought to life. They produced, therefore, a short document—four thousand words in length after four hundred hours of debate through a hot summer—whose ambiguities and vagueness it was left to the future to clarify. As Madison said, ambiguity was the price of unanimity. They wrought well, not primarily because they were constitutionalists—they were after all overturning one with some casualness—but because they had supreme faith in their own handiwork, in the new country, in the revolution they had led to victory, and in the future they glimpsed of their own resources and fortune. They were politicians of whom some were scholars, like Madison; some creative thinkers, like Hamilton; some, and not the least important, party managers and manipulators like John Beckley of Philadelphia; and like good politicians they had faith, most of all, in themselves. It was for the politicians that Franklin spoke on the last day of the Convention. There had been criticism of the omission of a Bill of Rights, defining the area in which an individual lived a life free from governmental constraint. There was criticism of the powers given to the central government. There was talk of summoning yet another and more representative Convention. Franklin met these challenges in a famous and characteristic plea:

> I confess that there are several parts of the Constitution which I do not at present approve, but I am not sure I shall never approve them. For having lived long, I have experienced many instances of being obliged by better information or fuller consideration, to change opinions even on important subjects, which I once thought right but found to be otherwise. It is therefore that, the older I grow, the more apt I am to doubt my own judgment and to pay more respect to the judgment of others. . . . Thus I consent, sir, to this Constitution because I expect no better, and because I am not sure that it is not the best. . . . On the whole, sir, I cannot help expressing a wish that every member of the Convention who may still have objection to it, would with me, on this occasion, doubt a little of his own infallibility, and to make manifest our unanimity, put his name to this instrument.

The major problem, however, on which compromise would be all but impossible, was the ratification of the Constitution. This involved a public debate outside the State House in Philadelphia and the approval of popularly elected state conventions. As we have seen, the Convention was, although in name only, amending the Articles. To do so required the unanimity of all thirteen states. In the absence of Rhode Island this was clearly unattainable. The Convention therefore took the high-handed view that the new document would become effective when ratified by nine states in specially summoned conventions.

The debate in the country was far more bitter than that in Philadelphia, and much less amenable to control. It was now that the "democratic" issue was most clearly raised and in the course of the debate that faction and party first appeared. Yet the opposition to the new document did not challenge its main themes; the Republic and its balanced government were fully accepted. Nor could it provide a clear leadership: Randolph hesitated and became a Federalist; Hancock in Massachusetts was won over by the expectation of rewards; Sam Adams was impressed by the support for the Constitution he found among the shipwrights of Boston at a carefully arranged meeting at the Green Dragon, and by the final compromise to include in it a Bill of Rights. The central theme of the Anti-Federalists was the fear of an encroachment on the rights of the states and on "liberty." This fear was stronger in the larger and more "democratic" states than in the smaller. The Delaware convention ratified promptly and unanimously; New Jersey a little less promptly but also unanimously. It took Pennsylvania a month of debate and some rather rough practices to come to accept it. They did so by 46 votes to 23; but the minority claimed that in the elections of delegates only thirteen thousand freemen voted out of seventy thousand entitled to do so; here was still a sharp divergence between the interests of Federalist Philadelphia and Anti-Federalist western Pennsylvania. In Massachusetts the Federalist victory was narrow: 19 votes out of 355. Not until June 1788 did the ninth state, New Hampshire, give its approval. At that point it was not clear that the two key states, Virginia and New York, had agreed to support the Constitution. In fact Virginia had approved it by a narrow majority of ten votes, 89 to 79, before learning of the action of New Hampshire. New York's majority was even smaller—30 to 27—when it came to its decision in July.

This result in New York was once again evidence of Alexander Hamilton's energy, political flair, and persuasive power. At Philadelphia he had been in a minority in his delegation; he attended only occasionally and his theories of centralization made him suspect. His colleagues, Yates and Lansing, who had finally withdrawn from the Convention on the grounds that it had exceeded its authority, were friends of George Clinton, governor of the state and a leading Anti-Federalist. Clinton expressed his fears in a series of articles under the pen-name Cato. New York's politics were personal and peculiar, and they were largely the mercantile politics of the City of New York. It commanded the trade of the whole country, and in 1787—as in 1776 and earlier—it preferred neutrality or even independence to coming down on the wrong side. To these motives of fear, of cupidity, and of commercial risk and profit as well as of public spirit, Hamilton appealed in the series of eighty-five essays that became, along with Madison's and Jay's, the *Federalist Papers*. There was small hope, he believed, for the future of the country so long as the government was powerless and was scorned by foreign traders, so long as it was handicapped by varied and conflicting state laws and currencies, and so long as it was incapable of paying its own debts or compelling the states to meet theirs. He won the New York convention to his views by the sheer force of his arguments.

The victory in New York was narrow. The nation as a whole, had it been polled individually, might well have been opposed to the Constitution. Charles A. Beard's figures, suspect though they now are, showed that only one in four of the adult males voted for delegates to the state ratifying conventions; probably not more than one in six of them ratified it. Hamilton thought that four sevenths of the people of New York were against the Constitution. Neither Rhode Island, which submitted it to its town meetings, nor North Carolina adopted the Constitution until the new government was in operation, when they had little choice. The extent of the opposition led seven states to accompany acceptance by a series of amendments, and in the first session of the new Congress twelve of these were agreed upon and submitted to the states. Ten were ratified and became the Bill of Rights. This was a concession by the Federalist leaders to their critics.

The Constitution was drafted and enacted by a group of determined men, very much a minority among their fellows and acting without legality; so it had been with the Revolution, and so it is with most great developments in human history. Neither the document nor the methods whereby it was made the fundamental law were the work of a majority; nor were they tributes to democracy, still an ideal of the future. The Federalists were nationalists; in nothing were they so skillful as in the name they chose, for their intention was unitary rather than federal. They were led by two masterful politicians, Hamilton and Madison. If Hamilton appears, in print as in his subsequent legislation, an apologist for the economic royalists, it is impossible not to see in his handiwork, as in his consistent purpose, a policy that had about it, at this stage at least, courage, foresight, and idealism. If Madison supplied the scholarship and the draftsmanship, Hamilton provided the drive and combative power that were even more necessary.

Of all aspects of the Revolutionary period, the motives that led to the drafting of the Constitution have become the most controversial. As the United States grew and prospered, it was natural that the Constitution as its basic law should become revered, and that its Founding Fathers should be seen as men of remarkable wisdom. This view was natural but has not gone uncontested in American history. The crisis of 1814, the Civil War of 1861, and the controversies over the legality of the New Deal were indications that the compromises of 1787 had not been final solutions for all problems. There has been in fact no "consensus," to use today's fashionable word, on the central theme of the American story—whether it is a *plures* or a *unum,* a federation or a centralized nation. Yet once the Civil War was won and nationalism was triumphant, Hamilton emerged as the patron saint of the American entrepreneur, and the Constitution was seen once more as a work of great prescience. It came to win approval abroad in the eloquent encomiums of Gladstone and of Bryce.

Nationalist historians such as Bancroft praised it still more lavishly. John Fiske, writing in 1888, accepted the Federalist arguments of a century before, to compose his study of *The Critical Period* and to portray the Founders as inspired and dedicated men who had brought order and security out of chaos.

It was natural that there should be a reaction from this patriotic view. And of it Charles Beard became the spokesman. Product of a Midwest that was then passing through the Populist and Progressive phase and of British politics in its Fabian heyday, Beard's *Economic Interpretation of the Constitution* (1913) was, as much as Fiske's book, a product of its time. To use a phrase used six years before by one of Beard's mentors, J. Allen Smith, in his *The Spirit of American Government*, Beard saw the Constitution as "a reactionary document," or at least as one that was counterrevolutionary. It was the product, Smith had said, not of democracy but of men who feared democracy, a "scheme of government . . . planned and set up to perpetuate the ascendancy of the property-holding class leavened with democratic ideas." Or as Burke had said of 1688, it was a revolution not made but prevented.

Beard argued, as did Merrill Jensen later, that the Federalists, the conservatives or nationalists of their day, had exaggerated the weakness of government in the decade before 1787, and that Fiske *et al*. had accepted their partisan indictments as statements of permanent truth. He pointed to the many fears the Federalists expressed of "democracy," their provisions guarding contracts and debts, their concern with a strong judiciary and the separation of powers as checks on majority rule. And he substantiated his argument by a massive analysis of the economic interests of the Founders, drawing heavily on the Treasury Department on lines that anticipated the cumulative-biography approach of Sir Lewis Namier toward British eighteenth-century politics. Not one of the Founders, he argued, was a farmer or an artisan; and five sixths of them stood to gain from the Constitution, since they owned securities or slaves or land for speculation. Far from being disinterested men, the patriots who came to the rescue of their country, Washington and Randolph, James Wilson and Rufus King, Oliver Ellsworth and Alexander Hamilton, Robert Morris and John Dickinson had such a large stake in its property and society that the document they drafted was inevitably biased toward their own economic interest. Their motive was the safeguarding of property rights. The value of their bond holdings appreciated by some forty million dollars when supported by the credit of the new government. Moreover, they were not popularly chosen and were a small but highly influential group. By controlling elections and manipulating conventions they put through an undemocratic document to which the majority of Americans were in fact opposed.

If Beard's analysis represents a piece of historical debunking, an expression in fact of militant Jeffersonian populism, it was brilliantly done and has left a profound mark on all subsequent writing on this period. It stimulated many state-by-state analyses; it greatly influenced the attitude of all later writers, some of whom, like V. L. Parrington, made contributions to American historical writing quite as significant as Beard's; it reinforced the trend toward the "new" and social emphasis in historical writing, evidenced in the work of Carl Becker, J. Franklin Jameson, and Arthur Schlesinger, Sr.; and, not least, many of the Founding Fathers at last emerged as explicable and human figures. They were not only human, they were capitalists and speculators. Beard was seeking to portray what he called the true "inwardness" of the Constitution. This was needed, he thought, expressly because the document gives no outward recognition of any economic groups in society, mentions no special privileges, and, as he puts it, "betrays no feelings." "Its language is cold, formal and severe." It could hardly be said to be either cold or noncontroversial after he had written.

The extent of Beard's impact is best evidenced by the scale on which his work has recently been attacked. For it was equally bitterly censured in his own time, not only for its economic determinism but for its demonstration that a work believed to be of near-divine ordering had been in fact the product of a very mundane self-interest. And much of the criticism then made was as weighty as that of our own day. E. S. Corwin in 1914 criticized Beard's exaggerations and faulted his figures; and he pointed out that one of the biggest property-owners of the Convention was Elbridge Gerry, who refused to sign the Constitution and opposed its adoption. R. L. Schuyler, in his excellently balanced study of the Constitution, while accepting that the two main groups were based principally on economic interests, stresses that there were many other motives; among the Federalists it was impossible to exclude patriotism, the wish to see the new country playing a dignified role in international affairs, the belief that only a strong and vigorous government would preserve the Union, experience in and respect for the Army rather than the Continental Congress; among critics, there was fear for liberty, strong state-right sentiments, and much sectional jealousy. The leaders, it was pointed out, were as much lawyers as businessmen and speculators; they were politicians also playing for power. It was Franklin who spoke of the United States as a "Nation of Politicians," and none could speak of the profession with more authority. Yet they were also, in some measure, idealists. They were affected, says Charles Warren, "by pride in country, unselfish devotion to the public welfare, desire for independence, inherited sentiments and convictions of right and justice."*

Economic determinism is persistent and unfashionable in the United States. And in recent years a new political attack has been launched on Beard's interpretation of the Constitution. Robert E. Brown has examined Beard's thesis in great detail and denied not only its validity but the research on which it was based. The records that Beard used date, he has argued, from several years after the Constitutional Convention. The holdings

---

* Robert L. Schuyler, *The Constitution of the United States* (1923); Charles Warren, *The Making of the Constitution* (1929).

of the Founding Fathers were in land far more than in securities. If their property was adversely affected by the situation before 1787, so were the property interests of the great majority of people, for the ownership of property was widespread. If they were selected by their state legislatures rather than popularly elected, such a method was the constitutional form under the Articles. If a man refrained from voting for delegates to the ratifying convention, this was more from indifference, and therefore presumably from contentment with the status quo, than from disfranchisement. And if both the Founders and the people acted as they did, it was as much for reasons of conviction as for reasons of economic self-interest.*

The same author in his *Middle-Class Democracy and the Revolution in Massachusetts 1691–1780* argues that there was no large working class denied the vote in Massachusetts and that the farmers in the western part of the state had as full representation in the legislature as the merchants of the east. Massachusetts, he believes, was already a democratic state. Not all the latest research accords with this interpretation, and it would indeed be revolutionary if similar views were to obtain of the southern states. But the emphasis is clear.

It has been driven home even more ruthlessly by Forrest McDonald in a name-by-name analysis of the Fathers and of the states, proving that they represented agriculture far more than commerce or securities, that many of them were lawyers with many varied clients to represent, and that their interests were far more diverse than Beard's categories revealed. Clearly, there was no sharp division between the interests of real and personal property.†

At this point one is tempted to recall Louis Hartz' remark: "But after all is said and done Beard somehow stays alive, and the reason for this is that, as in the case of Marx, you merely

---

* Robert E. Brown, Jr., *Charles Beard and the Constitution* (1956).

† Forrest McDonald, *We the People: The Economic Origins of the Constitution* (1958).

demonstrate your subservience to a thinker when you spend your
time attempting to disprove him."* What the critics are asserting,
however, is partly the superiority of recent research to Beard's
avowedly "fragmentary" methods, and still more the viewpoint
of the mid-twentieth century. The Fathers, they remind us, were
patriots after all, men with principles as well as pocketbooks. If
they represented property, they spoke for many constituents, for
there were many property-owners. They sought to create a strong
government not only, and perhaps not mainly, to curb democracy but also to create a new nation and preserve the gains of
the Revolution. For they had pride in both achievements. The
fashion today is to revere the Constitution almost as did Bancroft
and Fiske, and to see it as conserving a society that had already
gone far toward becoming a property-owning democracy. The
most remarkable characteristic of the political theory of the Revolution, says Clinton Rossiter, was "its deep-seated conservatism."
"The American future was never to be contained in a theory,"
writes Daniel Boorstin. "The Revolution was . . . a prudential
decision taken by men of principle rather than the affirmation of
a theory." Beard, despite his errors, has, it seems, been legiti-
mized; the Founders were not selfish; they were only wise. The
United States has come a long way, not only since 1776, but since
1913.

In his *Politics and the Constitution in the History of the
United States,* William W. Crosskey goes much further and contends that the members of the Convention were in fact seeking
deliberately to create a unitary national government which would
have the power of direct legislation in the fields of commerce and
welfare. The power to regulate commerce in its eighteenth-
century usage included, he contends, the whole range of economic activity. The Supreme Court was to be a national judicial
body which would create a uniform system of national law. In
his view, the Fathers were unsympathetic to state rights and

---

* *The Liberal Tradition in America* (1955), p. 28.

sought salvation in the centralizing of power. Moreover, the "United States," he holds, existed as a body politic before the states acquired what was, wrongly, called "sovereignty." This is an interpretation that has not yet won general acceptance.

Does any consensus emerge, then, from these conflicting views?

In contrast with the states of contemporary Europe, American society of 1787 was small in numbers, reasonably unified, and strongly democratic. If there were classes, they were much closer to each other than in Europe, and careers in America had long been open to talents, before the phrase became a slogan of European revolution. There was, as the French troops saw, a much greater degree of economic equality than in Europe. There prevailed in America what Franklin called a "happy mediocrity." If there were conservatives and radicals, they were not yet completely aligned in 1787, and not recruited from the same groups in every state. As Oscar and Mary Handlin have shown, the Federalists and Anti-Federalists of 1788 in Massachusetts do not correspond either politically or socially with the conservatives and radicals of a decade before.* Opinion was in flux. The revolutionary Patrick Henry ended up a conservative. Wealthy landowner George Mason was a radical who feared aristocracy, yet he opposed the suggestion that the President be directly elected on the unradical grounds that "it would be as unnatural to refer the choice of a proper character for chief magistrate to the people, as it would to refer a trial of colours to a blind man"; the people, he said, had not "the requisite capacity to judge." And the proposal that the chief executive should be directly elected was made by the conservative jurist James Wilson. Randolph, who helped to draft the Constitution, refused to sign it, then campaigned for its ratification on his

---

* "Radicals and Conservatives in Massachusetts after Independence," *New England Quarterly*, XVII (1944), p. 343. Robert Thomas has shown in similar fashion that the line between Federalist and Anti-Federalist in Virginia follows no clear pattern of property-holding. *Journal of Southern History*, XIX (1953), p. 63.

return to Virginia. Individuals can rarely be reduced to a pattern either of economic or of any other determinism. Nor indeed can states. The wealthy states like New York and Virginia hesitated longest over adoption. As Washington noted, the opposition to the Constitution came from "the men of large property in the South," not from "the genuine democratical people of the east."

Americans in 1787 were engaged in a great debate on government that had been in progress at least since the Albany Plan of 1754—if not since 1620 itself—of which the *Federalist Papers* and the Constitution were in a sense merely the latest expression. It is impossible to accept the gloomy view of V. L. Parrington when he says that little abstract political speculation accompanied the making and adoption of the Constitution, for the *Federalist Papers* are a classic statement of the issues that the Fathers faced, and of the ideals of the Whig style of politics. They enshrined a century and a half of experience, and much reflection on classical parallels.

But, in one sense, Beard and Parrington are right. The Fathers were lawyers and practical men, dealing with the problems of their day. They had discovered that, with Britain now removed and themselves facing acute local problems and frontier threats, there was need in America for a strong native executive power and for a President who was also Commander-in-Chief. A reading of Professor Farrand's compilation of the views of the framers of the Constitution reveals clearly that they saw their task as that of correcting the weakness of the Articles. But the appeals they were making were to interests much wider than Beard seems to have realized: to the public creditor, certainly, but also to the soldier, paid in bounty land that he could not obtain without a strong government, or in paper scrip that was almost worthless; to citizens as well as speculators in the West, who alike wanted protection from Indians and from foreign intrigues; to merchants trading abroad as well as manufacturers and workers seeking economic protection and security. "An assembly of the states, alone, by the terror of its power, and the fidelity of its engagements, can preserve a perpetual peace with the nations of Europe." The words were "Harrington's" in *The American Museum,* June 1787. There were very many who by 1787 had a stake in America's stability and its future, who in Hamilton's words were "anxious for the respectability of the nation." They were, in other words, good Whigs.

Equally, the Founders accepted the other dominant aspect of their world, that it was one of sectional interests. Federalism was not an invention but the translation into political form of geographic and economic facts, an expression of social and political reality. Not the least of the miracles wrought in Philadelphia was the settlement of the rivalry between small states and large —an issue that never again became a major problem. Localism remained, of course, a major issue. There was, in 1787, still little sentiment of nationalism to buttress the work of the architects in Philadelphia. And there was great variation. The democratic upthrust that occurred in Pennsylvania was not in evidence in Delaware or Maryland.

The greatest achievement, however, less willed by the Fathers' reason than product of their century and a half of political experience, was popular sovereignty. Given the need for a strong central government, whether for economic, nationalist, or idealistic reasons, or perhaps because they were simply persuaded of its necessity, both their history and their revolution taught them that it would be acceptable only if its roots went deep in some formula of consent. The higher the pyramid the deeper must be the local roots and the broader the base. In this sense what Federalists and Anti-Federalists accepted as common ground was far more striking than the controversy between them. There was no Thermidorean reaction; it was not needed. The men of property formed a party, although only slowly; they sought a stronger union than many, perhaps the majority, may have wanted. They sought it, however, as conservators of the Revolution. They came to Philadelphia from thirteen distinct states, but many had found in the Army a forcing-house of nationalism.

The strongest statement heralding Federalism had come from
Washington in June 1783, in his last circular as Commander-
in-Chief. It was a plea for "An indissoluble Union of the States
under One Federal Head." As Washington had again made
plain at Newburgh, the Federalists were as dedicated to republicanism as their opponents. They accepted, even accentuated, the
separation of powers: they erected barriers against potential executive tyranny with quite as much zeal as the radicals. They
did so, however, less from principle or from a reading of Montes-
quieu or Locke than from practice: it was but the form of
colonial government, of governor *versus* assembly, to which they
were accustomed.

Equally, the "democratic" movement was far removed from
Jacobinism. There was no need for any cry of "The land to the
peasants," for the land was abundant and was already fairly extensively owned; and few would have accepted the term *peasant*.
The seizure of Loyalist land was the closest approximation in
American history to the expropriation of the expropriators. They
did not need to go further. They were not expropriators, but in-
heritors. And their faith in what men could do with their own
property made some of them also—not always successfully—
entrepreneurs.

To some aspects of the modern state, of course, almost all
Americans in 1787 were quite blind. Some of their modern
admirers approve of their "principles." But what were they?
They were far from explicit in 1787. It is easier to define them
negatively; for they knew more clearly what they were against
than what they were for. They were hostile to tyranny, in all its
forms—of one man or of many, hostile to the concentration of
authority in any one man or institution, hostile to any unbalanced government. The essence of their fears was seen in
the bills of rights, incorporated in the state constitutions and by
1790 in the federal document. The liberties for which they had
fought were listed there, and the written documents gave them
precise form, protection, and, over the years, increasingly sanc-

tity But despite all its revolutionary advance, there is much that is missing, much that the Constitution did not say. It was not clear where lay the power to regulate industry, as Crosskey shows. Nothing was said on the acquisition of new territories, as Jefferson was to find. Political parties were not mentioned, apparently not even foreseen, despite the threat of faction. Least of all was anything said or glimpsed of the rights of a member state to secede from the new Union.

This is, however, but to say that the Constitution was drafted by politicians seeking to settle, if not to solve, the problems of their own age. "Experience must be our only guide," said John Dickinson. "Reason may mislead us." The work of lawyers, and of men influenced by their own British traditions, the strength of the document was its realism. There was little evidence in it of humanitarian sentiments and no nonsense about a world crusade. "Symbols of a world revolution," says Louis Hartz, "the Americans were not in truth world revolutionaries." Those with foreign experience, like Paine and Franklin, and those without it alike accepted the wisdom of isolation. Nearly all the constitutions, state and federal, contained some statement about equality but none of them suggested crusading for it abroad—or at home. There was little concern with the rights of man, and when Rufus King did use the phrase it was in a less exciting fashion than the French. There was no stress on tolerance; indeed many "democrats" were markedly intolerant men; in Pennsylvania and in the back country clearly so. None of them proclaimed the abolition of slavery or the granting of equal rights, in law or suffrage, to women as well as men. Some Protestants sought to limit the rights of non-Protestants. In Pennsylvania the radicals tried to curb the free expression of opinion. And by equality what was meant was equality before the law, not social justice or economic rights.

Extensive property-owning, then, meant a wide franchise; this in itself did not produce democracy. *Democracy* as a term was little used and in general greatly feared. It was a term completely absent from the Declaration of Independence and from the state and federal constitutions. Even Jefferson avoided it. Nor was a majority vote seen as a safeguard against tyranny. In the form of unicameral legislatures it was particularly feared. Under the Constitution there was to be, locally and at the center, a series of checks on arbitrary power, whether the power came from above or below. Elections were to be as indirect as possible, to allow time for reflection and for passions to cool. Few of the constitution-makers had any faith in simple majority rule.

The great debate of 1787 was successful in its outcome expressly because both groups held so many postulates and so many fears in common. There were men of property, as Beard argued, in the Federal Convention. There were many more outside it, as Brown argues. The Revolution over, all now had much to conserve.

8

The First President:
the Captive Federalist

THE CONSTITUTION was ratified with the adherence of New Hampshire in June 1788. There was a general expectation that Washington would be the first President, and the celebration of his fifty-sixth birthday in July became the occasion for the call to be launched. A toast was drunk at Wilmington, Delaware, to "Farmer Washington—May he like a second Cincinnatus, be called from the plow to rule a great people." Washington had his customary doubts; the electors had not. They were chosen in the different states on the first Wednesday in January 1789, and they met and cast their ballots on the first Wednesday in February. Some were chosen by voters, others by the state legislatures, those of New Jersey by the governor and council. Washington was unanimously chosen, with John Adams his Vice-President. On April 16, 1789, once again he left Mount Vernon at his country's call.

His journey to New York was a royal progress, through Philadelphia and Trenton. As he sailed up the Hudson, he was met by sloops on which choirs sang odes in his honor—one of them ironically set to the tune of "God Save the King." The peals of bells in the New York churches were drowned by the noise of thirteen-gun salutes from ship and shore batteries. At his inaugural on April 30, although he behaved nervously—his gestures awkward, his voice low, and his hands restless—he became the part, with his dress sword, his shoe-buckles of silver, and his canary-colored coach drawn by six horses. The manners became the man if not yet the office. If Fisher Ames thought his modesty "an allegory in which virtue was personified," he brought his own natural dignity to the presidency and the new nation.

When the first census was taken in 1790, the population of the United States was found to be just over 3,900,000, of whom some 750,000 were slaves. Virginia was the largest of the states, its population some 750,000, of whom 40 per cent were slaves.

The pattern of life was rural; compared with France, said Volney, the French traveler, in 1796, "the entire country is one vast wood." Land, however, was too fertile and too abundant to call yet for scientific agriculture; there was no general rotation of crops, the plow was crude, reaping and threshing were done by hand, the land was quickly overworked. But there was, if small scientific knowledge, a growing scientific interest. There were pioneer agricultural societies; new plants and fertilizers were discussed; the need for diversification and rotation of crops was accepted; there was growing correspondence among the larger farmers. In the South, the production of cotton was hindered by the need to separate the fibers from the seed by hand, and it was some time after Whitney's ingenious invention of the cotton gin that the door of opportunity was seen to be open. In 1791 the total cotton production of the whole United States was 400 bales. In 1810, it had become 178,000 bales.

In Washington's America life was more than rural, it was rustic. The cloth used was mainly homespun; Washington's fine homespun for his inaugural was made in Connecticut. Most articles were home-made as much for reasons of defense as for reasons of lack of opulence, to use Adam Smith's distinction. Cobbett noted that the appearance of the farm was neither so "neat" nor so "tight" as in England. Farther west, log cabins were the characteristic dwelling, standing in newly cleared fields that were full of stumps, or in the midst of dead and girdled trees.

Cities were still few, and Philadelphia with its paved streets and the beginnings of a water supply was still the most important. Its population in 1790 stood at close to forty thousand. It was, said John Adams, "the pineal gland" of the continent. There was small sign in 1790 of the future importance of New York, badly affected by the Revolution. Only 3 per cent of the population lived in the six towns of more than eight thousand (Philadelphia, New York, Boston, Charleston, Baltimore, and Salem). Although the wealthier citizens might live in brick houses of Georgian style, houses were mainly of wood, and lighted by candles. Glass for windows was rare: oiled paper was generally used. When the streets were lighted it was by oil lamps, and they were not used in moonlight or rain. Sanitation was primitive. And town life was scarred each summer by the recurrent epidemics of yellow fever; the outbreak of 1793 led to the mass evacuation of Philadelphia and 10 per cent of the population died. Again in 1797 there was a mood of panic in Philadelphia, and it was repeated in the epidemics in New York in 1798 and 1803. The "fevers" of high summer, not yet traced to the mosquito, seemed more menacing to the new Republic than an army of redcoats. Dr. Benjamin Rush's remedies, although they included sanitary reforms, were almost as menacing as the fever itself: he favored bleeding and purging.

Except in the vicinity of Philadelphia and in Connecticut, communications were still poor. There were no railways and few good highways, and not until the 1790s did the first steamboat appear—John Fitch's far-from-successful operation on the Delaware. Water communication was easier than that by land, and there were many canal projects, some of them fantastic. Until 1812 the shortage of capital was as much an obstacle to these developments as nature herself. Along the coast, travel by sea and river was favored. As a result, the roads that were built headed west. In the South, where capital went almost automatically into land and slaves, what road-building there was was done by the states; to federal action for internal improvements there were constitutional objections. And progress over the mountains was slow. In the North, however, private turnpike companies appeared, levying tolls; by 1800 there were seventy-two of them. There were even some private bridge companies. But it was ferries and fords that the Virginia Presidents had to use on their regular journeys to the North.

The lack of roads had many consequences. It cost thirty dollars and took at least four days to travel from Boston to New York. It took President Adams three days to reach the new Federal City from Philadelphia in 1800. Postal services were haphazard; postal rates were high and were paid by the recipient. It was not until 1800 that a regular mail route was in use from Maine to Georgia, taking twenty days. In this isolation, political issues stayed stubbornly local.

The trans-Allegheny country suffered most. It was little explored as yet. Here Nature, in Henry Adams' words, was still "man's master rather than his servant." The western farmer was cut off, remote from eastern cities, from political centers, and from markets. The obvious trade route was the Mississippi. This raised social and political issues. Until steamboat days the route was long and costly, the profits slight. Meat and grain went down river on flatboats, with small but tough crews addicted to such tough sports as rough-and-tumble fighting and gouging. The boats were broken up and sold as lumber in New Orleans and the crews returned home on horseback or on foot through hostile country where they had need of all their fighting spirit. Until the Pinckney Treaty of 1795, Spain had a stranglehold on this trade and used it to tempt from their American allegiance the colorful but utterly untrustworthy men living on the western waters.

The other expedient open to westerners was to transform their grain into whiskey and to transport this by pack horse to eastern markets. When Hamilton's excise tax, designed as a fiscal rather than a Puritan measure, imposed financial prohibition, the corn was fed to hogs, and hogs on the hoof were driven from Ohio and Kentucky to their destination back east. It is not for nothing that the highway, and the mobility it brought with it, is the central feature of American life, the keystone of its economy and of its capacity to survive as a federal society. Equally it is no accident that the isolation and remoteness that were nature's gift to the westerners made them independent and sturdy-minded, gregarious and unaddicted to privacy, rough and loud in manner but warm and egalitarian.

This society, scattered and diverse though it was, lived a common and largely a farming life. Manufacturing—except for iron —was on a small scale, short of capital and short of skilled craftsmen. It was as yet a primitive life, and European travelers, even as they saw America in the van of progress, noted the dirt, the lack of sanitation, and the poor roads. They noted too the monotonous if cheap and abundant food. The principal crop was Indian corn or rye, and the diet was based almost uniformly on rye or Indian bread, corn pone or hoecake, hasty pudding or hominy, and cod or salt pork. "Give me the children that's raised on good sound pork after all the game in the country," wrote Cooper in *The Chainbearer,* describing America in 1784. "Game's good as a relish, and so's bread, but pork is the staff of life."

The uniformity was even more marked of the beverages that went down with it. The water was often undrinkable. Chastellux noted in 1780 the popularity of coffee. But other beverages were more popular, and more native. The first temperance movement, some ten years later, was said to have been due to the disgust caused by the regular intoxication of ministers in their pulpits. Travelers in the South, like John Bernard, described with zest the "diurnal potations," the mysteries of mint sling and bumbo, apple toddy or pumpkin flip. James Madison, by no means a sociable figure and not reckoned a toper, regularly drank a pint of whiskey a day, a goodly share of it before breakfast. Cobbett thought drinking the national disease; at all hours, young men and "even little boys at or under twelve years of age go into stores and tip off their drams." Henry Adams, in commenting on this, notes that the mere comparison with Britain proves how great was the evil, for the English and the Scots were notoriously the largest consumers of beer and alcohol on the globe. Perhaps for this reason, few Americans lived long lives, and fifty was thought of as old age. Those like Jefferson who reached eighty-three, or like Adams who reached ninety-one, were indeed men of parts.

If art was not yet much in evidence, there was a growing interest in nature. The first generation of artists were imitators rather than creators; Feke and Smibert were mannered and clumsy; Peale, Copley, and Stuart were shaped more by London than by America. The architecture too was imitative, even if the South made of Georgian and Palladian styles as gracious in their new settings as ever they were in the old. The models remained for a while stubbornly English, and there were as yet few of the graces. But there were many signs of promise and an irrepressible optimism. "After the first Cares for the Necessaries of Life are over, we shall come to think of the Embellishments," wrote Franklin. "Already some of our Young Geniuses begin to lisp Attempts at Painting, Poetry and Musick."

The embellishments were likely to be increasingly native. "Had I come to Europe sooner in Life I should have known nothing but the Receipts of Masters," said Benjamin West. Americans were beginning to pioneer and to take pride in the pioneering. Linnaeus drew on the work of John Bartram of Philadelphia, whose research won him a European reputation. Jared Eliot of Connecticut found English treatises on agriculture unsuitable to New England and wrote his own. Jefferson showed his questing mind in his *Notes on Virginia* and challenged Buffon. It has long been fashionable to trace the origins of Jeffersonian republicanism—inaccurately, it now seems—to a famous "botanical expedition" up the Hudson River conducted by Jefferson and Madison in 1791. Cadwallader Colden also combined a taste for politics with an interest in natural history. John Winthrop set up a physics laboratory at Harvard. Benjamin Waterhouse pioneered in treating smallpox by inoculation. William Shippen and John Morgan had established the first American medical school at Philadelphia in 1762.

The note was critical; it was also practical. Franklin's interests were in stoves for homes and cures for smoky chimneys, in fire companies and colleges, courants and almanacs. Reflecting the Enlightenment as expressed through the philosophical societies that sprang up on both sides of the Atlantic, Franklin and his junto believed in the diffusion of useful knowledge.

The American people in 1790 lived close to nature. They had a strong sense of equality and a small sense of class. Their measuring rod was not tradition but utility, not status but worth. They were better informed by newspapers than were Europeans; and from their pulpits, their town meetings, and their county courthouses they were addicted to talk and debate. They were democratic-minded and argumentative, articulate and contentious.

The presidency of George Washington remains, surprisingly, among the most controversial of all the presidencies. Surprisingly, because it has been abundantly chronicled; indeed overabundantly. The hagiography that began with Parson Weems, his first adulatory biographer, has continued ever since, and no later writers have ever quite managed to shake themselves free from it. They have, happily, rarely been as naïve as he was.

But successive biographers have in their own ways been quite as careless with the facts. Sparks, in publishing the first edition of Washington's writings in 1837, did so only after a careful vetting and doctoring of his style. The most gifted of his nineteenth-century biographers, Washington Irving, writing in 1855-

59, portrayed him as a good churchgoer, which he was not, and denied that he married for money, which he did. The Washington portrait has been carved in marbled prose, lost to flesh and blood and temper.

It is only recently that Washington's biographers have had the temerity to point out his all-too-human sensitiveness, and his all-too-natural leaning to the cause of order and of nationalism, to which, largely at others' command, he had dedicated his life. The heavily magisterial tone of D. S. Freeman's six volumes, while rich in detail, contrives to leave the man interred in the achievement; in places his final (sixth) volume suggests that Washington never fully understood the broad intent of the Hamiltonian program. The final volume of Freeman's collaborators leaves many questions both unasked and unanswered. Irving Brant's comprehensive biography of Madison reveals how misled Washington was in 1795 in his view of Randolph, and how easy it was to mislead him. Some recent studies, like those of Alexander DeConde in foreign policy and the studies of party growth of the late Joseph Charles, reveal the limitations, the perplexities and the human traits of this very noble, if not highly articulate or intellectual, figure.*

To criticize the first President has always been akin to heresy; one might almost call it *lèse-majesté*. The assessment of the man has been made more difficult by his own lack of facility with words, both in speech and pen; he was heavily dependent on others, his "writing aides" as he called them, when he wrote dispatches or messages. His letters are conspicuously lacking in those statements of general ideas to which his contemporaries were so addicted. They are confined to specific matters; they are brief; and they are apt to be stilted in style. There is little in the way of analysis or of personal reflection and less still of gossip. His collected writings throw little light on the man himself.

The process of glorification was a quite deliberate, indeed an

---

* Alexander DeConde, *Entangling Alliance* (1958); Joseph Charles, *Origins of the American Party System* (1958).

inevitable, one. It was even more the work of artists than of writers. The Washington we know is the image popularized by Gilbert Stuart, who painted him at least one hundred twenty-four times. At three sittings the President gave in Philadelphia in 1795, four Peales set up easels around him: Charles, brother James, and sons Rembrandt and Raphaelle. In sculpture, Jean Antoine Houdon—his finest portrayer–and Horatio Greenhough made the image still more Roman and heroic. He was seen either as the Virginia colonel in buff and blue, or as the Roman imperator with sword and toga, or, at least with some concession to reality, as Cincinnatus at the plow. The creation of this public image was noted quite clearly by contemporary outsiders, like the British minister, Robert Liston, and his wife. Within five days of Washington's death, Henrietta Liston wrote to her uncle in Glasgow that the first President

> stood the barrier betwixt the Northernmost and Southernmost States. He was the Unenvied Head of the Army, and such was the magic of his name that his opinion was a sanction equal to law.

Her husband viewed the first birthday celebrations after Washington's death with more detachment.

> . . . these ceremonies tend to elevate the spirit of the people, and contribute to the formation of a national character, which they consider as much wanting in this country. And . . . Americans will be gainers by the periodical recital of the features of their Revolutionary war and repetition of the praises of Washington— The hyperbolical amplifications of the Panegyricks in question have an evident effect, especially among the younger part of the community, in fomenting the growth of that Vanity which to the feelings of a stranger had already arrived at a sufficient height.

The apotheosis of Washington is the more surprising in that it took place in an Age of Reason, dedicated to a strictly rationalist view of mankind; an age too of pamphlet wars and pamphleteering, when men like Cobbett and Callender and Wil-

liam Duane were prompt to blacken reputations. It is true that
the attacks on Washington in the last year of his presidency
greatly disturbed him, but they were never quite as vicious as
those on Jefferson and Burr, Adams and Hamilton. How in any
event did the popular opinion of him, the affection and trust,
emerge through the barriers of distance and etiquette that surrounded him, and which he in some measure encouraged? How
far was the popular legend accepted by his closest associates, how
far used by them for their own purposes? How far did Washington as a person come to be politically exploited before his
death as well as after it? And was he ever aware that he was
being exploited? These are the questions that still challenge the
modern historian of the Revolutionary period.

Washington's services are striking enough. There was, first, his
contribution as an organizer of the government. He inherited
from the Confederation only a handful of unpaid clerks and a
large number of debts; the outstanding paper money was worthless, and there were only three banks functioning in the country.
North Carolina and Rhode Island were not yet in the Union;
Vermont was still intriguing with Canada; Britain held on to
the western posts and was dangerously friendly with the Indians.
The American army had 840 officers and men; there was no
navy at all. Hamilton's view of the Constitution seemed nearer
reality than Washington's.

The Judiciary Act of 1789 set up the legal system that is
basically still in operation: district courts, circuit courts of appeal,
and a Supreme Court of one Chief Justice and five (now eight)
Associates. To ensure uniform legal interpretations throughout
the nation the Supreme Court was to rule on the constitutionality of state-court decisions. John Jay was appointed Chief
Justice, and the Court sat for the first time in February 1790,
resplendent in judicial robes, but without the white wigs of
their English counterparts.

Treaty-making was a more difficult matter. Washington took

quite literally the constitutional provision that treaties be made with "the advice and consent" of the Senate. He thought that on some occasions it should be possible for the President to appear before the Senate to explain the purpose of a treaty, and to obtain forthwith a "yes" or "no" on the points he raised. He thought of the Senate, that is, as a council of state. In order to settle the long-standing boundary dispute between the Creek Indians and the state of Georgia, Washington proposed negotiations with the Creeks, to attempt to wean them from the temptations of an alliance with the Spanish in Louisiana. In August 1789, with this in mind, he appeared before the Senate in person with a series of proposals; the most vigorous dissenter to them among the senators, William Maclay, asked that the treaty be deferred to a committee. According to Maclay, whose portraits were often etched with acid, Washington stalked out with a "discontented air," declaring that deferment "defeats every purpose of my coming here." He got the Senate's approval two days later, but the incident had important consequences: it became the rule for treaties to be presented to the Senate for approval after, and not before, they were negotiated; in the Senate the committee system began to develop; and the Senate made it clear that in its own estimation it was not a council of state but a legislative body, in no way subordinate to the President.

Increasingly, therefore, Washington turned for advice to his "Cabinet," the officers at the head of his three executive departments, State, Treasury, and War. They were not mentioned in the Constitution and they were responsible only to the President, not to Congress; they were denied the right to sit in Congress, to Hamilton's chagrin; they came, however, to be the originators of policy. And to the first two offices Washington appointed men of unusual capacity. Jefferson, who had been serving as minister in France since 1784, became Secretary of State, and youthful Alexander Hamilton, Washington's aide in the war and now a lawyer and a son-in-law of General Philip Schuyler of New York, became Secretary of the Treasury and Washington's major adviser. Henry Knox, the Secretary of War, continued in the office he had held under the Confederation—a more corpulent and genial, but a much less able, man than his colleagues. Edmund Randolph became Attorney-General.

The creation of the working administration, therefore, was Washington's achievement. But it was Hamilton rather than the President who gave what he himself called "executive impulse" to the administration. Hamilton was in 1790 and 1791, as in Philadelphia in 1787, the exponent of High Federalism, of authority in government, and of a sound system of public credit. His three great state papers were his reports on *Publick Credit* (January 1790), on *A National Bank* (December 1790), and on *Manufactures* (December 1791). He urged that all outstanding debts, foreign and domestic, whether of Congress or of the states, should be assumed at face value and paid by the federal government. The purpose was political as much as economic; not merely would creditors (and many speculators) be bound to the national cause, but that cause would be greatly strengthened both at home and abroad. "A public debt," he argued, "is a public blessing." The interests of the propertied classes would be tied up with the government; government stock would rise abroad and trade would be encouraged. The assumption of the debts of the states by the federal government would allow it to dominate the revenue sources of the country and consolidate national—and central—authority. A Bank of the United States should also be set up, to act as the fiscal agent of the government, and a system of tariff duties on imports and excises on home-produced liquor should be used to provide revenue. Hamilton emerged in fact as the first champion of protection in American history. He gave his reasons clearly in his *Report on Manufactures*: to encourage industries essential to the national defense, to diversify American economic life, and to develop a home market for agriculture. But even here it was less protection from foreign competition than incentive and energy at home that he sought. Bounties mattered far more than excises. Government

had in an infant state to promote immigration and reward invention. "The public purse must supply the deficiency of private
resource."

Hamilton's purposes were clear and persuasively expressed.
He was as much concerned with "energy in government" as with
"order in the finances." His own creative zest and overpowering
capacity for work made him impatient and autocratic. He had
little sympathy for democracy:

> All communities divide themselves into the few and the many.
> The first are rich and well-born, the other the mass of the people.
> The voice of the people has been said to be the voice of God; and
> however generally this maxim has been quoted and believed, it is
> not true in fact. The people are turbulent and changing; they sel-
> dom judge or determine right.

Government was a matter for the rich, the well-born, and the
able; to him they were apt to be synonymous categories. But he
was first and last a realist; he understood economic forces—as
Washington did not—and understood how to unleash them and
harness them to the new state; and more than any of his
contemporaries he had consuming energy and ambition.

Hamilton's highly partisan financial proposals were strongly
opposed by crotchety senators like William Maclay of Pennsylvania and suspicious congressmen like Madison of Virginia;
they disliked the rewarding of bondholders who were often
merely speculators, the penalizing of states which had already
tried to honor their obligations to their creditors, and the dangerously wide implied powers suggested by the setting up of the
Bank. His *Report on Manufactures* fell on deaf ears in Congress
and produced no legislation. Patrick Henry gave voice to an issue
that would gradually become a battle cry; he denied that the
Constitution gave any authority to the federal government to
assume the obligations of the states or to charter a Bank. There
was coming here to be a significant alignment of South *versus*
New England, of agrarian interests *versus* commercial and finan-

cial. In the end, by Jefferson's complaisance (which he later claimed to regret) a deal was made. The Hamiltonian program for the assumption of state debts would go through on condition that the Potomac should ultimately become the seat of the federal government. After a decade in Philadelphia (1790–1800) the capital was to be sited closer to the South and more amenable to its influence. Ten years later the Federal City, as it was then called, came into being near Georgetown.

In Washington's first term, therefore, if his services are obvious enough, the creative energy was Hamilton's. This very energy produced partisanship and factional strife.

From August 1790 onward the difference between Hamilton and Jefferson became sharper, on the excise and Bank proposals, on Federalism *versus* state rights, and increasingly on the issues raised by the French Revolution. By 1792 the tone of the public debate was reminiscent of 1775. Paine's *Rights of Man,* written in France, was dedicated to Washington; it was welcomed by Jefferson, reviled by Hamilton. A bitter press campaign of principles and personalities was unleashed; Fenno's *Gazette of the United States* was countered by Freneau's *National Gazette.* And the latter was again talking of social conflict—"Another revolution must and will be brought about in favour of the people." It began to train its guns not only on the Cabinet but also on its Head, to sneer at "the drawing Room," "those apparent trifles, birthday odes," and the Friday-evening levees. Senator Maclay, never an unprejudiced observer, accused Washington of "pushing the Potomac." "The President," he said, "has become in the hands of Hamilton, the dish-clout of every dirty speculation, as his name goes to wipe away blame and silence all murmuring."

As a result, Washington welcomed the prospect of retirement at the end of his first term. In the spring of 1792 he had a number of discussions with Madison on the shape of a farewell address. He found him a convinced opponent of the idea: the rise of party spirit, Madison urged, was a reason rather for staying on than for withdrawing; another four years would save the country from the risks of a new regime or the dangers of monarchy, and would give "tone and firmness." Hamilton, Knox, and Randolph endorsed this advice. In the summer of 1792 Jefferson too was urging Washington to consent to serve again, and used an argument that had influence—"North and South will hang together if they have you to hang on." The Farewell Address that Hamilton and Madison prepared was not used for another four years.

On March 4, 1793, Washington was inaugurated President for a second time. Already the European scene was darker; Louis XVI was guillotined in January; on February first France declared war on Britain, and a great European coalition was formed to resist the Revolution. In his handling of this, as in foreign policy in general, Washington was a more assured figure.

The French Revolution was a decisive event in American history. It has been seen, naturally enough, as important in exacerbating the partisan conflicts of Federalists and democratic Republicans. This it did. There were—for a time—outbursts of "Bastille fever"; Royal Exchange Alley in Boston became Equality Lane; for a time even honorific titles like *Judge,* to which later democratic America was to show itself curiously prone, went out of fashion. Even *Mr.* gave way to *Citizen;* one critic, angered by the excesses, suggested that *Biped* was preferable as it would suit men and women alike and thus be more fully democratic.

But the real importance for the United States of the French Revolution was far more significant than this passing excess of emotion. For within five years France was seen more as enemy than ally. What did not change were the facts of geopolitics. For more than twenty years Europe was convulsed by war, and the war was both international and civil, a war engaging the peoples of Europe as never before, a war of ideas. For the twenty crucial years of its own adolescence as a nation the United States was left in freedom and allowed to consolidate itself. Immigrants were strikingly few—some four thousand per year. They were no longer aristocratic adventurers like Lafayette, or advocates of revolution like Tom Paine, but refugees like Dupont de Nemours. The value of foreign travel was now seen as less important and all agreed on the need for education at home. The Atlantic became for a generation less a bridge than a barrier, a shield of the new Republic.

The situation of 1793 made explicit what had hitherto been implicit in Washington's attitude. When the Revolution broke out in 1789, the fact on which he had seized was American remoteness. "We, at this great distance . . . hear of wars and rumours of wars, as if they were the events or reports of another planet." At times, particularly in his letters to Lafayette, he expressed sympathy with the Revolution, but from the first he saw the threats that a war in Europe presented to America. He wanted, he had written in 1790, to be "unentangled in the crooked policies of Europe" and sought only the free navigation of the Mississippi. He sensed the tumult and the paroxysms of France, the "more haste than good speed in their innovations," and wanted no part in the attendant political disputes of Europe. These views were reinforced by the events of 1790–93, domestic as well as foreign, and by the alarms in Florida and New Orleans, in the Caribbean and in the Ohio country.

With the outbreak of war in Europe in 1793, the United States issued a proclamation (in April) declaring her intention to pursue "a conduct friendly and impartial toward the belligerent powers." It was drawn up by Edmund Randolph, the Attorney-General, and it did not contain the word *neutrality*—indeed, to Jefferson it was not a declaration of neutrality at all. The proclamation marks the real beginning of the break between President and Secretary of State. For Washington it was an expression of neutrality, in fact if not in word. Jefferson's view was more devious. Publicly, he argued that by holding back a declaration of neutrality the United States might induce the European powers to bid for it, and thus secure "the broadest privileges of neutral nations." Privately, however, he thought it pusillanimous, a "milk and water" instrument, which disregarded American obligations both to the cause of France under the alliance of 1778, and to the larger cause of liberty. When "Pacificus" Hamilton came out in support of the proclamation, Jefferson encouraged "Helvidius" Madison to attack him—"For God's sake, my dear Sir, take up your pen, select the most striking heresies and cut him to pieces in the face of the public." However much idealism lay behind Jefferson's methods, they appear less noble and infinitely less discreet than Washington's.

Washington was convinced of the wisdom of neutrality. His purpose, he later declared to Henry, was

> to keep the United States free from political connexions with *every* other country, to see them independent of all and under the influence of none. In a word, I want an *American* character, that the powers of Europe may be convinced we act for *ourselves* and not for *others*.

He admitted a friendship for, even some obligation toward, Lafayette. Gouverneur Morris, the American minister in Paris— himself as indiscreet on the other side as Jefferson—was instructed to convey informally to the French the regard of Americans for Lafayette, and to Madame de Lafayette to convey "all the consolation I can with propriety give." When Henry Lee informed Washington that he was considering enlistment in the French army and requested advice, the reply was impeccable and magisterial—

> As a public character, I can say *nothing* on the subject. . . . As a private man, I am unwilling to say much. Give advice I shall not. All I can do, then . . . is to declare that if the case which you have suggested was mine, I should ponder well before I resolved, not only for private consideration, but on public grounds.

And then, just to be sure, he advised Lee to burn the letter. If Lee failed to act on one piece of advice, he saw the point, however guarded, of the other.

The problems posed by the war in Europe were not just matters of personal alignment and personal sympathy. Some three quarters of America's trade was with Britain, and 90 per cent of her imports came from there. But it was still hard for the friends of Britain in America to raise their voices; Britain on the seas and in the western posts was still an arrogant power.

The first real challenge to the Federalist quest for neutrality was presented, however, by the arrival of Edmond Charles Genêt as the French minister to the United States. France could hardly have selected a more tactless ambassador. As luck would have it his ship was blown out of its course, and he landed, in April 1793, at Charleston, in "Democratick" territory. His twenty-eight day journey, by easy stages, to Philadelphia, was a procession which evoked an enthusiasm reminiscent of the President's own, four years before. It gave him a quite false notion of his popularity and of his role. Genêt was deterred neither by the announcement of neutrality nor by a chilly reception from Washington in Philadelphia. With the support of the Jeffersonians, he proceeded to act in most undiplomatic fashion. As he lyrically reported to his changing masters in Paris, "I provision the Antilles, I excite the Canadians to free themselves from the yoke of England, I arm the Kentuckians." He organized expeditions against Florida and Louisiana; George Rogers Clark found himself "Commander-in-Chief of the French Revolutionary Legion on the Mississippi River." He sent out privateers and he sponsored Jacobin Clubs.

By June, even Jefferson was alarmed at this—"indefensible" . . . never "was so calamitous an appointment made. . . . Hotheaded, all imagination, no judgment, passionate." By August he was, thought Jefferson, "absolutely incorrigible," and the Cabinet unanimously demanded his recall. The responsibility however was not Genêt's alone; it was also Jefferson's, who had at first abetted his schemes. For by 1793 Madison and Jefferson were becoming afraid that behind the mask of neutrality lay "a secret Anglomanny." Jefferson's five years in Paris had left him with no love of the English—"those rich, proud, hectoring, swearing, squibbling, carnivorous animals who live on the other side of the Channel"—or of those in America who admired their institutions or imitated their ways. And he thus for a time encouraged Genêt in his rashness.

Washington was kind to Genêt but resolute in his neutrality. He believed that "the defensive alliance" with France had come to an end when the treaty of peace with Britain was signed in 1783. His first obligation was to the United States, and to the facts of a revolution in Europe from which, if possible, the United States must be protected. This, he told Congress in December 1793, necessitated firmness and strength as well as subtlety.

> There is a rank due to the United States among nations, which will be withheld, if not absolutely lost, by the reputation of weakness. If we desire to avoid insult, we must be able to repel it; if we desire to secure peace, one of the most powerful instruments of our rising prosperity, it must be known that we are at all times ready for War.

The Genêt affair added zest to the domestic party battle. Years later, in correspondence with Jefferson and with memory blurred, Adams wrote of the "thousands" in the Philadelphia mobs who threatened to drag Washington from his house and to bring the government down. He was convinced that revolution was averted only by the coming to Philadelphia in the late summer of a still more deadly scourge—yellow fever. After it had passed, the political temperature stayed high. The "Marseillaise" and "Ça Ira" were now the marching songs of Anti-Federalism. To the Jeffersonians the Federalists were "British boot-lickers" or worse. To Fenno, to British exile William Cobbett, and to the Federalist *Gazette of the United States* the Republicans were "Demo-

craticks," "filthy Jacobins," "frog-eating, man-eating, blood-drink-
ing cannibals."

The Democratic Societies or Jacobin Clubs, the *National
Gazette* (edited by Freneau), and the *Philadelphia Aurora*
(edited by Duane), were now the instruments of a party of
which Jefferson was the obvious leader. It was coming to be
based on an alliance of Virginia with New York; its chief
figures, after Jefferson, were Madison and William Giles of Virginia, Maclay and Gallatin in Pennsylvania, Sam Adams and
Hancock in Massachusetts, Clinton in New York, and stormy
Matthew Lyon in Vermont. Now even foreign policy fed the
the flames of faction.

The pattern of the future was becoming clear. By 1794, Washington's idea of good government was almost identical with
Hamilton's. The identity was never complete. Hamilton was
bolder and brasher than Washington, with a gift of words and a
grasp of finance—and of intrigue—far surpassing the President's.
Washington, though less intellectual, was infinitely superior to
Hamilton in judgment. Jefferson's range was wider than that of
either of them, his cast of mind more contemplative and contradictory. But Washington could have little sympathy with
Jeffersonian ideas, and the man of affairs found himself much
more attuned to the administrative emphasis and to the concrete
program of the Hamiltonians. From 1789 to 1794 he was above
party, an enemy of what he called "faction," a Federalist. By
1794 he went further and became a Hamiltonian. The partisanship spread; Madison went the other way, and Jefferson resigned
the Secretaryship of State on December 31, 1793, to be replaced
by Edmund Randolph.

The Hamiltonian influence was now clearly visible. When in
1794 open rebellion against the excise tax broke out among the
farmers of western Pennsylvania, federal Treasury officials, like
State officials before them, were driven back. Under Hamilton's
persuasions, Washington saw in the rebellion "the first *formidable* fruit" of the Democratic Societies, and of "their diabolical

leader, Genêt." Unless it was broken, "we may bid adieu to all government in this country, except mob and club government." There were no federal police to enforce the law, but the Constitution empowered the federal government to call out the state militia when necessary. Would the states acknowledge this authority? Washington put the matter to the test, called out the militia, and talked of leading it in person over the mountains. Hamilton accompanied the troops as a kind of political commissar. By the time the militia appeared and fifteen thousand turned out at the call, the rebellion had come to an end. Having displayed the power of the federal government and satisfied conservative opinion as much as he alarmed Jeffersonian, the President in July 1795 pardoned the insurgents. For him firmness, again, was allied to clemency.

The same Hamiltonian policy led Washington to attempt a settlement of the disputes with Britain. Anthony Wayne's victory over the Indians at Fallen Timbers in 1794 opened up the Ohio country and weakened British influence over her forest allies. Britain still held the fur posts, drawing from them a trade estimated at a hundred thousand pounds a year, still excluded American ships from her West Indian ports and still dickered over the boundary with Maine. She was countering the revived and lucrative American trade with the French West Indies by invoking the Rule of 1756 (that trade closed in time of peace could not be opened in time of war), and, under its cloak, seizing American ships. She claimed the right also to search American ships for British deserters at a time of lax naturalization laws and inadequate proof of citizenship. This interference was particularly resented in New England, the Federalist stronghold; and in the debates in the House of Representatives in 1794, New England and the middle states seemed in process of aligning on this issue with the South. Despite the unpopularity of any suggestion of rapprochement with Britain, Washington felt that an effort should be made to settle these outstanding problems, and that it should be done by a special mission and a treaty requiring only Cabinet and Senate approval. Accordingly, in April 1794 he dispatched John Jay as special envoy to London.

When the news of the treaty signed by Jay (November 1794) reached the United States the following March, Washington's popularity at home was given its severest test. Jay knew that his work would meet with opposition but thought that the terms were the best that could be obtained. Britain agreed to evacuate the fur posts by 1796 and to open her East Indian ports to American ships; she agreed to open her West Indian ports also, but only to vessels under seventy tons; the United States agreed not to export sugar, molasses, coffee, cotton, or cocoa; joint commissions were to settle the Maine boundary dispute and claims for damages arising from seizures, but nothing was said about impressment, the trade of neutrals with France, or Indians. Washington did not pretend to like these terms and kept the treaty for four months before submitting it to the Senate. The Senate ratified the treaty after long discussions, in June 1795, by the minimum number of votes necessary, but rejected the West Indian clauses and the ban on exports.

When the terms of the treaty leaked to the press they met a wave of popular protest. "The cry against the Treaty," Washington wrote to Hamilton, "is like that against a mad-dog; and every one, in a manner, seems engaged on running it down." There was worse than this waiting for Hamilton, whose support for the treaty led to his being stoned in the streets. For a time the House refused to appropriate the money called for by the Treaty and requested a copy of Jay's instructions. Washington refused: "The nature of foreign negotiations requires caution, and their success must often depend upon secrecy." This was, he claimed, the reason for vesting the treaty-making power in the President, acting with the advice and consent of the Senate. Washington saw the dispute not as one on the merits of the treaty alone, but on the treaty-making power, and the Constitution itself. It was only "the Colossus of the President's merits with the people," wrote Jefferson, that had allowed the "Anglomen" to get their handiwork enacted, after months of wrangling. The President signed the treaty in August 1795.

Though the Treaty of 1795 failed to make clear what were the rights of neutrals, and he had his reservations about it, Washington was right in thinking that it was the best treaty that could be won at the time. It represented, on however small a scale, the beginnings of arbitration in Anglo-American disputes. Spain became so alarmed at the prospect of an even closer Anglo-American accord that she proceeded to negotiate a settlement of her own disputes with the United States in the Godoy-Pinckney Treaty, the Treaty of San Lorenzo. This treaty got little attention and less applause, but it was a complete diplomatic success for Pinckney. Spain granted to the United States the rights of navigation on the Mississippi and the right of deposit at New Orleans free of duty for ocean-going American goods; she recognized the thirty-first parallel as the northern boundary of Florida and agreed to try to restrain the Indians from border raids. The treaty helped the United States retain the fluctuating loyalty of the Kentucky and Tennessee area, now becoming states; it pointed the way south and west; and for a generation it made the nation Mississippi-minded.

By 1795 the domestic scene, however, like so much in the handling of foreign policy, had become completely partisan. Randolph, who had succeeded Jefferson as Secretary of State in 1793, was dismissed in 1795 on the doubtful grounds of receiving bribes from France. Hamilton returned to the practice of law in order to maintain a steadily increasing family. Henry Knox, too, resigned: a good general, he had become "a furious Federalist" but an administrator of only modest capacity. By 1796 the government was completely recast; conscientious and combative Timothy Pickering at the State Department, the efficient and self-effacing Oliver Wolcott at the Treasury, the inefficient Irishman James McHenry as Secretary of War. New men—and by now an avowed principle. "I shall not," Washington wrote to Pickering, "whilst I have the honour to administer the government, bring a man into any office of consequence knowingly, whose political tenets are adverse to the measures, which the general government are pursuing; for this, in my opinion, would be a sort of political suicide." Washington had come to a position he disliked, and for which the Constitution gave no warrant; the pattern of party rivalry in the United States, like the pattern of government itself, stems from the years of his administration.

The partisanship of the press made Washington's last year in Philadelphia one of acute misery. He was particularly hurt by a reference of Jefferson's to the "men who were Samsons in the field and Solomons in the council, but who have had their heads shorn by the harlot England." He was being compared, he said, to a Nero, or even to a common pick-pocket; after forty-five years of public service he was tired of being "buffeted in the public prints by a set of infamous scribblers." He now looked forward eagerly to his retirement.

The decision was not one of principle. Washington was physically and mentally a tired man. And no one so sensitive to his reputation could long continue in a post now vulnerable to partisan attack, to innuendo, and to public censure.

Over the authorship of his Farewell Address (September 1796) there has been much debate. Washington had always sought secretaries who, as he put it, would "possess the soul of the General"; if he left the writing of the Address to others, and especially to Hamilton, it incorporated—as he insisted it should —much of Madison's draft of 1792, and he went over it carefully himself. It is a Federalist document, the nearest approach in his writings to a declaration of the Washington *credo*—that unity of government is primary; sectionalism and partisanship open the door "to foreign influence and corruption." More than anything else, Washington counseled against "the insidious wiles of foreign influence." It was not so much a policy of isolation from Europe that he advocated as the exclusion of Europe from America, and the maintenance thereby of an American national character. The "primary interests" of Europe and America were quite distinct. There should be no independent "permanent inveterate antipathies against particular nations, and passionate attachments for others," but constant vigilance, preparedness, and, if necessary, temporary alliances on extraordinary occasions.

Washington, though bequeathing a legacy and no doubt fully conscious of it, was also speaking in a particular situation—deploring the meddling of Genêt and his successors Fauchet and Adet in American affairs, the intrigues of Jefferson and Freneau, and advocating that the United States have the strength to resist insults, whether from the Barbary pirates or the French revolutionaries or the captains of British frigates. He was speaking as a realist out of long experience, and concluded that nations, like men, must depend in the end on themselves alone; this was the lesson of all revolutions, the goal of all national movements. "There can be no greater error than to expect, or calculate upon real favours from Nation to Nation." Not isolation for all time, then, but independence; not sectionalism or partisanship, though it appeared to be "inseparable from our nature," but loyalty to the national cause; not party controversy, but "strength and consistency" to give the country "the command of its own fortunes": this was the legacy of 1776 as well as of 1796. Like all else it set a precedent, and one of the wisest. The passing of the years has made Washington's Farewell Address almost as important a bequest of the first President as the drafting of the Constitution itself. It is read in both the Senate and the House of Representatives at noon on each February 22, as a tribute and as a reminder.

Washington's last speech to Congress was delivered on December 7, 1796. In it he pressed the case for a naval force, for a military academy, and for a national university. It was dangerous, when revolution ran through Europe, to send young Americans abroad at their most impressionable age. In a Republic they should be taught "the science of government" and taught it at home. On this, as on many other points, Washington's view was shared by Jefferson. The latter thought French a useful language, but Canada the best place to learn it. "While learning the language in France, a young man's morals, health and fortune are more irresistibly endangered than in any country of the universe." The French, Jefferson was now stressing, lacked patience and experience. He had from the first seen the risks if man was studied only in books and not in the real world. Even the ideologue was a realist at heart. And by 1796, despite all the bitterness of party spirit, Monticello was not so far away from Mount Vernon.

The role of Washington as President remains difficult to assess. It is clear that he began with a belief (shared by John Adams) in an independent executive, but that he moved steadily toward the Hamiltonians in his sympathies, especially after 1793; on financial matters he was completely dependent on Hamilton's guidance. Yet to the end Washington deplored the growth of parties; one reason he cited for refusing to consider a third term was that by 1796 party bitterness prevented universal acceptance of the President. He sought to remain a chief of state and to exalt the authority of government only to find that the country would be no more united by him than by anyone else.

It is clear that for Washington this was a bitter blow. To be above the battle—if above it he was—was not, he found, to escape public censure. Washington was both hurt and baffled by the attacks of the rascally Freneau and by the savagery of Tom Paine's open letter from Paris in 1796. He had learned the hard way the truth of Fisher Ames' analogy: "A monarchy is like a merchantman. You get on board and ride the wind and tide in safety and elation but, by and by, you strike a reef and go down. But democracy is like a raft. You never sink, but, dammit, your feet are always in the water." A much later President had a still more vigorous comparison. "If you can't take the heat," reflected ex-President Truman, "you should get out of the kitchen."

In the domestic field, he was not a forceful leader in his own administration, once he had managed to set it up. He provided few ideas; the problems that aroused him were those in which he had direct personal experience—relations with the Indians, military affairs, defense of the frontier, the maintenance of national unity. His Farewell Address says nothing about "the rights of man" and nothing about slavery, the basic threat to those rights in the next two generations. Its theme is Washington's own, even if the language is Hamilton's—the need for union and the danger of foreign entanglements. He moved away steadily from a Virginian to a national, at times a nationalist, position; the break was not only with Jefferson, but with Madison as well, with Monroe and with Henry, despite the talk of nominating the latter for Secretary of State in 1795. The break with Mason had taken place long before. His system, he said, was to overlook all personal, local and partial considerations, and "to contemplate the United States as one great whole."

It now appears surprising that Washington did not foresee the likelihood of the rise of party spirit. But Adams did not see it either or, if he did, refused to face the consequences. He too tried to act as though the Executive were above party, representing the national interest, and paid the price in 1800. In Washington's case, the attitude is explicable enough: he was no theorist; his concern was with sound administration—of his estates, of the Army, or of the nation. He could hardly be expected to know how bitter and irresponsible the press charges would be or how savagely they would treat his concern with "respectability." "I was no party man myself," he wrote to Jefferson in 1796, "and the first wish of my heart was, if parties did exist, to reconcile them."

What he did understand was the threat of sectionalism, and of state rights, to the unity won in 1783, and the threat of international revolution to the institutions of 1787. In this he was remarkably farsighted. He was in modern history the first leader of a successful national revolt against imperialism, but for him, unlike Jefferson and Monroe and Paine, America's national revolt was not part of an international revolution. It was not part of a crusade to be launched across the world but the product of a particular situation in America in 1776. By 1797 the new and free country had to be protected against revolution, as the Constitution protected it against democracy. The America that became the guide to Latin America in the 1820s, to Greece and Hungary, Italy and Ireland, was Jefferson's—not Washington's—America. There was no response from Washington to Miranda's appeal to lead a second liberation movement in Latin America.

Yet the decision to cut the country free from Europe's entanglements was of profound importance. Sheltered by three thousand miles of ocean, the United States was left free to settle her frontier disputes with Britain and Spain far more smoothly than would otherwise have been possible. She was able to declare herself neutral toward Europe and to erect neutrality into a "Great Rule." She was able by 1798 to end the entangling alliance of 1778. She was able, without commitment by herself, to have new republics growing up in the Americas to the south in place of the old Spanish Empire. And she was able, at a lucky moment in 1803, to buy out the French holdings in the trans-Mississippi West without firing a shot. The French Revolution was as pregnant a development for the United States as the fact of her own independence, for more than anything else it made it permanent. It permitted the United States to develop along her own natural, distinct, non-European lines. It was in the fact of her isolation that American nationalism at last began to grow.

At home, the legacy of Washington's two terms was administrative rather than political. He was a gifted and experienced administrator—and the federal government, after all, had fewer employees in 1790 than did Mount Vernon. As discipline was the soul of an army, so, he said, "system to all things was the soul of business." System involved industry, integrity, impartiality, and firmness. "No man," said John Adams, "has influence with the President. He seeks information from all quarters, and judges more independently than any man I ever knew." His standards for appointments were very high—higher than those in contemporary Britain or France, higher than those of most of his successors. He sought, and found, men who "would give dignity and lustre to our National Character."

He was helped by a rising standard of living. Though not an era of good feelings, his presidency was an era of good times. One reason for the popularity of the Constitution was the fact that it coincided with an upswing of prosperity. All sections of the nation and all ranks of society shared in it, and the federal government, regardless of the party group in control, was the beneficiary.

In foreign affairs, too, Europe's agony was America's advantage; the situation in Europe facilitated the settlement with Britain and Spain, it eased the tension on the western border, and it made closer the ties between the Tidewater and the trans-Allegheny country. There were associated problems: the French Revolution gave further impetus to American democracy, and foreign refugees and foreign ideas brought the risk of dangerous involvement in Europe. But in its prosperity at home and its policy of peace abroad, the Washington administration laid a sound foundation for the new Republic. Never before had a republican government attempted to organize so vast an area on a federal pattern. Rarely before had an executive been so directly responsive to the popular assemblies. Rarely has an office, one that was to grow into the most important executive office in the world, been given the stamp so clearly of one man's character.

Washington sensed that Europe's distress could be for America destiny as well as advantage. "Sure I am," he wrote, "if this country is preserved in tranquility twenty years longer, it may bid defiance in a just cause to any power whatever; such in that time will be its population, wealth and resources."

9

The Second President:
Federalism High and Low

WITH JOHN ADAMS it was no longer possible to maintain the theory of a President above partisanship, for by 1796 it was obvious that the contest for the presidency had become the most important aspect of the now-virulent party battle. In that year the Democratic Republicans had high hopes; their candidate for President was Jefferson, and Aaron Burr of New York was put forward for the vice-presidency; their case was strong, thanks to the financial measures of Hamilton and the forceful suppression of the Whiskey Rebellion. Federalism was out of favor in the West and in the South. It was possible to use Jay's treaty to present the Federalists as pro-British; they could equally appear as a party of overriding centralization and of high finance behind whom were the insidious wiles of a hated foreign influence. Not merely Hamilton in his nationalism, but the Supreme Court, in Chisholm v. Georgia, in upholding the right of the citizen of one state to sue another, seemed to be riding roughshod over the rights of the sovereign and still self-conscious states.

If the clash of parties and issues was clear enough, the choice was not. Washington did not publish his Farewell Address until September 19, and it did not appear in many newspapers until October. A number of Federalist electors were still thinking of

Washington rather than of Adams until the late summer. This handicapped Adams, but it hurt Jefferson still more, particularly in New England, where he was less well known and very much less well liked. Until the Twelfth Amendment was passed, the rule was simply that the candidate with the most votes in the Electoral College became President, and the runner-up Vice-President, whatever their allegiance might be. The Constitution, in its innocence, had not recognized parties.

Hamilton, who was aware of Washington's decision to retire at least a month before it was public knowledge, exerted what pressure he could on the electors, with the hope that John Adams' running-mate, Thomas Pinckney of South Carolina, fresh from his diplomatic triumph, would in fact emerge as the first choice. But Hamilton miscalculated the extent of the support for Adams in New England. The result was that while Adams secured seventy-one votes, Pinckney got only fifty-nine, and Jefferson, with sixty-eight, became not only leader of the opposition, but Vice-President, although no one had voted for him as anything but President. What Adams had seen as a remote possibility but "a dangerous crisis" in January had now come to pass. President and Vice-President were in opposite boxes.

Of all the Founding Fathers, honest John Adams has waited longest for recognition. There is no monument to him in Washington, D.C., not slow to salute its citizens, or even in Massachusetts, for which he drafted a state constitution that is still in force. He himself sensed and predicted the neglect. Writing to Benjamin Rush in 1809, he said "Mausoleums, statues, monuments will never be erected to me. . . . Panegyrical romances will never be written, nor flattering orations spoken to transmit me to posterity in brilliant colors." The neglect is the more surprising in that Adams was the one prominent New Englander in high federal office, and that few of the Founding Fathers, many of whom appreciated their role in history and faithfully kept their records to prove it, were quite so zealous in preserving their papers, keeping their diaries, or caring for their books. The tide has now turned. His correspondence with Jefferson has been carefully edited and published; several biographies have appeared; and there was launched in 1955 an impressive scholarly project, the *Adams Papers,* in which L. H. Butterfield is proposing to publish the complete correspondence of John Adams and of the family in definitive form.

The tribute so long overdue has already shown him to be far more significant than previous histories have implied. As a political thinker he was perhaps the most original and, with Madison, the best read in constitutional history and law of all the Founders. He was remarkably self-contained and, if neither objective nor unemotional, he had a marked capacity for forming an independent and dispassionate judgment on events; and he had, we can now see, political courage of an unusually high order. His own prickly and unmalleable Yankee personality, however, made him hard to harness to a party. Like Robert Peel, he was "a difficult horse to go up to in the stable"; as were his son, grandson, and great-grandson after him. He never had a party or a personal following, and until the end he made it plain how superior a lack he thought this was. "I am determined to support every administration whenever I think them in the right," he wrote in 1808. "I care not whether they call me Federalist, Jacobin or Quid." In a political society one pays a high price so to indulge in one's own integrity. J. Truslow Adams, the historian of the family, called him simply "bull-headed." He carried his rectitude like a banner; and he stopped now and then to salute it. *Amicus Plato, sed major veritas.*

In 1797 John Adams was sixty-two. It is ironic to reflect that he had, thirty years before, been offered by Britain the post of Advocate-General in the Court of Admiralty—a post he promptly rejected; that he had successfully defended the British troops involved in the Boston Massacre; and that in 1771 he had given up his legal practice in Boston because of what he thought was failing health. In 1774 he had begun a second career on a larger stage. He had been an enthusiastic, almost naïve, member of the Continental Congress; "the Atlas of Independence," he had served with grim conscientiousness during the war on at least eighty committees and presided over twenty-five of them; he had represented the new Republic in Paris, London, and The Hague; he had helped to draw up the Treaty of Paris, and he had then, from 1785 to 1788, schooled himself to the difficult task of being the first minister to Britain.

He had thus a rich experience of domestic, and a rare knowledge of foreign, affairs. He was able and scholarly; he was highly critical of himself, as of others; and he was all too conspicuously honest. But despite his experience he was in many ways a political innocent, incapable of dissembling. His candor and transparency left him in fact without defenses and easily hurt. Outspoken and indiscreet, engrossed in himself, jealous and suspicious, he was without finesse in the handling of men. Senator Maclay has left a savage portrait of him as President of the Senate:

> He takes on him to school the members from the chair. His grasping after titles has been observed by everybody. Mr. Izard, after describing his air, manner, deportment, and personal figure in the chair, concluded with applying the title of ROTUNDITY to him. I have really often looked at him with surprise mingled with contempt when he is in the chair and no business before the Senate. Instead of that sedate, easy air which I would have him possess, he will look on one side, then on the other, then down on the knees of his breeches, then dimple his visage with the most silly kind of half smile which I can not well express in English. The Scotch-Irish have a word that hits it exactly—smudging. God forgive me for the vile thought, but I can not help thinking of a monkey just put into breeches when I saw him betray such evident marks of self-conceit.

But Jefferson's verdict on him in 1787 is probably closer to truth:

> He is vain, irritable and a bad calculator of the force and probable effects of the motives which govern men. This is all the ill

which can possibly be said of him. He is as disinterested as the being who made him; he is profound in his views and accurate in his judgment, except where knowledge of the world is necessary to form a judgment. He is so amiable, that I pronounce you will love him if ever you become acquainted with him. He would be, as he was, a great man in Congress.

Adams' presidency was ill-starred. His Cabinet was inherited from Washington; of its members, Timothy Pickering as Secretary of State, Oliver Wolcott at the Treasury, and James McHenry as Secretary of War were far more loyal to Hamilton than to the new President; Jefferson saw them as only a "little less hostile" to Adams than to himself. Nor were any of them, including Charles Lee (the Attorney-General), men of stature. Washington had found it a difficult, indeed a humiliating, task to recruit to the administration after Jefferson's and Hamilton's resignations. Adams was aware of this; he had written in 1795 to Abigail bemoaning it:

> The expenses of living at the seat of government are so exorbitant, so far beyond all proportion to the salaries, and the sure regard of integrity . . . is such obloquy, contempt and insult, that no man of any feeling is willing to renounce his home, forsake his property for the sake of removing to Philadelphia, where he is almost sure of disgrace and ruin.

The circumstances of his election did not make it likely that Adams would be any more successful a recruiting sergeant than Washington. There was in 1796 no precedent for a change of officials with a new administration. Nor did Adams favor the principle of rotation in office. He wanted a strong and disinterested executive and the good will of his aides. He got neither.

From Adams' inaugural until the summer of 1798 the differences smoldered; Cabinet comments were those of Hamilton at second hand. But much as he disliked Hamilton, he was not yet aware of treachery; so long as Adams breathed firmness in foreign policy the differences did not come to the surface.

Adams' dilemma lay in France. Under Washington, relations with Spain and with Britain had improved. This was not only the result of the Pinckney and the Jay treaties; it was due also to shrewd diplomacy. In private correspondence with Grenville, Jay sought to persuade him to discontinue impressment of American seamen; Robert Liston, the urbane British minister, reinforced the pleas. But with France relations had deteriorated. Genêt, Fauchet, and Adet were singularly indiscreet in their behavior in America; Gouverneur Morris' haughtiness had made him *non grata* to the French; James Monroe's republican zeal made him *non grata* to the Federalists; his overoptimistic assurances to the French made the Jay Treaty inexplicable to them, and they were naturally surprised and indignant. They regarded it as proof of a deep Anglo-American understanding; and indeed, having accepted the British view of neutral rights, the United States was now ordering French privateers to leave her ports. In Paris, said Monroe, the United States was seen as "a perfidious friend." The Directory announced the termination of the 1778 alliance; by June 1797, three hundred American merchant ships had been seized and their cargoes confiscated; Monroe's successor, C. C. Pinckney, was refused recognition and told to leave the country.

Adams sought particularly to avoid a clash by sending three commissioners (Pinckney, John Marshall, and Elbridge Gerry) to Paris; the news of the efforts of the Directory—or of Talleyrand's underlings—to extort *pourboires* before beginning discussions produced a fierce reaction in the United States. Pinckney's rebuke "It is no; no, not a sixpence" was inflated into the legendary "Millions for defense but not one cent for tribute." The *XYZ* affair—the initials given to the euphonious but unpronounceable names of the French agents—still reads like a piece of fiction. Even if bribery was usual in eighteenth-century European diplomacy, the contempt for the United States implied by the dubious approaches of Hottingeur, Bellamy, and Hautevel was hard for sensitive Republicans to stomach.

The Directory, of course, was in aggressive mood, reasserting a traditional rather than a revolutionary view of the dominance of France in Europe; it was surrounding itself with vassal states; only Britain and the United States remained aloof from its influence. It was bringing pressure on Spain to cede the Floridas and Louisiana to France; there were French agents in the Mississippi country and along the Canadian line; Milfort, the half-breed leader of the Creeks, was commissioned a brigadier in the armies of France. During the negotiations, there were hints at the existence of a French "party" in the United States. Bribes apart, it was quite impossible for the Federalists to consider the French request for an American loan without running the real risk of war with Britain. And in fact Hamilton was himself pressing hard throughout 1797 and early 1798 for steadily closer relations with Britain. In March 1798 Adams announced to Congress the failure of his peace mission. On June 21, he went further:

> I will never send another minister to France, without assurances that he will be received, respected and honored as the representative of a great, free, powerful and independent nation.

Behind these patriotic banners the Federalists could rally. Many Republicans rallied too—"Trimmers dropt off from the party," wrote Fisher Ames of the Republicans, "like windfalls from an apple tree in September." War fever increased. Congress declared all treaties with France null and void, ordered the construction or purchase of new ships, and created a Navy Department. And as no unimportant dividend of national unity and belligerence, the Federalists triumphed in the congressional election of 1798—their very last triumph.

Adams endorsed these steps as necessary measures for defense and for diplomatic maneuver. He hoped to avoid war, although he would accept it if it were declared by France. To Hamilton, however, 1798 was like the Whiskey Rebellion of 1794: an opportunity to be used. War could destroy the Republicans, unite the country behind the Federalists, and—not least—strengthen the government. Adams did not share these extravagant enthusiasms. He disapproved particularly of the extent of congressional plans for enlarging the Army. The civilian President suspected one who had, four years earlier, so obviously played the role of the man on horseback leading an expeditionary force. The Army was to be increased to twenty thousand, but Hamilton hoped to raise these figures much higher; it was—and remains—proper to ask for what so large a force was intended in 1798: coastal defense against an invasion which then seemed unlikely, or adventure against New Orleans, the Floridas, or the Louisiana country? It seems clear now that Hamilton had not forgotten earlier approaches to Washington to act the part of liberator; and it was rumored that the Venezuelan patriot-adventurer Miranda hoped, in collusion with the British fleet, to free the Spanish Main.

Adams' suspicions of Hamilton came to a head when Washington, whom he asked to act as commander-in-chief, requested that Hamilton be appointed second-in-command and be the actual chief of operations in the field. Adams believed in seniority; Lincoln, Morgan, and Knox came before Hamilton. On Washington's threat of resignation, however, Adams yielded; but his suspicions of his Cabinet were now no longer dormant. He preferred to trust to a navy for defense; he became worried by Hamilton's enthusiasm in his role of Inspector-General in recruiting officers and men; Pickering's opposition to the appointment to the Army of Adams' son-in-law, William S. Smith, added to the tension.

The year 1798 saw the emergence of a group of High Federalists, of which Hamilton was the undisputed leader and policy-maker. They included his aides in the Cabinet, Fisher Ames and Theodore Sedgwick of Massachusetts, Uriah Tracy of Connecticut, Robert Goodloe Harper of South Carolina, Rufus King and George Cabot, both in London. The essence of High Federalist policy was war with France; partly because, like Ames, they shuddered at the prospect of anarchy on the frontier; partly because, like old General Schuyler or Senator Sedgwick, they wanted to destroy the Jeffersonians; partly because, like Hamilton himself, they believed that order and stability in government were essential and that they could only be guaranteed by a standing army. As Gouverneur Morris later put it, after Hamilton's death, "Our poor friend Hamilton bestrode his hobby to the great annoyance of his friends, and not without injury to himself. . . . He well knew that his favourite form [of government] was inadmissible, unless as the result of civil war; and I suspect that his belief in that which he called 'an approaching crisis' arose from a conviction that the kind of government most suitable in his opinion, to this extensive country, could be established in no other way."

The martial spirit of 1798 and 1799 had three aspects, and in each the rift between the High Federalists and the Low was clear. The first aspect was domestic and party-political, and its authors were the Federalists in Congress, the party of the black cockade. The French ally of 1778 was forgotten; *Jacobin* and *Democrat* became terms synonymous with *traitor,* and America suffered its first wave of political hysteria. Although immigrants were not numerous, many of them were French or Irish, and they were often radicals; French agents were at work in the West; some of the newcomers were conspicuous recruits to Republicanism as editors and pamphleteers, and it was easy to brand them unpatriotic, or worse.

Three major laws were enacted. The Naturalization Act, designed to halt the recruitment of new voters by the Republicans, raised the residence requirement for citizenship from five to fourteen years. The Alien Act empowered the President to deport or imprison "dangerous" aliens. The Sedition Act made it a crime to publish false or malicious writings against the government or its officers. The effect of these measures was not as ugly as might have been feared, partly because many leading Federalists, including Adams, deplored them. The only act to be seriously invoked was the last, under which ten Republican editors and one member of Congress, Matthew Lyon, were convicted, and a number of individuals prosecuted for overindulgence in free speech. As Adams had foreseen, they promptly became martyrs. And the Kentucky and Virginia Resolutions, drafted respectively by Jefferson and Madison, declared that these acts were unconstitutional, that they violated the Bill of Rights, and that the states were the proper judges of constitutionality and could, if they chose, act to nullify such laws. If the protests were as much propagandist as were the laws themselves, they at least raised a major issue. And if Adams and Hamilton differed on many matters, they were both as alarmed as Jackson was to be by the dangerous talk of nullification, or as Lincoln was to be by the more dangerous fact of secession.

Paradoxically, it was the Republicans who stood for localism and for federalism; the High Federalists in fact were centralists and nationalists. At this stage Adams was of their company. While making no direct recommendation to Congress on these measures, he made his contribution to the high spirit of the times by his intemperate replies to the addresses that poured in upon him. Only the Republicans gained by the unwisdom and unpopularity of this legislation. If the Fries' rebellion in western Pennsylvania against the federal property tax levied in 1798 was suppressed, one consequence was that this area became thereafter solidly Republican in character.

The second aspect of 1798-99 was the fact of an undeclared war with France. In two years, French commerce in the West Indies was in large measure destroyed. Privateering had a rebirth. Jingoist sentiment now inclined to the idea of a standing army, an alliance with Britain, and dominion over the South American states. There were here, thought Adams, dreams of conquest scarcely less grandiose than those of the Pizzaros. Rufus King reported from London in February 1798 that the Spanish colonial empire would disintegrate when France invaded Spain; Miranda, backed by Britain, would lead an expeditionary force; the United States must aid Britain lest France re-establish her

American empire. The new Republic's best defense, it seemed, was not only offense, but empire on her own in the West, and, in the Caribbean, protection for the newer republics of whom she might be mentor. Guns captured from French ships were donated by Britain to the United States for the defense of Charleston—an act of such gratuitous international kindness as to be diplomatically highly suspect. Anglophile sentiment ran high, particularly in Rufus King and Robert Goodloe Harper, and it was discreetly abetted by Robert Liston, the British minister. If the High Federalists had had their way, the Great Rule of Washington would have been abandoned before it had been fully established, and a foreign policy of adventure abroad might have permanently replaced the principle of isolation.

Finally, through this crisis Adams, unlike Hamilton, sought to hold off the dogs of war in the Cabinet and Congress. He was supported by Wolcott—on this at odds with Hamilton—and by Benjamin Stoddert, his new Secretary of the Navy. He deplored the warlike mood the Hamiltonians induced. He disliked the idea of a standing army and the political ammunition it provided for the Republicans. In this he was far more shrewd than Hamilton. He was unable to curb Congress, however. Dr. Logan had already gone to Paris in his solitary but highly suspect efforts to keep the peace with France; Congress, by passing the Logan Act, promptly made his peaceful crusade a misdemeanor—a charge that still holds if an American citizen is rash enough to seek to intervene in a dispute between the United States and a foreign government. The same ugliness attended even the President's own efforts, and it was on this fundamental note that the final break with the High Federalists came.

Through Gerry, and William Vans Murray at the Hague, Adams was informed that Talleyrand wished to renew diplomatic intercourse. Reports from John Quincy and from Rufus King confirmed this. The French put out soothing statements about *XYZ*, alleging that the American commissioners had innocently allowed themselves to be imposed upon by charlatans.

Although preparations for war went ahead, the President sought with dogged courage to keep the doors open to negotiation. By his influence in his party, in Congress, and indirectly in the Cabinet Hamilton pressed as hard for war. To the horror of the Senate, Adams recommended, first, in February 1799, the appointment of Murray as minister to the French Republic, and then, when the Senate showed violent objection, the appointment of a three-man peace commission—with advice that it should not sail until there was evidence of real French good will.

This step, taken entirely on his own initiative, rallied opinion to him. Diplomatically, it was wise; economically it was sound, for as many were profiteering from trade with the French West Indies as were likely to profit from war, and the federal military program had doubled the cost of government; and, as political tactics, it was not only shrewd but necessary. To have permitted war with France in 1799 would have been tantamount to permitting the risk of civil war at home and to the acceptance of government by militarism. For Adams, peace was a necessity. Such was the Federalist split, however, that, also of necessity, it brought a widening of the gulf between the High Federalists and the President. Adams' refusal to dismiss Pickering and McHenry, even though he was aware of their intrigues against him, and his long absence at Quincy in the summer of 1799, like his similar absence in the previous year, were acts of unwisdom. On his return in October—his Cabinet met at Trenton because of the fever in Philadelphia—he acted once more on his own authority and ordered the mission to sail. At this point the two groups broke apart. As in 1792 and 1796, the High Federalists began their now-customary intrigues to deny office to the man who, almost unaided, had kept his country out of war.

For one with a sharp sense of his own importance, and who, on the broad question of peace or war, was remarkably mature, John Adams was curiously longsuffering. Indeed, he appeared never to suspect Wolcott's intrigues at all. In the end McHenry resigned, after a stormy interview, and not even his friends mourned his departure. Pickering was, in May 1800, at last dismissed from office. The Federalist leaders, at odds with each other, now openly campaigned against the President, and Hamilton, using information provided by Wolcott, produced his *Letter Concerning the Public Conduct and Character of John Adams.* He described Adams as unfit for the presidency and revealed Cabinet secrets. It appeared in the last week of October, too late to permit of a reply before the elections.

The legacy of this rivalry and dissension was twofold. On September 30, 1800, peace with France was concluded at Morfontaine; it was Adams' own achievement. In October, as his thanks, he was defeated in the electoral college, gaining sixty-five votes to Jefferson's and Burr's tied seventy-three. The last months of office were months of gloom and petulance; the midnight judges were appointed, and in the cold dawn of March 4, 1801, a few hours before Jefferson's inaugural, Adams made an angry, unforgiving and ungracious exit from the still uncompleted presidental mansion in the far from completed Federal City.

It is, however, much too simple to explain these four years in terms of a personal vendetta. Certainly the two men were utterly different in temperament and attitude, and there was personal dislike and mistrust. Adams was much older than Hamilton and lacked his flamboyant and mercurial driving force. He saw Hamilton as one who attached himself to the great, linked by service to Washington and by marriage to Schuyler; he saw him as clever, arrogant, and a libertine; he saw him, to Hamilton's particular disgust, as an outsider, "the Creole adventurer," "the Creole bastard," isolated by origins and by birth; he was one, he thought, who would almost inevitably be passed over for posts of real responsibility. In 1809 Adams excused Hamilton's errors on the grounds that he was "not a native of America," "he never acquired the feelings and principles of the American people." Hamilton was by 1797 aware of this himself, and his gloom and frustration grew with the years: "Every day proves to me more and more that the American World was not made for me."

It was due to Hamilton, Adams believed, that he had obtained less than half the electoral votes for Vice-President in 1792; it was Hamilton who conspired against him with his own Cabinet; it was Hamilton who thwarted what chances he had of a second term, by publishing a pamphlet condemning the negotiations with the French as "capricious and undignified," and attacking the President's "extreme egotism." Adams later wrote:

> In this dark and insidious manner did this intriguer lay schemes in secret against me, and like the worm at the root of the peach, did he labor for twelve years, underground and in darkness, to girdle the root, while all the axes of the Anti-federalists, Democrats, Jacobins, Virginia debtors to English merchants, and French hirelings, chopping as they were for the whole time at the trunk, could not fell the tree.

If Adams cannot be thought impartial, Noah Webster, a staunch Federalist, equally deplored Hamilton's wrecking of the party. In his *Open Letter to General Hamilton,* in 1800, he said, "your ambition, pride and overbearing temper have destined you to be the evil genius of this country." Abigail Adams saw the trend even more sharply. "That man," she said, "would become a second Bonaparty if he was possessed of equal power!" The charge was valid; Hamilton's hero was Julius Caesar.

But behind the clash of dour, crusty, and family-rooted Yankee and versatile, illegitimate, and ambitious West Indian lay a deeper clash of principle. Hamilton was the true monarchist, and of all the Revolutionary leaders the man who qualified best for the title of man of "Little Faith." For him the Constitution was always a second best, and his doubts about its durability continued until the day he died. He described it in 1802 as "a frail and worthless fabric which I have been endeavouring to prop up," "a shilly shally thing of mere milk and water." What he admired were discipline and authority in government; what he

preached was mercantilism. He subsidized those who invested
in manufactures and public securities; he taxed the landed interest. He favored a "hereditary" chief magistrate, representing
the "permanent will" of society and capable of curbing the
"turbulent and uncontrouling [*sic*] disposition" of democracy. He
wanted the "Officers of the General Government" protected by
the courts. He wanted a permanent army. He wanted to increase
the legal power of the federal government over the states, and
the larger states to be reduced in size. He wanted federal roads
and canals built throughout the nation. He wanted an upper
house chosen for life on a property basis. "Our real disease," he
wrote on the night before he was shot, "is democracy."

His economic-cum-political views were shaped, in fact, less by
America than by his youth in the store in the lush sugar islands,
where prosperity depended—hurricanes permitting—on an elaborate trading system, and where society was hierarchic. He had no
sympathy with Jefferson's farmer-democrats. The rich, the well-
born, and the able were to be given every encouragement, and
the fluidity of a free society would allow them to be creative, not
destructive.

This was not Adams' view of Federalism. For one thing, he
was a farmer's son and, if a lawyer by vocation, he remained an
agrarian in background. He was far more a Physiocrat than a
mercantilist. There was a simplicity and frugality in Adams'
code, a taste for "a frock and trowsers, a hoe and a spade." If
he shared the belief in order and status and leaned for a time
to monarchism, the emphasis was very different. To him the federal Constitution was "the greatest single effort of national de-
liberation that the world has ever seen." He did not in fact share
Hamilton's view that the executive should be exalted above faction, a constitutional monarch. While to Hamilton the "rich"
were the capitalists, to Adams land was the most desirable form
of property. He accepted the trading system and the assumption
of state debts as necessary, but he disliked the use of assumption
in order to reward speculators. He was thus far more typical of

the conservative farmers and small traders than was Hamilton. He accepted the need for a national bank of deposit, but he had a Jeffersonian horror of local banks issuing paper far beyond the amount of their own capital—"the madness of the many for the profit of the few." He had no taste for the speculators in land or in paper. When the High Federalists spoke with awe of "the wise, the good and the rich," Adams respected only the first two categories. He deplored plutocracy. He deplored also the sense of adventure on which the Hamiltonian system, like the Hamiltonian career, was based. His standpoint was unblushingly civilian; there was no taste for military glory in Adams.

As the years passed, Adams' virulence increased. "The trading system and the banking system which are the works of the Federalists," he wrote in 1809, "have introduced more corruption and injustice . . . than any other cause." By this time he was moving away from a now-wrecked Federalism and, perhaps because he was in part the architect of the disaster, his language had a pungency unusual to seventy-four-year-olds:

> As Hamilton was the Sovereign Pontiff of Federalism, all his Cardinals no doubt will endeavour to excite the whole Church to excommunicate and anathematize me. Content. It was time for a Protestant Separation.

Neither Adams nor Hamilton was consistent. The former moved from revolutionary causes through realism to conservatism; a not unfamiliar transition. Hamilton's inconsistencies were more heinous. In *The Federalist* (Nos. 12 and 21) he thought that "the genius of the people" hates excises, yet they were an essential part of his revenue system in 1791, and in 1794 he was employing force to crush the resistance to them of the Whiskey Rebels in Pennsylvania; the advocate of isolation (in *Federalist*, 11) became in 1794 the notorious Anglophile of the Jay Treaty; the supporter of free elections and free choice in 1787 threatened to use force in 1800 to nullify the people's will. He claimed in 1787, and in 1791–94, to "think continentally," yet by 1800 he was the not fully avowed leader of the High Federalists, at odds with President Adams and wrecking both Adams' administration and his own party.

Increasingly he advocated the use of armies: in 1794 to crush Pennsylvania farmers; in 1798, when he became Inspector-General, to go to war with France or perhaps to embark on a great crusade as a liberator in Spanish America; in 1800 to preserve Federalist power in New York. "In times like these," he told John Jay, "it will not do to be over-scrupulous." He split with Adams because the President kept peace with France. He thought Jefferson ought to go to war to gain Louisiana, but when Jefferson achieved its purchase in a staggering diplomatic triumph, Hamilton wrote:

> the advantage of the acquisition appears too distant and remote to strike the mind of a sober politician with much force. . . . It . . . must hasten the dismemberment of a large portion of our country, or a dissolution of the Government.

The passionate nationalist could become the most bitter and irrational of partisans. He was brilliant and farsighted, driven by great qualities, perhaps the most creative personality in the age of the American Revolution; but he was not made for politics, or for the tact and the compromises that politics demands. His own life, which held out so much promise, was tragic. His ideas triumphed a century later.

As always when a governing party splits into two, the opposition inherits power by default. The decline of the Federalists was paralleled in these years by the rise of the Democratic Republicans. They profited from the errors of the Federalists. They were strong in the South and in the West. They became the exponents of state rights, and in the Virginia and Kentucky Resolutions of 1798 they expressed their own political philosophy almost as clearly as did Hamilton and the early Madison in *The Federalist Papers*. They were by 1799 well organized in particular states, with Madison, it is now clear, even more their mastermind than Jefferson. They too had a personal rivalry to settle—that between Jefferson and Burr; it was Hamilton's role in settling it, by swinging the votes of the states in the House of Representatives against Burr, that put Jefferson in the White House, and earned for Hamilton Burr's dangerous enmity.

The presidency of John Adams, like that of Jefferson after him, revealed the strength and the weakness of the scholar as politician. Despite all his travel, his reading, his pessimistic Puritan strain, and his shrewdness, he who was a skeptic in the study could not make himself a cynic in the Cabinet, and it is from this dichotomy that he often appears in action as naïve. A big man on the big issues, like peace with France, he found it hard to be forceful or creative or even at ease in his dealings with individuals. What he lacked were not so much the human qualities of warmth and comradeship, though these were not conspicuous, but cynicism about the motives and knowledge of the ways of the men around him. These might have allowed him to guess at the perfidy of some of his associates and thus have averted the ruin of his party.

As Jefferson had said, Adams was a "bad calculator." While he had no illusions about Hamilton and saw himself as a very wise student of affairs, in practice he treated Hamilton's lieutenants with quite unmerited charity and with unusual patience. In his closing months of office, when, to Jefferson's chagrin, he filled the judicial places with his own appointees, he rewarded not only John Marshall, who had replaced Pickering for a few months as Secretary of State, but also Wolcott. Even in the years of bitter harvest that followed, it was only to Hamilton and "Tim Pick" that he refused forgiveness, although by 1818 he was telling Jefferson that in a future world he might overcome his objections to meeting even them, "if I could see a symptom of penitence in either."

What must, however, be stressed here is that the story is not merely a personal one. Party spirit was the real novelty. Adams felt as alien to it and as disturbed by it as had Washington. In their view, there was no place for it, and they saw its existence as evidence of human wickedness, or of foreign intrigue, rather than as the expression of a different point of view. Federalists saw in Republicans men opposed not merely to the administration but to the Constitution, and dupes of France. To Republicans the Federalists were "Anglomen." It was still the springtime of party history, and if such charges were later the small change of party controversy, in 1798 and 1799 they were, to many, matters of belief and bitter hatred, convictions and not yet conventions. There was an unusual acrimony in debate, as politicians learned to accept the paradox that a healthy democracy necessitates keen, and often violent, partisanship. Adams suffered acutely: from the charge that the executive was head of a party, which in his eyes degraded the office; from the immoderates in both groups, none of whom respected the middle way; and from the fact that his own partiality was not only for Low Federalists, but for Old Whigs, his comrades of 1776, like Gerry and Benjamin Rush. He suffered for his faith—a curiously unrealistic one—in the possibility of an independent executive.

Even if one concedes, however, that the fault did not lie in himself, it is incontrovertible that he contributed to his own debacle: by inheriting Washington's Cabinet and not forcing the issue with it, or its gray eminence, much earlier; by losing good will over his failure to oppose the Alien and Sedition acts, hard though he tried later to deny responsibility for them; by failing to match intrigue with firmness; and by failing to build up a following of his own. For one who favored a strong executive he was a surprisingly weak President. And he had—always—too many scruples. By 1800 the most conspicuous feature of American politics was the extent and virulence of partisan spirit. It made Washington's last year, and Adams' whole term, miserable and unproductive.

Yet the services of John Adams cannot be minimized. If his distrust of democracy, a distrust he shared with the High Federalists, was as substantial as his distrust of faction, out of it emerged his decision to use the interval between November 1800 and March 1801 to make the judiciary staunchly Federalist. If the motives were partisan and suspect, the long-term results were to prove beneficial; the powers not only of the courts but of the federal government as well were enhanced; loose construction and judicial review were part of the Adams legacy. Not the least of his services was that he gave John Marshall to the Supreme Court.

More than this, he could claim with justice to have kept the peace with France, to have curbed the foreign policy of adventure abroad advocated by Hamilton, and to have strengthened the Great Rule of Washington. He had been, in 1774, one of the first to see that isolation was a logical consequence of the Revolution. He held to it through all the tensions of 1798 and 1799, and, by keeping the peace with France, he unknowingly made it possible for his successor to acquire the Louisiana Territory and the West by simple purchase. Although as much a man of impulse as Hamilton, he had a basic understanding of the value to the new country of peace and stability. And on this he was more consistent than Hamilton. Isolation from Europe was not only a political advantage for America, it was a moral distinction; he shared the faith of 1776 in New World values. Hamilton was a High Tory; John Adams, in all his changing moods, was an Old Whig.

10

What Then Is the American, This New Man?

THAT A BETTER WORLD lay across the Atlantic was a recurrent fancy in eighteenth-century Europe. It took the form of the conceit that "genius" moved from east to west in the course of historic development—a conceit that has continued to fascinate historians. It was the theme of Bishop Berkeley in 1726:

> There shall be sung another golden age,
>   The rise of empire and of arts,
> The good and great inspiring epic rage,
>   The wisest heads and noblest hearts.

> Not such as Europe breeds in her decay:
>   Such as she bred when fresh and young,
> When heavenly flame did animate her clay,
>   By future poets shall be sung.

> Westward the course of empire takes its way;
>   The first four acts already past,
> A fifth shall close the drama with the day;
>   Time's noblest offspring is the last.

Fifty years later, the Abbé Gagliani of Naples told Mme D'Épinay: "Everything hastens to renew itself in America . . . do not buy your house in the Chaussee D'Antin; you must buy it in Philadelphia." The decay of Europe is the repeated theme of liberal Europeans like Condorcet and de Chastellux, and of liberal Americans: Jefferson, Franklin, Paine, John Adams. Jonathan Edwards said that Providence had marked America to be "the glorious renovator of the world." "It was the fashion in 1777," said Ezra Stiles, "to talk high for American liberty." Franklin and Adam Smith foresaw the shift of power across the Atlantic. "This people," wrote Turgot to Dr. Price in 1778, "is the hope of the human race. It may become the model."

It was in 1777, while serving as a chaplain in the revolutionary army, that Timothy Dwight, a grandson of Jonathan Edwards and a future president of Yale, expressed his hopes for the future of his country in his "Columbia":

> To conquest, and slaughter, let Europe aspire;
> Whelm nations in blood, and wrap cities in fire;
> Thy heroes the rights of mankind shall defend,
> And triumph pursue them, and glory attend.
> A world is thy realm: for a world be thy laws,
> Enlarg'd as thine empire, and just as thy cause;
> On Freedom's broad basis, that empire shall rise,
> Extend with the main, and dissolve with the skies.

In the years from 1776 to 1779 Washington too widened his view of his "country" from the Northern Neck to the new and shaky Federation; in 1779 he was first saluted as *Pater Patriae;* the fact of a common army, sharing a bitter experience as they were driven across state lines, was a powerful basis on which nationalist sentiment could grow. This was noted by the first historian of the American Revolution, David Ramsay of South Carolina, who, writing in 1789, noted how in the course of the war local jealousies abated, intermarriage became more frequent, and religious bigotry was weakened—"a foundation was laid for the establishment of a nation, out of discordant materials." By 1783, however discordant the elements, *country* was being used not for the little platoon one belonged to but for the whole, the new, the united nation.

> Where happy millions their own fields possess,
> No tyrant awes them, and no lords oppress.

American success in the War of Independence coincided in 1782 with the classic statement of the vernal view of the new society. It came from Hector St. John de Crèvecoeur in his *Letters from an American Farmer,* when he asked "What is an American?" He gave his answer:

> Here are no aristocratical families, no courts, no kings, no bishops, no ecclesiastical dominion, no invisible power giving to a few a very visible one, no great manufacturers employing thousands, no great refinements of luxury. The rich and the poor are not so far removed from each other as they are in Europe. . . . We are a people of cultivators scattered over an immense territory, communicating with each other by means of good roads and navigable rivers, united by the silken bands of mild government. . . . We are all animated with the spirit of an industry which is unfettered and unrestrained, because each person works for himself. . . . A pleasing uniformity of decent competence appears throughout our habitations. . . . *He* is an American, who leaving behind him all his ancient prejudices and manners, receives new ones from the new mode of life he has embraced, the new government he obeys, and the new rank he holds. He becomes an American by being received in the broad lap of our great *Alma Mater.* Here individuals of all nations are melted into a new race of men, whose labours and posterity will one day cause great changes in the World. Americans are the western pilgrims, who are carrying along with them that great mass of arts, sciences, vigour and industry which began long since in the east; they will finish the great circle.

The idea was expressed by Paine in 1776: England belongs to Europe, America to itself. It has been put more recently, and more forcibly, by Wallace Stevens: the American moon came up, cleansed clean of lousy Byzantium.

In the nineteenth century, this image of the United States was not fully accepted, either abroad or at home. Heinrich Heine, an admirer of the New World, had his doubts:

> Sometimes I am bound to see
>   Revolution's glorious sequel:
> America, the great, the free,
>   Land where everyone is equal.
>
> But how could I love a land
>   Where the mob is monarch really,
> Where there are no King-pins, and
>   People chew and spit so freely?

Henry Adams, writing in 1891, has left an equally famous but far less lyrical picture than Crèvecoeur of the American scene in 1800:

With the exception that half a million people had crossed the Alleghenies and were struggling with difficulties all their own, in an isolation like that of Jutes or Angles in the fifth century, America, so far as concerned physical problems, had changed little in fifty years. The old landmarks remained nearly where they stood before. The same bad roads and difficult rivers, connecting the same small towns, stretched into the same forests in 1800 as when the armies of Braddock and Amherst pierced the western and northern wilderness, except that these roads extended a few miles farther from the seacoast. Nature was rather man's master than his servant, and the five million Americans struggling with the untamed continent seemed hardly more competent in their task than the beavers and buffalo which had for countless generations made bridges and roads of their own.

Even by water, along the seaboard, communication was as slow and almost as irregular as in colonial times. The wars in Europe caused a sudden and great increase in American shipping employed in foreign commerce, without yet leading to general improvement in navigation . . . the voyage to Europe was comparatively more comfortable and more regular than the voyage from New York to Albany, or through Long Island Sound to Providence. . . .

The valley of the Ohio had no more to do with that of the Hudson, the Susquehanna, the Potomac, the Roanoke, and the Santee, than the valley of the Danube with that of the Rhone, the Po or the Elbe. Close communication by land could alone hold the great geographical divisions together either in interest or in fear. The union of New England with New York and Pennsylvania was not an easy task, even as a problem of geography, and with an ocean highway; but the union of New England with the Carolinas, and of the seacoast with the interior, promised to be a hopeless undertaking. Physical contact alone could make one country of these isolated empires, but to the patriotic American of 1800, struggling for the continued existence of an embryo nation, with machinery so inadequate, the idea of ever bringing the Mississippi River, either by land or water, into close contact with New England, must have seemed wild.

An image does not need to be true, however, to possess emotive force. By 1800 the United States had neither reached a full sense of nationhood—it did not do so until 1815—nor fully escaped from problems similar to those in Europe. The same historian, F. J. Turner, who saw in the frontier the distinctive feature of American history and the progenitor of American nationalism, also saw the significance of sections. What had made for difficulty in 1754, in 1774, and in 1787 was still a source of dissension in 1800. New England's fear of the Southwest is a constant theme in these years. "It has been said," said Morris in 1787, "that North Carolina, South Carolina and Georgia only will in a little time have a majority of the people of America. They must in that case include the great interior country and everything is to be apprehended from their getting power into their hands." Fears about the future of the West are the recurring theme of the dispatches of British minister Robert Liston (1796-1800) and came to the surface with the Spanish Conspiracy of 1797 and the Burr adventure of 1803-1806. By the Louisiana purchase, said Fisher Ames, "we rush like a comet into infinite space."

As the elaborate statistics of Nathan Dane revealed, and as the proposals of the Hartford Convention of 1814 confirmed, the fear of New England was concentrated on Kentucky and Tennessee, the growing points of the Southwest. This was no longer a Hamiltonian fear of democracy, but a fear on the part of the commercial states of those other states which invested almost exclusively in land and slaves, and which, if they became members of the Union, would, in the eyes of New England, destroy its balance and impugn its moral worth.] By 1812 Gouverneur Morris was, he said, losing his sense of loyalty to what he had helped to build in 1787. Sectionalism is even more striking a feature of independent America in 1800 than of the colonies in 1763. The Constitution had not been able to determine whether the state or the new nation could, in the last analysis, demand a citizen's ultimate loyalty. The tightrope between national and federal so skillfully walked by Madison in 1787 called in 1812 for a dexterous tread. It still does.

The vast extent of the country was as much stimulus to sectionalism as to nationalism; as Tocqueville said later, these were "like two distinct currents flowing in contrary directions in the same channel." The size of the Republic brought on the one hand pride and prosperity; it brought on the other diverse climates, economies, and social patterns under a single political framework. What at one stage were embryo territories became, within a generation, sections with policies of their own, so that compromises had continually to be remade, with heart-searchings and alarms.

Yet if nationalism met difficulties in the New World, it was aided by many factors: by distance and isolation from Europe; by a common language, a common spelling book in 1783, and common institutions; by a hard-won victory in war; by the long interval of European revolution which kept the Old World preoccupied; by the stimulus this gave to an "American System"; by the role of the first President as a symbol of the country's unity and purpose; by Hamilton's financial policies; and by the uniform pressure on each section of common problems. Whether the threats were seen as coming from French or Spanish or British agents, or from Indians on the frontiers, Americans as well as foreigners were now recognizing national characteristics and had a real sense of sharing a common destiny. The limits of their country from the St. Croix to the Suwannee were still ambiguous, as in 1763, and to the west they were about to be extended. But a new nation had been built. As with other embryo nationalisms, its first expressions were extravagant and xenophobic—

> Can we never be thought to have learning or grace
> Unless it be brought from that horrible place
> Where tyranny reigns with her impudent face?

asked Freneau. In Noah Webster's speller, and his later dictionary, in the paintings of John Trumbull, in Morse's *Geography,* and in Barlow's *Vision of Columbus* it was expressing its character, its pride, and something of its adolescence.

Yet if this is the first striking characteristic of these forty years, the second is that the nation made by war and independence, in an age of revolution, was not by 1800 a revolutionary nation. In 1789 Washington described the destiny of republican government as an "experiment entrusted to the hands of the American people." It soon came to appear that it could be trusted to no other, and that it was a fragile plant that must be sheltered from Old World storms. The years from 1793 to 1800 are in this sense quite as important as 1776 or 1787. In 1793 the ally of France refused to stand by its ally of fifteen years before, not because France had a revolutionary government—a fact that the United States was in no position to deplore—but because of a sense of distance—physical, political, and psychological—between the Old World and the New, and because also of a rather sensitive distaste for revolutionary meddling in American domestic affairs—forgetful of France's not dissimilar, but more conspicuous, meddling in what had been in 1778 a British domestic affair. Washington's decision in 1793, however arrived at, was fundamental: a decision to be neutral and isolated.

The neutrality seemed doubtful when the terms of the Jay Treaty were revealed, and by 1798 both neutrality and isolation were severely challenged by the High Federalist campaign of 1798–99. But the great rule held, and it became as binding a part of American mythology as the personality of Washington or the phrases of the Declaration of Independence. It was the achievement of John Adams to hold to this view of the peculiar distinctness of the United States and to avert intervention in Europe; within a decade he found his policy being reinforced by the embargoes of Jefferson; in this as in so much else the third President was right to say, in his first Inaugural, "We are all Republicans, we are all Federalists." If in 1812 both isolation and neutrality were abandoned, to many the War of 1812 was fought with the wrong enemy. At Springfield, Massachusetts, in 1812 a meeting could declare "We hold in utter abhorence an alliance with France, the destroyer of old republics."

Having fought its war for independence with European help, having established a Republic vaster in territory than had ever been attempted before, having in most states set up a property-owning democracy that was far in advance of anything in Europe, having scorned the many doubts about its capacity to survive that were voiced by Hamilton, by Colonel Nicola who in 1782 had offered Washington a crown, by the Society of the Cincinnati, and by Europe, the nation turned away in 1793 from all further foreign adventures. The principles of 1776, it said, had not been those of 1789. After reading and translating the long article on the two revolutions by the young Friedrich Gentz that appeared in 1800 in the Berlin *Historisches Journal,* the still younger John Quincy Adams wrote to Gentz (June 1800) congratulating him on having vindicated the American Revolution from "the imputation of having originated or been conducted upon the same principles as that of France." By 1800 the United States had opted out of revolution. Miranda in 1806 fought the fight unaided. That her cause was no longer the cause of all mankind America demonstrated by her later rejection of Tom Paine. He who had first used the words "the United States of America" was in 1806 denied the right of being an American citizen.

But if by 1800 no longer revolutionary, American republicanism and democracy were strikingly successful. The census of 1800 indicated a population of 5,308,473—double that of 1775 and one third greater than the population in 1790. Most of this was by natural increase; in much of it there was a remarkable degree of racial intermixture. If industrial development was small, and dependent still on the importation of the illicit skills of people like Samuel Slater, and if the volume of foreign trade exceeded that of interstate traffic, there were signs of change. By 1800 there were fifteen thousand miles of post roads. Three new states had been added to the original thirteen, and those on the threshold of statehood in the old Northwest were permanently to exclude slavery. The experiment of a republican and federal form of government on the scale of a continent seemed to be successful—although the tests of 1803 and 1812 lay ahead. Democracy was not yet fully established. Even the "revolution" of 1800 was led by an aristocrat, and the New England Federalists were still seeking to check the trend toward universal manhood suffrage; Chancellor Kent of New York argued that America was not, after all, a peculiar society; democracy, he argued, had always brought trouble to the Old World, and a wide suffrage jeopardized both property rights and liberty. Freedom was not yet established—for women, for Negroes, or for indentured servants. It was, however, an open society, property-owning and entrepreneurial; and property, like trade and commerce, prefers reform to revolution.

More striking than its emergent nationalism or its growing but cautious democratic temper was American rationalism. It too was not yet fully victorious, and it was stronger in the Jeffersonian circles in Philadelphia, and after 1800 in Washington, than in Boston or the West. But it was a powerful force and a destroyer of many conventions. The Constitution was one of its embodiments; a document drawn up by ordinary men, devoid of appeal to kings or deities; a product of human compromises, not of social mysticism. There were many other signs. The steady decline of Puritanism into a cold formalism continued, and the campaign of Jonathan Edwards had failed to revive it. Congregationalism was being affected, and in places undermined, by Unitarianism; as, within a decade, Harvard Divinity School was to show. In 1782 Harvard Medical School began its work. New schools opened their doors: the Phillips academies, Dickinson College in Pennsylvania, St. John's at Annapolis, Hampden-Sydney in Virginia. In 1784 Judge Tapping Reeve opened his famous and fecund law school at Litchfield, Connecticut. The prestige of the French Army during the War of Independence had made rationalism and deism fashionable. Jefferson's campaign for religious freedom in Virginia was reflected in the attitude of Tom Paine—whose attacks on the Bible in *The Age of Reason* did more to alienate sympathy from him than did his political opinions—and in the materialism of backwoodsmen like Ethan Allen, whose *Reason, the Only Oracle of Man,* published in 1784, threw a new light on the frontier hero of Ticonderoga and the Green Mountains. To Timothy Dwight he was a "clodhopping oracle," but Allen was a significant figure in whom deism was an aspect of Americanism.

Yet here again there was conflict and challenge. After 1800 Jefferson turned away from deism and it became increasingly identified with the *illuminati* of Paris and their excesses. Timothy Dwight, seeking on the one hand to bring the new science of chemistry to Yale, campaigned on the other against deism as a disruptive force in society as well as in the churches. The revivalism of 1800 in Connecticut and along the frontier saw the growth of many Protestant groups, especially of Methodists, Baptists, and more fundamentalist sects. Bishop Francis Asbury traveled some 250,000 miles and crossed the Alleghenies sixty times on horseback in the course of a lifework of converting 300,000 to Methodism and ordaining 4000 preachers. The Great Revival of the early nineteenth century was only in small part a counter-revolution; it affected mainly the frontier areas, which were not likely to have been the seedgrounds for deism. It was an effective check on infidelity, however, and it had long-term results of a liberal kind: political activity became emotional and democratic; party conventions were cast in the mold of revivalist camp meetings—a character they still retain; a stimulus was given to the antislavery movement, to missionary work among the Indians, and to those humanitarian crusades for the relief of the insane and of criminals that had a result in the days of Jackson.

If the rationalism of the Jeffersonians had by 1800 only a modest success, there was a real faith in reason and in experiment; America was "the empire of reason," wrote Enos Hitchcock in 1799. The émigrés from Europe were now less revolutionaries than refugee scientists, like Dr. Priestley, Thomas Cooper, or Dupont de Nemours. The American Philosophical Society, reborn in 1769 as a merger of the older society with Franklin's Junto, was modeled on the Royal Society and was the center of much inquiry. The objective was still that of Franklin, not speculative but useful knowledge. Members were instructed, in the preface to the first volume of the Society's *Transactions,* to "confine their disquisitions, principally, to such subjects as tend to the improvement of their country, and advancement of its interest and prosperity."

The core of the Society was the Jeffersonian circle. Benjamin Rush was America's first professor of chemistry, a prosperous doctor, a signer of the Declaration of Independence, a penal and temperance reformer. He was enlightened, active—and opinionated. He believed in bleeding, holding that all diseases were caused by spasms in the blood vessels. Yet his *Medical Inquiries and Observations upon the Diseases of the Mind* was also a pioneer work in psychiatry. The Quaker David Rittenhouse was, said Jefferson, "second to no astronomer living"; beginning with optics—he supplied Washington with spectacles—he became a self-taught astronomer, plotted the transit of Venus in 1769, and in 1793 discovered a new comet. He helped to manufacture munitions in the war; he became the first director of the United

States Mint. His nephew Benjamin Smith Barton was the greatest American botanist of the age, who shared Jefferson's own interests in flora and fauna and whose *Elements of Botany* (1803) went through several American and English editions, and was even translated into Russian. Charles Willson Peale was the artist and curator of the group. He was in fact a more genuinely native painter than Gilbert Stuart, and his portraits of Washington, if less accomplished than Stuart's and less stylized, are probably more accurate representations of the Father of the Country. These men were as much empiricists as philosophers; all except Barton, who was too young, had played their part in helping to win the war and to serve the state; they all advocated state-financed schools, believing that democracy depended on an educated people; their philosopher-king of course was Jefferson.

In the Friendly Club, New York had its own rival junto, with William Dunlap, Elihu Hubbard Smith, and Charles Brockden Brown as its stars. They were a less philosophic, but more literary, group than Philadelphia's; indeed, for 1800 they were almost bohemian. And in the Hartford Wits there was a New England junto, to whom the word *bohemian,* had it been understood, would have been anathema.

Benjamin Rush's ideas on education are particularly significant of the Jeffersonian viewpoint. "The great design of a liberal education is, to prepare youth for usefulness here, and for happiness hereafter." Students should be taught to understand the reality of change; fixed and traditional courses should be avoided; a course in "the art of forgetting" should be compulsory for teachers, judges, and all who influence opinion. He opposed the teaching of Latin and Greek, which, he thought, was like pursuing butterflies to the neglect of more useful knowledge. Students should learn to speak German and French; the grammar should come later. But there were lessons to be drawn from the past: "Above all, let our youth be instructed in the history of the ancient republics, and the progress of liberty and tyranny in the different states of Europe." There should be established a federal university as a national center of learning, as much concerned with research as with teaching, and with a principal who would inspire students "by occasional public discourses with federal and patriotic sentiments. Let the principal be a man of extensive education, liberal manners and dignified deportment." After it had been established for thirty years, Congress should require that no one could hold public office without a degree from the university. "We are restrained from injuring ourselves by employing quacks in law; why should we not be restrained in like manner, by law, from employing quacks in government?"

In 1800 it was Philadelphia rather than Boston, despite its Academy of Arts and Sciences, that was the hub of the American universe. But the Jeffersonian circle had no monopoly of scientific interest or of ideas. Benjamin Silliman was about to start his distinguished career as chemist and natural historian at Yale. Eli Whitney produced his cotton gin in 1793. John Fitch had built a steamboat, but it was another decade before it became of practical service. Samuel Bard and David Hosack were active in medicine and botany in New York. In part under Scottish stimuli—for many of the early teachers of medicine were Edinburgh graduates—medicine was treated as a branch of higher learning, no longer a trade for apothecaries. The interest in science was reflected in the interest in geology and natural history—in Bartram and Jeremy Belknap, Hosack and Jefferson. If there was a God in the Jeffersonian heaven, it was nature's God; "In meaner works discovered here, No less than in the starry sphere," as Freneau wrote. There was a sense of awe and majesty in their view of America's topography and resources; but they were challenged, not frightened, by what they saw. It is expressed not only in Freneau's poems or Jefferson's *Notes on Virginia*, but also in William Bartram's *Travels* (1791)—the result of a five-year expedition through the Carolinas and Georgia into the Creek country. The book seemed to confirm the European images of the New World; a place where the inquirer was humane, rational, and poetic, where the savage was noble and where nature was benign. Chateaubriand drew heavily on Bartram, as did Wordsworth and Coleridge. Bartram seemed to speak for the New World when he wrote: "My chief happiness consisted in tracing and admiring the infinite power, majesty and perfection of the great Almighty Creator, and in contemplation that through divine aid and permission, I might be instrumental in discovering and introducing into my native country some original production of nature, which might become useful to society."

The contrast between rational man and the grandeur of nature emerges in the literature of this period. It touches sensuous and lyrical heights in Bartram. But literature was almost exclusively the servant of politics and rarely rose above pamphleteering. If the American Revolution was a patriotic stimulus to Francis Hopkinson, John Trumbull, or Philip Freneau, and if for Freneau the French Revolution was even more stimulating, their poetry was almost always partisan. It was certainly prolific. Freneau wrote twelve hundred pages of verse, strongly nationalistic and romantic in tone. Nor were the high standards of Franklin's prose, deceptively easy as it seemed to be, maintained by his successors. The journalism of the Aurora, of Fenno, or of Joseph Dennie lacked the sparkle and polish that were the marks of Franklin's long apprenticeship. And crudity had replaced his salaciousness.

In the writing of novels, the models were English and the results imitative, like W. H. Brown's *The Power of Sympathy* or Susanna Rowson's *Charlotte Temple*. An era of marked political isolation from Europe was also an era of marked cultural dependence on Europe—and of interdependence. For the Romantic school in Britain, like Chateaubriand in France, drew heavily on New World material. Only in Charles Brockden Brown's radical novels is a new note struck, from which a line of descent can be traced to Poe and Melville. Brown's ideal was Godwin, and it is from Godwin that he draws his high-minded figures, half-villain, half-hero—Welbeck in *Arthur Mervyn* or the ventriloquist Carwin in *Wieland*. "The world is governed," he wrote, "not by the simpleton, but by the man of soaring passions and intellectual energy. By the display of such only can we hope to enchain the attention and ravish the souls of those who study and reflect." Moreover, his stories had a real setting, on the Indian frontier (in *Edgar Huntly*) or in fever-swept Philadelphia (*Arthur Mervyn*). If he liked to strike terror, it was conventional that the novel should do so, and he drew on new formulae. In his pages, the Gothic has a new authenticity: mischievous demons abound; so does abnormal psychology. Keats' comment on him is apt: "Powerful genius—accomplished horror."

For a live tradition in the theater the censorship on plays was a serious discouragement, especially in Boston and Philadelphia, where the ban was tighter than in New York. What were produced on the stage were English classics, often improvingly disguised, like *Improper Education* (*She Stoops to Conquer*) or *Filial Piety* (*Hamlet*), or patriotic plays like Mercy Warren's *The Group* or Royall Tyler's *The Contrast*. Beginning a long run with the younger Hallam's company in 1787, the last of these, in its ridicule of Britain, did not a little to ensure the dominance of republican thinking in New York City. The first professional theatrical manager, William Dunlap, wrote sixty plays, and they led him remorselessly into bankruptcy. He wanted the theater to be the vehicle for the expression of republican virtues. Yet he showed some sophistication, and some waning in nationalist fervor, when he wrote

> From Europe shall enriching commerce flow,
> And many an ill attendant, but from thence
> Shall likewise flow blest Science; Europe's knowledge
> By sharp experience bought, we should appropriate;
> Striving thus to leap from that simplicity,
> With ignorance curst, to that simplicity,
> By knowledge blest; unknown the gulf between.

The dependence on Britain was even clearer among American artists. The Americanism of West and Copley was insubstantial, and Stuart and Trumbull too spent much of their lives in Britain. For these men the Revolution was indeed a civil war; they worked for American independence but their roots remained in Europe. It is striking that, although Trumbull never forgot—or allowed others to forget—that he was a colonel and a staff officer in the revolutionary army, he left America before the war was won, as he did again in the War of 1812: and he did so because America had no one who could teach him anything. Yet as portrait painters and iconographers Peale, Stuart, and Trumbull took full advantage of their journalistic opportunity. To-day's image of the Revolutionary War and of the Founding Fathers is almost entirely their work. In the worship accorded their subjects, their own reputation has grown.

In 1800 the United States of America was at once preindustrial, prenational, and predemocratic. Its leaders, Federalists and Republicans alike, were agrarians, however commercial-minded the High Federalist group might be, and they were gentry, albeit self-made. The political doctrines of the Fathers were Whig, with a strong overtone of the Commonwealth. They advocated the separation of powers, a balanced Constitution, a wide if not yet an open franchise, religious toleration, and a more secular education. None of these ideas was novel, or exclusive to America. It was not until after the close of the War of 1812 that a strong sense of distinct nationality emerged; but by 1800 the national characteristics were implicit. There was a Franklinesque emphasis on hard work, on utility, ingenuousness, and human shrewdness. There was more concern with plain living than with high thinking. Indeed, there was a certain Rousseauist distaste for the intellectual and an emphasis on the solving of practical problems that has always marched a trifle self-consciously, but assertively, in North America alongside the concern with education. A virgin nature reinforced this by demanding the pioneer virtues. The emphasis was on a republican simplicity; Jefferson spoke of "the unquestionable republicanism of the American mind"; and when Sarah Franklin Bache found her children being treated as "young ladies of rank" she replied with hereditary verve that "There is no rank in this country but rank mutton." Not all agreed with her, for Mrs. John Jay in New York and Mrs. William Bingham in Philadelphia sought to queen it over the drab republican courts that came into being in both cities. The Puritan inheritance on the one hand and the disappearance of a landed aristocracy on the other, however, made for an aridity and unimaginativeness that as yet hindered the flowering both of New England and the South; yet alongside this was a religious revivalism that spoke of the failure of the Puritan code to curb the whole man or woman.

The frontier conditions and habits of provincialism, of rough manners and rougher sports—from bear-baiting to gouging—and of personal isolation, contrasted with (and often caused) gregariousness at festivals and fairs, at barn-raisings, and harvests. The availability of land produced extensive land-grabbing and land speculation at all social levels, and at the same time reinforced a Whig belief that property, so easily acquired, was basic to political stability; extensive property ownership made American democracy possible in the eighteenth century and was to be its major source of conservatism in the twentieth. Being abundant, land was abused; just as no society in history has been so rich in resources as the United States, so none was for a century so prodigal with its wealth. Conservation came late in American development, and the American economy has long been geared not only to abundance but also to waste. This is one European impression of America that has stayed constant through the years.

If a legal-minded, it was not yet a particularly law-abiding society; neither was it a very cultured or a very tolerant one. Toleration triumphed in the end, as always, not from conviction but from necessity; it emerged from the clash of mutual intolerances of race or creed. The cultural leadership came, as always, from the aristocracy of talents, who had in this environment an easier road to the top, but who, being an elite, were never quite so fully respected as in Europe. And acceptance of the law—the last art to be learned, and the most sophisticated—came, as always, slowly, as men and women learned the most difficult art of all, how to live at peace with one another inside a common political system.

It was not in 1800 a society that believed in equality—any more than it had in 1763. But it was clearly a society that believed that no one was entitled to expect deference from others. Nor did it in 1800, any more than in 1763, believe in notions of social justice or social reform. It was a society of free individuals, standing on their own feet, on native ground. Those who were not free had at least the opportunity to become so. It did believe in liberty, and liberty in 1800 it enjoyed as it had not forty years before. It was discovering that with independence there came problems not so different from those faced by the Old World: of capitalist *versus* agrarian, of debtor *versus* creditor, of town *versus* rural frontier, and of party controversy. If not yet a democracy, it had destroyed all vestiges of foreign control and of an imposed upper-class system. It had raised the fabrick of freedom —the phrase is Freneau's—and buttressed it by a faith in constitutional processes that was, far more than slavery, its peculiar institution. Strong in numbers and rich in territory, it was even stronger and richer in optimism; sheltered by the ocean, it looked to the west, and to the future, in brash and racy confidence.

Bibliographical Essay

The most recent and the fullest description of the situation
of the colonies in, and just before, 1763 is in Lawrence H. Gipson's monumental *The British Empire before the American
Revolution,* of which nine volumes have thus far been published
(since 1936). This is a work of loving scholarship, detailed and
descriptive and handsomely presented. Not the least of its merits
is that it sees the American colonies in a world setting. It has
not yet reached the years of controversy and is thus almost
nostalgically imperialist in tone. Professor Gipson was a pupil of
Charles Andrews, and the standpoint from which he surveys the
colonial scene is that of London rather than Boston. It was so
also in Andrews' own dry but brilliantly detailed institutional
studies, *The Colonial Period of American History* (4 vols.,
1934–38) and *The Colonial Background of the American Revolution* (1931). Andrews, however, was a colonial rather than a
revolutionary historian. His chapter on the Board of Trade in
the fourth volume of his *Colonial Period,* while still of value,
needs modification in the light of the work of L. A. Harper,
The English Navigation Laws (1939) and O. M. Dickerson,
The Navigation Acts and the American Revolution (1951).
Another student of Andrews, Leonard Labaree, has written a
definitive study of colonial governors in his *Royal Government
in America* (1930) and supplemented it by editing *Royal Instructions to British Colonial Governors 1670–1776* (2 vols.,
1935), a quite indispensable work. For the development of a

colonial aristocracy see his *Conservatism in Early American History* (1948).

The states and regions have all had their historians; among the best of these studies are T. P. Abernethy, *From Frontier to Plantation in Tennessee* (1932); H. T. Lefler, *North Carolina History told by Contemporaries* (1934); Dixon R. Fox, *Yankees and Yorkers* (1940) and A. C. Flick, ed., *History of the State of New York* (10 vols., 1933–37); J. T. Adams, *Revolutionary New England 1691–1776* (1923) and his provocative *New England in the Republic 1776–1850* (1926); and Clement Eaton, *A History of the Old South* (1949). *The American States During and After the Revolution* (1924), by Allan Nevins, is an invaluable handbook.

There are several excellent colonial-history textbooks, particularly C. P. Nettels, *The Roots of American Civilization* (1938), despite its strong feelings, and Max Savelle, *The Foundations of American Civilization* (1942). The early chapters of Harvey Wish, *Society and Thought in Early America* (1950), while stronger on literature and the frontier than on economic conditions, give a vivid picture of social life.

But all of these works now need supplementing from two other sources. The first is the monographic or biographical literature that has become available on each section and topic during the last twenty years. For New England, S. E. Morison's *The Puritan Pronaos* (1935), reissued 1936 as *The Intellectual Life of Colonial New England,* is written with a felicity that makes him perhaps the most readable of all living American historians; Perry Miller's *The New England Mind: From Colony to Province* (1953) is equally distinguished. On the Middle Colonies, W. F. Dunaway, *A History of Pennsylvania* (1935) and *The Scotch-Irish of Colonial Pennsylvania* (1944)—the latter with an excellent bibliography of monographs—are very useful. So is Carl Bridenbaugh, *Rebels and Gentlemen: Philadelphia in the Age of Franklin* (1942) and C. A. Barker, *Background of the Revolution in Maryland* (1940).

In the last twenty years there has been a vast amount of writing on and from the South. The South is now coming to be the most productive field for—and nursery of—historians. It has been fortunate in the last decade in the work and stimulus of the Institute of Early American History and Culture at Williamsburg, which has helped to publish the *William and Mary Quarterly,* whose third series (since 1944) has made it the leading journal in the field and whose own publications are of outstanding quality. Among works of value published by the Institute or on its behalf are A. E. Smith, *Colonists in Bondage, white servitude and convict labor in America 1607-1776* (1947), Louis Morton, *Robert Carter of Nomini Hall* (1945), C. S. Sydnor, *Gentlemen Freeholders: Political Practices in Washington's Virginia* (1952), and F. B. Tolles, *Meeting House and Counting House, The Quaker Merchants of Colonial Philadelphia* (1948).

Particularly valuable in this field are the social studies produced by Carl Bridenbaugh, one-time director of the Institute, especially his *Cities in Revolt: Urban Life in America 1743-1776* (1955), *The Colonial Craftsman* (1955), and *Myths and Realities: Societies of the Colonial South* (1952). Not everyone agrees with some of Professor Bridenbaugh's judgments—his view of some southern aristocrats as "sports" in the biological sense was not everywhere received with pious acceptance south of the Mason-Dixon line—but he has done great service to the objective study of colonial social and political history.

The Institute has also helped with the second main source of material, the provision of new editions of contemporary history or chronicle. Among these are Robert Beverley's *The History and Present State of Virginia,* originally published in London 1705, republished, ed. L. B. Wright (1947); *The Journals and Letters of Philip Vickers Fithian* (ed. Farish, 1943); and Alexander Hamilton's *Itinerarium 1744* (ed. Bridenbaugh and published in 1948 as *Gentleman's Progress*). The *Secret Diaries* of William Byrd (3 vols.) were published in 1941, 1942, and

1958, the first two by the Dietz Press in Richmond, the third by Oxford University Press. A new edition of William Bradford's *Of Plymouth Plantation* was edited by S. E. Morison in 1952. To these should be added Louis B. Wright's *The First Gentlemen of Virginia* (1940); his lucid if somewhat selective *The Colonial Civilization of North America 1607–1763* (1949), emphasizing the closeness and durability of colonial links with Britain; and the early chapters of his *Culture on the Moving Frontier* (1955), where the thesis is pushed to somewhat extravagant lengths; F. C. Rosenberger's evocative *Virginia Reader* (1948); and two other contemporary sources: *The America of 1750: Peter Kalm's Travels in North America* (2 vols., 1937) and *Burnaby's Travels Through North America* (ed. R. R. Wilson, 1904). Of the various collections of sources, the two best are S. E. Morison's *Sources and Documents Illustrating the American Revolution* (1929) and Merrill Jensen's detailed and carefully annotated collection *American Colonial Documents to 1776*, published as Vol. IX of the *English Historical Documents* series (1955).

Among other monographs of value on particular topics are W. T. Baxter, *The House of Hancock: Business in Boston 1724–1775* (1945) and J. B. Hedges, *The Browns of Providence Plantations* (1952); W. W. Sweet, *Religion in Colonial America* (1942) and *Religion in the Development of American Culture 1765–1840* (1952); and the varied papers collected in R. B. Morris (ed.), *The Era of the American Revolution* (1939). On Negro slavery Ulrich Phillips, *American Negro Slavery* (1918) presents a highly readable, elegant but unreconstructed view; the best modern work, refreshingly critical, is J. H. Franklin, *From Slavery to Freedom* (1947). No student should omit a basic work that throws a new light on slavery and on many other things: Lewis H. Gray, *History of Agriculture in the Southern United States to 1860* (2 vols., 1933). And no reader can fail to find delightful Dixon Wecter, *The Saga of American Society: A record of social aspirations 1607–1937* (1937).

CHAPTER 2

The now-classic analysis of British politics in the early part of the reign of George III is that of L. B. Namier, *The Structure of Politics at the Accession of George III,* published in two volumes in 1929 and republished in 1958 as a single but substantially unchanged work. Namier broke completely with the view of George III as a tyrant, dominated by his mother and Bute, seeking to overthrow the constitution. After meticulous research on the five hundred volumes of the Newcastle papers in the British Museum, he produced an analysis of Parliament in terms of "interest," "connection," and patronage that was at once revolutionary and seminal. In 1930 he published *England in the Age of the American Revolution.* In 1951 he revived a cooperative enterprise, *The History of Parliament,* that had had an abortive start in the thirties, a vast biographical project on which a number of editors and researchers in the University of London and elsewhere are now engaged. And as by-product of this, new volumes are appearing from a group of historians who are Namier's disciples and who have been working on the large quantities of manuscript material in the British Museum or that have come into the hands of local record offices in recent years, mainly as an indirect result of the social changes since 1945. *England in the Age of the American Revolution* is now a project, not a single volume, and two studies under that general title have already appeared: John Brooke, Professor Namier's chief lieutenant, published *The Chatham Administration, 1766–68* in 1956, and Ian Christie followed with *The End of North's Ministry 1780–82* in 1958. In 1957 Dr. Owen published *The Rise of the Pelhams.* Other volumes are scheduled to fill the gap from 1754 to 1784. Those published so far confirm the master's findings; all are admirably written; all are "historians' history," detailed and heavily biographical, but in general eschewing analysis. There have been, from A. J. P. Taylor and Professor Butterfield, some criticisms of the Namier thesis, especially in the latter's

article in *Encounter* (April 1957), elaborated in his *George III
and the Historians* (1957) and in his article in *History* (Febru-
ary 1958). The work of the late Richard Pares in his studies of
colonial conflicts and business enterprise, *War and Trade in the
West Indies 1739–1763* (London, 1936), *Colonial Blockade and
Neutral Rights 1739–1763* (London, 1938), *Yankees and Creoles*
(London, 1956), and still more in his Ford Lectures *King
George III and the Politicians* (Oxford, 1953), broadly confirms,
however, the theses of the Namier school. So do G. H. Guttridge,
English Whiggism and the American Revolution (1942) and Sir
Keith Feiling, *The Second Tory Party 1714–1832* (London,
1938).

It is impossible to overemphasize the contribution of these
historians. They have brought to their writing a minutely detailed
knowledge of men in the setting of their own times; they base
every statement on precise and accumulated evidence; they convey a welcome sense of the vivacity and immediacy of the age
of George III.

Two criticisms, however, of this new and now dominant
historiography can be advanced. The first is that although it
was the study of the imperial problem during the American
Revolution that first suggested the enterprise to Professor
Namier, the colonies play a very small part in his analysis. He
was himself preoccupied with the "political nation" at home in
the years 1760–65, and even his followers in emphasizing connection and place (and perhaps minimizing "issues"?) make
small and only incidental reference to the American problem.
This is true even where, as in Christie's volume, the "political
nation" can only be studied against the background of events in
South Carolina and Virginia. Thus far America has been
treated as only one section in Professor Namier's *England in
the Age of the American Revolution,* a section that he con-
fessed needed much more attention than he could then give it.
See also his essay on Charles Garth in the *English Historical
Review,* 1939. In this sense the Namier volumes are not studies

of the American Revolution, and their general title is misleading.

The second criticism that might be offered is this: It is impossible to study the reign of George III without concluding that there was a sense in which Burke was speaking not for posterity but for his own times. While no doubt not a party in the modern sense, the Rockinghams did have leaders who held fairly regular meetings; they had in the end a policy for the colonies in 1765–66; they had a following so much larger than the other groups as to constitute almost a different animal; after some uncertainty in 1766 they acted as an opposition to the Chatham–Grafton ministry; they attached importance to consistency; and they survived long enough to take office in the final bankruptcy of the policy they had always opposed. It is true that they did not go into opposition in 1766 to resist the allegedly unconstitutional power of the King or to secure more liberal treatment for the American colonists. But the American war, as Brooke admits (p. 61), gave the Rockinghams "a policy and a cause, which brought them posthumous renown in the nineteenth century." By 1782, if not before, there were issues in politics that were strong enough to break factions if not yet to make parties: American independence, the Yorkshire movement, radicalism, the character of Indian government, electoral reform itself. Sir Lewis, by confining himself to the political nation, omitted important elements wielding no little influence. Where America was concerned, the omissions are crucially important: dissenters, manufacturers, and shopkeepers were highly sympathetic to the colonies. There is little in his pages of the politics of the City of London or of Westminster or of the Yorkshire freeholders; there is even less of that half-world of politics in which Wilkes and Lord George Gordon moved, of the emotions in politics that led Fox and the Duchess of Devonshire to sport the buff and blue of Fairfax County. Men are not moved by self-interest alone, least of all when they face the fact of revolution. It is one of the most curious of current historical paradoxes that the emphasis on "connection" and empiricism and the distaste for principle that mark British study of the eighteenth century should be paralleled by the emphasis in the United States that their own Revolution was the result of principles, issues, and an emerging sense of national unity.

The work of the Namier school has revised all previous estimates of British politicians and of the King. George III is now seen as an obstinate man but not a tyrant, "the first among the borough-mongering, electioneering gentlemen of England," an industrious, constitutional, but unpliant King. He can perhaps be seen most vividly in his *Letters to Lord Bute 1756–66* (ed. Romney Sedgwick, 1939) and in his *Correspondence 1760–1783* (ed. Sir John Fortescue, 6 vols., 1927–28); to which should be added Sir Lewis Namier's *Additions and Corrections* (1937).

The researches of the Namier school have been particularly hard on Burke, seen by them as little more than a great and gifted rhetorician, whose defense of the Old Whigs and use of the word *party* are held responsible for much of the false doctrine of George III's tyranny. There is a further paradox here; the hero of American conservatism is seen by some British writers as the bête noire of British politics. A recent biography by Sir Philip Magnus emphasizes that Burke was suspect in his own time for other reasons, and that he never held major office. Older studies of him all need revision, however, in the light of the *Burke Correspondence,* of which Professor T. W. Copeland is general editor, a major enterprise of the University of Chicago. A complete edition of all Burke's writings is planned under a team of editors, based largely on the Wentworth-Woodhouse manuscripts now housed in the Sheffield Public Library; until this is done and a rounded picture of the great Irishman emerges, some of the more extreme views of him that are now current should be treated with reserve. One of the best recent studies of Burke, and the first scholarly assessment of his role in American politics, is by Professor Ross Hoffman of Fordham University, *Edmund Burke, New York Agent* (1956), which makes clear how circumscribed that role was. He did not see his post as

Colonial Agent for New York as that of an ambassador to the British government, as Franklin did. He put his task as M.P. well to the forefront. Associated with the most conservative colony, he remained blind to the growing radicalism in America and convinced until the war actually began that conciliation was possible. This view—of the moderation of American demands—harmonized with the aristocratic views of the Rockingham group. As in France, so in America, Burke's sources were tainted and partisan; in both he sought to prevent revolution.

There are many studies of Chatham, from Basil Williams' big biography (2 vols., 1913) to the late Sir Charles Grant Robertson's useful brief sketch *Chatham and the British Empire* (1946), Miss Hotblack's *Chatham's Colonial Policy* (1917), and the third volume of O. A. Sherrard's biography, *Lord Chatham and America* (London, 1958). Mr. Sherrard insists that the confusion of domestic politics in the 1760s was not primarily Chatham's responsibility, and adduces much evidence, even if he does not fully convince.

The best study of Charles Townshend is Sir Lewis Namier's all-too-short Leslie Stephen Lecture (1959). Shelburne needs a modern biography; E. G. P. Fitzmaurice's life (3 vols.) was written in 1875–76, and his American, especially his western, interests are inadequately treated. The best and most sympathetic study of his imperial policy is in Vincent Harlow, *The Founding of the Second British Empire 1763–93,* Vol. I (1952), especially chapters v–viii. There are two excellent articles on his earlier western policy by R. A. Humphreys, "Lord Shelburne and British Colonial Policy 1766–68" (*E.H.R.,* Vol. L [1935]) and "Lord Shelburne and a Projected Recall of Colonial Governors in 1767" (*American Historical Review,* Vol. XXXVII [1931–32]).

Recent research, in its emphasis on Parliament, has minimized the work of the "back-room" boys. Andrews' *Colonial Background* and *The Colonial Period,* Vol. IV, are valuable. They need supplementing by D. M. Clark, "American Board of Customs 1767–85" in *A.H.R.,* XLV (1940); L. A. Harper, *The*

English Navigation Laws (1939); O. M. Dickerson, *The Naviga-
tion Acts and the American Revolution* (1951); Ella Lonn,
Colonial Agents of the Southern Colonies (1945); Carl Ub-
belohde, *The Vice-Admiralty Courts and the American Revolution* (1960); M. M. Spector, *The American Department of the
British Government 1768–1782* (1940); and A. H. Basye, "The
Secretary of State for the Colonies," *A.H.R.,* XXVIII (1922).
Equally valuable is Chester Martin's *Empire and Commonwealth* (1929) for his assessment of William Knox—see also
Knox's "Controversy Reviewed (1769)," *Old South Leaflet* No.
210, and *Historical Manuscripts Commission,* various, Volume
VI (1909). There is a workmanlike biography of Thomas Pownall by J. A. Schutz (1951). Valuable raw material is in Edward
Channing and A. C. Coolidge, eds., *Barrington-Bernard Correspondence* (1912); Carl Van Doren, ed., *Letters of Franklin
and Richard Jackson* (1947); V. W. Crane, ed., *Franklin's Letters to the Press 1758–1775* (1950); and J. W. Barnewell, ed.,
"Correspondence of Charles Garth," in *The South Carolina Historical Magazine* (1925, 1927–1930). C. F. Mullett, "English Imperial Thinking 1764–1783" in *Political Science Quarterly,* Vol.
45 (1930), pp. 548–79, is stimulating. So is Klaus Knorr, *British
Colonial Theories 1570–1850* (1944). If the work of Andrews has
demonstrated that the Empire, while being run from London,
was run as a great mercantile association, and Dickerson has
gone farther and said that the Navigation Acts were the basis
of colonial prosperity, Lawrence Harper and Louis M. Hacker
have reminded us of the existence of exploiters in this as in all
periods.

Thus far historical research has tended to neglect the geographic context in which the Revolution took place, especially
the strategy in the West. Valuable pioneer work was done by
Clarence Alvord and by C. F. Carter in *Great Britain and the
Illinois Country 1763–74* (1910), and *The Critical Period 1763–
1765, The New Regime 1765–67,* and *Trade and Politics 1767–69*
(ed. Alvord and Carter, Illinois State Historical Library *Collec-*

tions, British Series, Vols. X, XI, and XVI [1915-21]). Alvord's *The Mississippi Valley in British Politics* was published in 1916. See also the work of T. P. Abernethy, *Western Lands and the American Revolution* (1937), of J. R. Alden, *John Stuart and the Southern Colonial Frontier* (1944), and his biography of Gage, and of S. M. Pargellis in his military studies, *Lord Loudoun in North America* (1933) and *Military Affairs in North America 1748-65,* a useful collection of documents from the Cumberland Papers in Windsor Castle (1936). There is still a wealth of new material to be explored in the Johnson *Papers,* the Gage *Correspondence,* the Draper MSS collection in the State Historical Society of Wisconsin, and in the *Cahokia Records* (1907) and *Kaskaskia Records* (1909), ed. C. W. Alvord. Most of the studies of the half-legendary frontier figures are patchy. Older works, like W. L. Stone's life of Brant (1838) and R. G. Thwaites' *Boone* (1902), are, however, still useful. A. Pound's *Johnson of the Mohawks* (1930) is very valuable; J. W. Lydekker's *The Faithful Mohawks* (1938) less so. It is wise to look at this problem from the standpoint of the Canadian as well as the American frontier, in books like J. B. Brebner, *The North Atlantic Triangle* (1945); A. L. Burt, *The United States, Great Britain and British North America from the Revolution to the Establishment of Peace after the War of 1812* (1940); G. S. Graham, *British Policy and Canada 1774-1791* (1930), and Arthur Lower's salty *Canadians in the Making* (1959).

CHAPTERS 3 AND 4

The causes of the American Revolution are among the most controversial of all historical topics. Thus far, there have been in fact three distinct stages in the historiography of the Revolution. Stage one, when the myths were shaped and the heroes given their togas, ran from "Parson" Mason Weems' hagiography of Washington to George Bancroft's great saga (*History of the United States,* in ten volumes, 1834-1874). This was history as an act of patriotic faith professed by a Jacksonian Democrat. Freedom grew naturally on American soil, it held; only the best Britons migrated; the navigation system was wicked, and George III was especially so. This has become the epic and stylized view of American history, reflecting the assumptions of the nineteenth century—assumptions not confined to the United States—that history is, as it was to Acton, the story of liberty. This view, still highly readable in the pages of Parkman, still enshrined where the Constitution is concerned in Fiske's *The Critical Period* (1888), was the work of historians who were amateurs—and perhaps superb historical writers for being so.

The second stage saw the development of a group of professional historians who were highly critical of this emphasis. Product of German thoroughness in research, interested in the development of institutions, and sticking closely to the newly opened sources of the Public Record Office in London, their most striking exponents formed a school of imperial historians —Osgood, Beer, and particularly C. M. Andrews. If not British-oriented they were certainly London-oriented, for not the least of Andrews' services was his work as an explorer of British archives and as a cataloguer; they were non-nationalist and politically unengaged; they emphasized that the Revolution was a political and constitutional movement, a conflict of sovereignties rather than a class war; and in the work of Labaree and Gipson their influence can still be discerned.

On Andrews' death in 1943, a third stage begins. It sees the writing of many monographs; there is much ultraprofessional inquiry and controversy, as in the debate on Beard; and there is now much greater precision in research. It is early to say that any one "pattern" is emerging. Indeed most contemporary writers would, one hopes, deny that they write to any predetermined pattern at all. Yet the emphasis today is striking and is both domestic and nationalist. Deriving in part from Beard and in part from the earlier monographs of J. F. Jameson, *The American Revolution considered as a social movement*

(1926), reprinted as a paperback (1950); Carl Becker, *The History of Political Parties in the Province of New York 1760–1776* (1909), and A. M. Schlesinger, Sr., *The Colonial Merchants and the American Revolution* (1918), there has been a growing interest in social and intellectual history—best seen recently perhaps in the work of Bridenbaugh. It was natural that in the 1930s this economic interest should be stressed. Perhaps the sharpest statement of the view that the Revolution was caused by economic grievances, especially among manufacturers, came not from Beard but from Louis Hacker, in "The First American Revolution," *Columbia University Quarterly*, XXVII, No. 3 (September 1935). Even then, however, it did not pass unchallenged (as by Andrews). This interest has naturally been, with one or two exceptions, strongly domestic; since the death of Clarence Alvord there appear to be few contemporary American historians other than Gipson working in the "imperial" field as Andrews knew it. To stress the clashes in the colonies, especially the conflict of class interests, was naturally to minimize the clash with Britain. Becker was responsible for this view of the Revolution as a struggle over who should rule at home; and Jameson stressed the extent of the reforms that were won at home, even if, in the opinion of F. B. Tolles, he exaggerated their significance ("The American Revolution as a social movement, a re-evaluation," in *A.H.R.* Vol. LX [October 1954]).

This preoccupation with the domestic achievement of the Revolution has gradually widened. The social conflicts are now given less emphasis, and the building of a new and distinct society is seen as the major feature. This is best evidenced in the writings of Daniel Boorstin, *The Genius of American Politics* (1953), *The Americans: the colonial experience* (1958), and *The Lost World of Thomas Jefferson* (1948); Edmund Morgan, *The Stamp Act Crisis* (1953) and *The Birth of the Republic 1763–1789* (1956); Max Savelle, *Seeds of Liberty* (1948); and Clinton Rossiter, *Seed-Time of the Republic* (1953) and a number of essays on conservatism. It is impossible here not to be struck by the note of national pride in the Revolution, its achievements, and its significance. Boorstin's emphasis is on its "given-ness" in an American environment. The liberalism that grew in the New World was no mere transplanted flower, growing in richer soil; much of the force that fed and nourished it was, he argues, indigenous. Even if the Virginians were, in Boorstin's word, "transplanters," the squirearchy that grew up was Virginian, not English. Utility, pragmatism, and compromise were the American hallmarks; in Boorstin's writing they acquire almost a theological sanction. Morgan stresses that the Stamp Act was really burdensome, and that the objection to it was a matter of principle; this, far more than the emergence of leaders or organizations, was its essence. Democracy was widespread in Massachusetts and probably elsewhere, says Robert E. Brown, Jr., in his *Middle-Class Democracy and the Revolution in Massachusetts 1691–1780* (1955); there was no sharp class conflict, at least in Massachusetts, he argues; independence was in the main inevitable sooner or later, since British imperial policy threatened an existing middle-class democratic society, and was both a democratic and a national "good." Much of the controversy aroused by recent revisionism is in fact a controversy over terminology; and a twentieth-century preoccupation with words as weapons—not least words like *class, democracy,* and *conservatism*—has crept into the argument. But at least the pendulum is swinging back; and if the pride is now in the extent of American democracy, in its "middle-class" character and in the smoothness of the changes between 1776 and 1787—pride, one feels, less in having a revolution than in having it on conservative lines—the emphasis on distinction, on uniqueness, on concern for "principles," on being a peculiar if not a chosen people, is closer to Bancroft than to Andrews. Bancroft, says Professor Morgan, at least addressed himself to the central question, "How did the United States come into being as a nation dedicated to principles of liberty and equality?"

This is not to say that there is a "school" of historians holding these views, or that the emphasis is universal. Clarence Alvord did not share it; Michael Kraus and L. B. Wright emphasize that the Atlantic was a cultural bridge even when it was a political barrier; Dickerson has revealed how far colonial interests were themselves involved in the maintenance of the imperial tie. But nationalism is certainly seen today as one of the central issues in the Revolution. Works that should be studied here are Merle Curti, *The Growth of American Thought* (1943); Michael Kraus, *International Aspects of American Culture on the Eve of the Revolution* (1928), and Hans Kohn, *Nationalism* (1959), chapter 1.

Revolutions are of course synonymous with controversy—both at the time and in academic retrospect. The controversies no doubt will continue. Of recent studies the following are essential as guides to the main topics. On the Stamp Act, Edmund and Helen Morgan's *The Stamp Act Crisis* (1953) is excellent. It should be read in the light of Franklin's role in London (Carl Van Doren, *Benjamin Franklin* [1938] is still the best biography, but it will need revising as the projected forty-volume *Franklin Papers* emerge from Yale) and of the work of the London merchants (for Barlow Trecothick see an unpublished thesis in Sheffield University library by B. R. Smith, "The Committee of the Whole House to consider the American Papers, January–February 1766," based on the Wentworth-Woodhouse papers). Bernhard Knollenberg, *Origin of the American Revolution 1759–1766* (1960) is a work of distinction, based on profound research, that sees these seven years as the decisive ones. It tends to become, inevitably perhaps, a catalog of British errors. On the constitutional question, see Julian Boyd's *Anglo-American Union* (1941) for the Galloway Plan of 1774, and R. G. Adams, *Political Ideals of the American Revolution* (1922), reissued as a paperback (1958). All American writers on this topic, however, are apt to exaggerate both the ease of nation-building and the possibility of finding a solution in federalism. The last was quite impossible in the light of the necessary British emphasis in the eighteenth century on the King-in-Parliament.

The years 1767 to 1773 are best seen as they appeared to the participants, in the correspondence of John Adams, Washington, Jefferson, Richard Henry Lee, and others, and in Burnett's edition of the *Letters of Members of the Continental Congress* (8 vols., 1921–38). To these should be added the editions of "lesser" —but often more puzzled—men: *The Writings of John Dickinson* (ed. P. L. Ford, 1895), *Some Political Writings of James Otis* (ed. C. F. Mullett, 1929), *The Letter Book of John Watts* (N.-Y. Hist. Society *Collections,* Vol. LXI, 1928) and *The Bowdoin and Temple Papers* (Mass. Hist. Society *Collections,* 6th series, Vol. IX, 1897; 7th series, Vol. VI, 1907).

The role of the merchants is well portrayed in Schlesinger. On the importance of propaganda and the press, see J. C. Miller, *Sam Adams: Pioneer in Propaganda* (1936, republished 1960); Philip Davidson, *Propaganda and the American Revolution* (1941); A. M. Schlesinger, Sr., *Prelude to Independence, the newspaper war on Britain* (1958), and Bruce Ingham Granger, *Political Satire in the American Revolution 1763–1783* (1960).

For the two years of crisis, 1774–1776, there is a rich mass of material in print. Peter Force, ed., *American Archives* . . . 4th series (6 vols., 1837–46) and 5th series (3 vols., 1848–53) cover these two years in detail. See also Hezekiah Niles, ed., *Principles and Acts of the Revolution in America* (1822). Two good secondary sources are: C. P. Nettels, *George Washington and American Independence* (1951) and Carl Becker, *The Declaration of Independence, a study of the history of political ideas* (1922, reprinted 1942). The first of these is stimulating and original; the second is a delight to read.

If any one single volume had to serve as an introduction to this period, there are three to choose from: L. H. Gipson, *The Coming of the Revolution 1763–1775* (1954), for its emphasis on the Anglo-American relationship; John C. Miller, *The Origins of the American Revolution* (1943, reissued 1960), for its happy and balanced blending of the main political causes into a single readable whole; or E. B. Greene, *The Revolutionary Generation 1763-1790* (1943), for its excellent summarizing of economic and social history.

CHAPTER 5

The voluminous material on the War of Independence can be grouped into seven main sections.

First, there are the "political" sources: the war as seen by the man in Congress—or in London. In addition to Burnett's *Letters of Members of the Continental Congress* (8 vols., 1921–38) there are the thirty-four volumes of the *Journals of the Continental Congress 1774–1789* (1904–37). There are useful recent biographies of a number of "secondary" figures—Elias Boudinot (by George Boyd, 1952), Thomas Mifflin (by Kenneth Rossman, 1952), Joseph Reed (by J. F. Roche, 1954), Robert Morris (by Clarence L. Ver Steeg, 1954), James Bayard (*The Federalism of James A. Bayard* by Morton Borden, 1955), and John Jay (by Frank Monaghan, 1935).

On the British side, there is rich material in some of the reports of the Historical Manuscripts Commission, especially the Carlisle Papers (*H.M.C.*, 15th Report, Appendix IX, Part IV), the Dartmouth Papers (14th Report, Appendices, Part X, Vol. II), the Hastings Papers (*H.M.C.*, Vol. III), and the Stopford Sackville Papers (*H.M.C.*, Vols. I and II). *The Journal of Nicholas Cresswell, 1774–1777* (1924) presents a picture that does not flatter the colonists. There is still no adequate study of British politics in the years 1776–1783, as affected by the Revolution: C. R. Ritcheson's *British Politics and the American Revolution* (1954) will serve as introduction.

Second, there are the views of the commanders in the field. Washington's *Writings* (39 vols., ed. J. C. Fitzpatrick) were published 1933–1944; his role in the war has been chronicled, almost day by day, in Douglas Southall Freeman's *Life* (7 vols.; Vols. 3, 4, and 5 are indispensable for the war). *The Lee Papers*

(4 vols.) were published by the New-York Historical Society (*Collections,* Vols. IV–VII [1872–75]). Von Steuben was studied by Albert Faust (published by the Steuben Society of America, 1927) but more carefully by J. M. Palmer in his *General Von Steuben* (1937). Louis Gottschalk has performed another pious but admirable scholarly duty in writing his life of Lafayette, the second and third volumes of which cover the American years (1937, 1942). The George Rogers Clark papers were edited by James A. James, *Illinois Historical Collections,* Vols. VIII and XIX (1912, 1926), and he also wrote the best life of the colorful frontiersman (1928). For Hamilton's journal (ed. Barnhart), see *Henry Hamilton and George Rogers Clark in the American Revolution* (1951).

The Clements Library at the University of Michigan has become a storehouse of British manuscript material; it houses the papers of Lord George Germain, Shelburne, Gage, and Clinton, as well as those of Nathanael Greene and of a number of Hessian officers. For Gage, see J. R. Alden's life and C. E. Carter, *The Correspondence of General Thomas Gage 1763–1775* (2 vols., 1931–33). In 1954 William B. Willcox edited Clinton's *Narrative* of his campaigns, entitled *The American Rebellion.* In 1957 Bernard A. Uhlendorf published the Baurmeister letters in his *Revolution in America.* But one of the most vivid accounts of a Hessian's view of the war is printed in the first part of J. G. Seume's "Memoirs of a Hessian Conscript" (*William and Mary Quarterly,* 3rd series, V, No. 4), which reveals that many were the innocent victims of the Landgrave of Kassel, "the great trader in human beings of that day and age," and that they included students, lacemakers, magistrates, cashiered majors, and "a monk from Würzburg." "One had to live somewhere, somehow. . . . Then too the idea of crossing the ocean was rather inviting for a young fellow." Many years earlier, in 1827, the worthy Baroness von Riedesel published her *Letters and Memoirs relating to the American War of Independence,* permanently damning Gentleman Johnny Burgoyne. Howe's own *Narrative* and Burgoyne's *A State of the Expedition from Canada,* neither marked by modesty, appeared promptly—in 1780. Banastre Tarleton's *History of the Campaign of 1780–81* was seven years later in appearing, but what it lacked in timeliness it made up for in even more striking conceit.

For the Navy, S. E. Morison's life of John Paul Jones (1959) is stirring reading. On the British side, the best sources are the Navy Records Society publications, especially *The Barham Papers,* ed. J. K. Laughton (2 vols., 1906, 1912), *The Barrington Papers,* ed. C. K. Bonner (2 vols., 1937, 1941), and *The Private Papers of John, Earl Sandwich 1771–1782,* ed. G. R. Barnes and J. H. Owen (4 vols., 1932–38).

Third, and perhaps the most valuable of all, are the accounts of participants who were not in command, officers or other ranks, who could use candor and curses. On the British side: E. H. Tatum, Jr. (ed.), *The American Journal of Ambrose Serle, Secretary to Lord Howe, 1776–1778* (1940); *The Diary of Frederick Mackenzie* (2 vols., 1930); Lieutenant Thomas Anburey's *Travels through the Interior Parts of America* (2 vols., 1789); *Letters from America, 1773–1780* (being the letters of Sir James Murray) ed. E. Robson (1951); E. A. Benians (ed.), *A Journal by Thomas Hughes 1778–1789* (1947); G. D. Scull (ed.), *Memoirs and Letters of William Glanville Evelyn, 4th. Foot, 1774–76* (1879) and, not least, R. Lamb, *Memoir of his own life* (1811). There are richer and more racy revelations on the American side in Ethan Allen's delightful and utterly unreliable *Narrative* of his captivity (1846); Alexander Graydon's *Memoirs of his own time* (1846); Joseph Martin's *A Narrative of some of the Adventures, Dangers and Sufferings of a Revolutionary Soldier* (1830); Albigence Waldo's famous "Valley Forge 1771–1778 Diary," *Penn. Mag. Hist.,* XXI (1897), and James Collins, *Autobiography of a Revolutionary Soldier* (1889).

Fourth, there is the material on the Loyalists. The only single study is by C. H. Van Tyne, *The Loyalists in the American Revolution* (1902), which now needs a thorough revision. The most valuable raw material is in Lorenzo Sabine, *Biographical Sketches of the Loyalists* (2 vols., 1864) and H. Egerton (ed.), *The Royal Commission on the Losses and Services of the American Loyalists 1783–1785* (1915). They have been studied state by state; among the best of these studies are A. C. Flick, *Loyalism in New York* (1901), I. S. Harrell, *Loyalism in Virginia* (1926), Robert O. De Mond, *Loyalists in North Carolina during the Revolution* (1940), and William Siebert, *The Loyalists of Pennsylvania* (1920) and *Loyalists in East Florida* (1929). The story of the Tory Rangers has been told with vigor by Howard Swiggett in *War Out of Niagara* (1933). The story of *The Queen's Rangers* was told by Sir J. G. Simcoe, himself a leader of them, as early as 1787. Jonathan Boucher left an autobiography, published as *Reminiscences of an American Loyalist 1738–89* in 1925. So did Samuel Curwen in *Journal and Letters* (1842), a moving story. A. G. Bradley's *United Empire Loyalists* (1932) is the story of the great trek to Canada. Loyalist dilemmas have been described with much sympathy in a number of short sketches: Lewis Einstein, *Divided Loyalties* (1933); Catherine Fennelly, "Governor William Franklin of New Jersey," *William and Mary Quarterly,* VI (1949); E. H. Baldwin, "Joseph Galloway," *Penn. Mag. Hist.,* XXVI (1902), and J. E. Alden, "John Mein, Scourge of Patriots," *Col. Soc. Mass. Publications* XXXIV (1942). Leonard Labaree's essay "Nature of American Loyalism," *Proceedings of the American Antiquarian Society,* new series, LIV (1944) is also worth noting.

Fifth, there are a number of specialized studies on the strategy, tactics, and campaigns of the war. Edward Curtis, *The Organization of the British Army in the American Revolution* (1920) and L. C. Hatch, *The Administration of the American Revolutionary Army* (1904) are standard works. See chapter 3 of Walter Dorn's *Competition for Empire 1740–63* (1940) for comments on the quality of the recruits. Troyer S. Anderson's *Command of the Howe Brothers During the American Revolution* is an able analysis. A. H. Bill's two studies are vivid—*Campaign of Prince-*

ton 1776–1777 (1948) and *Valley Forge: The Making of an Army* (1952). For Arnold, see Carl Van Doren, *Secret History of the American Revolution* (1941), based on the manuscripts in the Clements Library at Ann Arbor, and proving conclusively that Arnold embraced treason entirely for the financial rewards it would bring; James T. Flexner, *The Traitor and the Spy* (1953) and W. M. Wallace, *Traitorous Hero* (1954). For Yorktown, see Chastellux, *Voyages* (1786); Richard Oswald's *Memorandum,* ed. W. Stitt Robinson (1953); William B. Willcox, "The British Road to Yorktown: a study in divided command," *A.H.R.,* LII (October 1946), and R. G. Adams, "A View of Cornwallis' Surrender at Yorktown," *A.H.R.,* XXXVII (October 1931). Many of the pamphlets produced in the course of the Yorktown "debate" were collected and printed by B. F. Stevens in *The Campaign in Virginia 1781* (1888). For tactics see J. F. C. Fuller, *British Light Infantry in the Eighteenth Century;* Sir John Fortescue, *History of the British Army,* Vols. II–VI (1899–1910); Eric Robson, *The American Revolution* (1955) and "The Raising of a Regiment in the War of American Independence," *Journal of the Society for Army Historical Research,* XXVII; and J. Wright, "The Rifle in the American Revolution," *A.H.R.,* XXIX, and "Corps of Light Infantry," *A.H.R.,* XXXI. There are admirable maps in the *West Point Atlas of American Wars* (ed. Esposito, 1959).

Sixth, there is the diplomacy of the war. The classic study is by Samuel Flagg Bemis, *The Diplomacy of the American Revolution* (1935), supplemented by Carl Van Doren's *Franklin* (1938) and by chapters II and III in R. W. Van Alstyne's *The Rising American Empire* (1960). For Silas Deane, see T. P. Abernethy in *A.H.R.,* XXXIX, p. 477; for Arthur Lee, see B. J. Hendrick in *The Lees of Virginia* (1935). For the Carlisle Commission, see Alan S. Brown, "The British Peace Offer of 1778," *Papers of the Michigan Academy of Science, Arts and Letters,* XL (1955), and William B. Willcox, "British Strategy in 1778," *Journal of Modern History,* XIX, No. 2. For the French alliance, see E. S. Corwin, *French Policy and the American Alliance of 1778* (1916) and for a revised and controversial view of it, Alexander DeConde, *Entangling Alliance* (1958); but Henri Doniol, *Histoire de la participation de la France a l'établissement des Etats-Unis d'Amérique* (5 vols., 1886–92) is still a basic work. So is Francis Wharton, *The Diplomatic Correspondence of the American Revolution* (6 vols., 1889).

Seventh, there are several secondary histories, among the best of which are Willard M. Wallace, *Appeal to Arms, a Military History of the Revolution* (1951); Christopher Ward's detailed *War of the Revolution,* ed. J. R. Alden (2 vols., 1952); John C. Miller, *Triumph of Freedom 1775–1783* (1948); John R. Alden, *The American Revolution* (1954); and Lynn Montross' racy but sound *Rag, Tag and Bobtail* (1952). The best studies of the early stages of the war are by Allen French, *The Day of Lexington and Concord* (1925), *General Gage's Informers* (1932), and *The First Year of the American Revolution* (1934). In *Rebels and Redcoats* (1957) George F. Scheer and Hugh F. Rankin produced an "eyewitness" account by collecting the letters, diaries, and reports of participants and linking them by an editorial narrative. In *The Spirit of Seventy-Six* (2 vols., 1958), H. S. Commager and R. B. Morris performed a similar task on a bigger scale. Both works are admirable and vivid. Among the "secondary" but classic studies are Sir John Fortescue, *History of the British Army* (13 vols., 1899–1930) and Admiral A. T. Mahan, *The Influence of Seapower upon History 1660–1783* (1890), reissued in paperback (1957).

CHAPTERS 6 AND 7

For social conditions in the new states, the most useful guide is Allan Nevins, *The American States During and After the Revolution* (1924). Over the last thirty years many historians have been concerned with the question posed by Carl Becker— who should rule at home?—as the writings of Beard and Becker,

Jameson and A. M. Schlesinger, Sr., testify. To Jameson particularly, the Revolution was a social upheaval that had rich democratic consequences, in the abolition of slavery in many states, the disappearance of primogeniture and entail, the disestablishment of the Anglican Church, the break-up of Loyalist estates, and the reduction of property qualifications for the suffrage. "The stream of revolution" tended to produce, he believed, "a levelling democracy."

While few historians today would deny that important social reforms were won by the Revolution, Jameson's *simpliste* view has been seriously qualified by recent research. What was true of one state did not hold of another. In Maryland, the Revolution was closer to a contest between two groups of aristocrats than to a social clash (P. Crowl, *Maryland during and after the Revolution* [1943]). What was true of eastern Massachusetts was not true of western, nor were the political divisions of the years before 1776 the same as those that followed (L. H. Newcomer, *The Embattled Farmers* [1955]; Oscar and Mary Handlin, "Radicals and Conservatives in Massachusetts after Independence," *New England Quarterly*, XVII (1944), p. 343). Robert E. Brown, Jr., argues that all adult males in Massachusetts had the vote already; both Charles Sydnor and Dumas Malone argue that there was a considerable participation in Virginian elections. In his article "The American Revolution considered as a Social Movement: a Re-evaluation," *A.H.R.*, LX (1954), pp. 1–12, F. B. Tolles draws together these researches to offer a major revision of the Jameson thesis.

A similar re-examination of the political arguments of Charles Beard has also been under way. Beard's thesis has been challenged by Robert E. Brown, Jr., *Charles Beard and the Constitution* (1955) and by Forrest McDonald, *We The People* (1958). Brown argues that Massachusetts certainly—and probably America in general—was in large measure already a free society, with wide manhood suffrage and much freedom of opinion. McDonald establishes that the Founders formed no consolidated economic

group, and that no consistent relationship can be established between their votes on key questions and what have hitherto been
seen as their economic interests. The delegates from the small
states had a host of reasons for seeking a Constitution. The
states that hesitated longest—Virginia and New York—or opposed ratification of the Constitution—North Carolina and
Rhode Island—thought they could stand alone and came in only
because of local issues or because of the devoted efforts of the
Federalist persuaders. No single economic theory will explain the
very mixed motives of men.

Despite this brilliant and sustained piece of research, there are
historians who, for the most part, continue to follow Beard's
thesis and see the forces at work after 1787 as being also in
large measure counterdemocratic. Merrill Jensen does so, in his
The Articles of Confederation (1940) and *The New Nation*
(1950). Jackson T. Main reviewed McDonald's thesis critically
and searchingly in *The William and Mary Quarterly,* 3rd series,
Vol. XVII, No. 1 (January 1960). And Elisha P. Douglass, in
his *Rebels and Democrats, the struggle for equal political rights
and majority rule during the American Revolution* (1955), while
demonstrating that only in Pennsylvania and North Carolina did
real democratic advance take place, believes that what emerged
were "republics of equipoise." "The Whig governments were
prevented from becoming narrow, selfish oligarchies only by the
gradual recognition of equality demanded by the democrats."

This debate, while it is seen at present as central by many
American historians, bears rather on what might be called the
"significance" than the "causes" or the "results" of the Revolution; many historians, in dealing with it, seem more concerned
with the "meaning" of the Revolution for today than for the
eighteenth century. Moreover, if much of the recent research is
satisfyingly factual, it is more successful in disproving Beard's
evidence than in constructing a convincing alternative that can
hold for all the thirteen new states. Even for Massachusetts, the
conclusions drawn by Robert J. Taylor in *Western Massachusetts*

in the Revolution (1954) are not easy to reconcile with those of Brown. The decisive social forces inside one state were not likely to be identical with those in another; while both Boston and the Regulator country were angry in the 1760s, it was for quite different reasons, and the anger was visited on different enemies. It seems most improbable that the democratic thesis Brown advances for Massachusetts will hold for any state south of Pennsylvania. And almost all American historians minimize the fact that very many of the social changes were the automatic result of the defeat of Britain in the war, rather than the success of a Whig or a counter-revolutionary argument. Victory itself weakened the case for any more violent change; forfeited royalist estates as much as cheap land helped democratic advance; success in war ended the planter's indebtedness to Britain; the war, and the critical period from 1781 (or in fact 1776) to 1787, permitted (indeed encouraged) great freedom of debate in all the states.

One issue that was common to almost all of them was frontier *versus* Tidewater. The best recent study of the form it took in South Carolina—the Regulator movement—is in Richard J. Hooker's edition of Charles Woodmason's journal, *The Carolina Backcountry on the Eve of the Revolution* (1953). William K. Boyd edited in 1927 *Some Eighteenth-Century Tracts Concerning North Carolina,* in which he printed some of the writings of Herman Husband and George Sims. Much Regulator material is printed in W. L. Saunders, ed., *The Colonial Records of North Carolina,* Vols. VII–X (10 vols., 1886–1890), and Merrill Jensen has extracted some vivid illustrative material from it in his *English Historical Documents,* Vol. IX, Part VI (1955). The best sources for a study of the similar democratic ferment in Massachusetts are the returns of the towns on constitutional questions between 1776 and 1780—material well used by Douglass. *The Journal of the Convention 1779–1786* was published in 1832. A good recent study is Oscar and Mary F. Handlin, *Commonwealth; a study of the role of government in the American economy: Massachusetts 1774–1861* (1947), stressing the urge for change that came—in Massachusetts as in the Carolinas—from the back country.

Pennsylvania, most democratic state of all, has been extensively studied and described. There is much contemporary material in the *Pennsylvania Magazine of History and Biography,* in Graydon's *Memoirs,* and in the various biographies of Franklin, Reed, Mifflin, and Charles Thomson. There are some useful secondary studies of Pennsylvania politics: Charles H. Lincoln, *The Revolutionary Movement in Pennsylvania 1760–76* (1901); J. Paul Selsam, *The Pennsylvania Constitution of 1776* (1936); R. L. Brunhouse, *The Counter-Revolution in Pennsylvania 1776–1790* (1942); and H. M. Tinkcom, *The Republicans and Federalists in Pennsylvania 1790–1801* (1950). It was, says Tinkcom, the pressure of national issues that gave cohesion to the political groupings in Pennsylvania. Not until the alignment over the Jay Treaty were there two distinguishable political "parties." An excellent article by Brooke Hindle, "The March of the Paxton Boys," in *The William and Mary Quarterly,* 3rd series, Vol. III, No. 4 (1946), should also be noted.

Of the life lived in the new West, there are some admirable and entertaining studies. If there was less certainty that the *Men of the Western Waters* would adhere to the new nation in 1781–94 than Dale Van Every suggests in his study of them (1956), it is a vivid story he tells. There are excellent political analyses of the frontier areas by Abernethy and by Billington; and by Brebner, too, in his *Explorers of North America* (1933). There is an authoritative study of the struggles of the "civilized tribes" by R. S. Cotterill, *The Southern Indians* (1954). K. P. Bailey, *The Ohio Company of Virginia* (1939) and G. E. Lewis, *The Indiana Company* (1941) are good on the land companies, despite the confusion of their claims. And A. T. Volwiler, *George Croghan and the Westward Movement* (1926) and Nicholas B. Wainwright, *George Croghan, Wilderness Diplomat* (1959), the latter drawing on recently discovered papers in Philadelphia, reveal the somewhat shady motives of those who were ultimately to appear, in Turner's later telling, as heroes and pioneers. Turner's first three chapters in *The Frontier in American History* are still excellent reading.

The major source book for the Federal Convention is Max Farrand's edition in four volumes of the *Records* (1937). C. C. Tansill, *Documents Illustrative of the Formation of the Union of the American States* (1927) is a useful single-volume edition. The work of the Convention is very well described by A. T. Prescott in his *Drafting the Federal Constitution* (1941), in which he regroups Madison's notes to bring out clearly the discussion on each topic that arose. Consult also, of course, *The Federalist* (many editions). Jonathan Elliot, *The Debates in the Several State Conventions on the Adoption of the Federal Constitution* (5 vols., 1836–45), reprinted in 1941 in facsimile from the second edition, needs a new edition but is of great value.

Of the secondary works, Beard's famous study has received frontal assaults in recent years. Merrill Jensen's two books, mentioned above, are important and valuable developments of Beard. A. M. Simons, *Social Forces in American History* (1911) went even farther than Beard and offers a Marxist interpretation. Fred Rodell, *Fifty-Five Men* (1936) reflects a Beardian point of view. But Charles Warren, *The Making of the Constitution* (1929) shows that fear of disunion began long before 1787 and that the idea of union—if not of nation—was at least as old as the idea of independence. There are some good but older studies of the state conventions: Hugh Blair Grigsby, *The History of the Virginia Federal Convention of 1788* (2 vols., 1890–91) worth supplementing by the account in A. J. Beveridge, *The Life of John Marshall* (Vol. I, 1916); S. B. Harding, *The Contest over the Ratification of the Federal Constitution in the State of Massachusetts* (1896); J. B. McMaster and F. D. Stone, *Pennsylvania and the Federal Constitution 1787–88* (1888), and C. E. Miner, *Ratification of the Federal Constitution by the State of New York* (1921). To understand the alignment of the sections.

however, the indispensable source is O. G. Libby, *The Geographical Distribution of the Vote of the Thirteen States on the Federal Constitution 1787–1788* (1894). Irving Brant, *Madison* (6 vols., 1940–61) is now the definitive biography. There are some useful articles in the *William and Mary Quarterly* (3rd series), especially Cecelia Kenyon, "Men of Little Faith: the Anti-Federalists on the Nature of Representative Government" (Vol. XII, No. 3), J. R. Pole, "Suffrage and Representation in Massachusetts: a statistical note" (Vol. XIV, No. 4), with a comment by R. P. McCormick (Vol. XV, No. 3), and R. B. Morris, "The Confederation Period and the American Historian" (Vol. XIII, No. 2).

Chapters 8 and 9

John C. Fitzpatrick has edited Washington's very laconic *Diaries* (4 vols., 1925) and his *Writings* (39 vols., 1931–44). There are one-volume selections from these compiled by Saxe Commins, *Basic Writings of George Washington* (1948) and by Saul Padover, *The Washington Papers* (1954).

There are many biographies of Washington, beginning with those of Parson Weems and John Marshall. There is an entertaining study of the first biographer of all in Harold Kellock, *Parson Weems of the Cherry-Tree* (1928). The monumental biography is by Douglas Southall Freeman, in six volumes (1948–54), completed for the controversial last six years of Washington's life by two of Freeman's associates, John A. Carroll and Mary Wells Ashworth, as *George Washington, First in Peace* (1957). The whole work is strong on Washington as soldier and as Virginian, but less successful in evoking the man behind the myth. Rupert Hughes' three volumes (1926–30), also incomplete, are the all-too-readable work of a "debunker." There is a competent but somewhat uncritical study by N. W. Stephenson and W. H. Dunn (2 vols., 1940). There are single-volume assessments by Marcus Cunliffe (1959) and Esmond Wright (1957).

There are admirable biographies of Jefferson. One of the best insights is provided by the old but often republished study by his great grand-daughter, Sarah N. Randolph, *The Domestic Life of Thomas Jefferson* (1871, republished 1939); and Henry S. Randall's *Life* (3 vols., 1863), without pretending to objectivity, is rich in material. Gilbert Chinard's *Thomas Jefferson; The Apostle of Americanism* (1929) is good despite its title, but it evades any real assessment of Jefferson *qua* politician. Dumas Malone's *Jefferson and the Rights of Man* (1951) is the second volume of what promises to be a definitive biography. *The Jefferson Papers* (ed. Julian P. Boyd, since 1950) are indispensable.

Hamilton, less appealing and less tortuous than his rival, has not been as fortunate in his biographers. Nathan Schachner's study (1946), till recently the best, is now surpassed by J. C. Miller, *Alexander Hamilton, Portrait in Paradox* (1959), shrewd, frank, and highly readable. Broadus Mitchell is engaged on what promises to be a major biography. The article by Rexford Tugwell and Joseph Dorfman, "Alexander Hamilton, Nation Maker," *Columbia University Quarterly,* XXIX (December 1937), is perceptive. So is William Brock's essay, "The Ideas and Influence of Alexander Hamilton," in *British Essays in American History* (ed. Allen and Hill, 1957). There is a valuable anthology of Hamilton's writings, with a lucid commentary by the editor, in R. B. Morris, ed., *Alexander Hamilton and the Founding of the Nation* (1957). Columbia University is now preparing a new and complete edition of the papers of Alexander Hamilton.

Two valuable studies of Revolutionary finance are (*passim*) in Joseph Dorfman, *The Economic Mind in American Civilization* (1946) and Bray Hammond, *Banks and Politics in America from the Revolution to the Civil War* (1957). Racy Anti-Federalist views can be found in William Maclay's *Journal,* ed. E. S. Maclay (1890), in William Manning's *The Key of Libberty,* ed. S. E. Morison, *William and Mary Quarterly,* 3rd series, Vol. XIII, No. 2 (1956), and in Charles Warren, *Jacobin and Junto: or Early American Politics as viewed in the diary of Dr. Na-*

thaniel Ames, 1758–1822 (1931). Pungency on the other side occurs in George Gibbs, ed., *Memoirs of the Administration of Washington and Adams from the Papers of Oliver Wolcott* (2 vols., 1946). If quite false as history, this is a valuable source for Federalist letters, which are not easy to find.

The most interesting development of recent years, however, has been the close study of the origins of the American party system. It has been well analyzed in E. P. Link, *Democratic Republican Societies 1790–1800* (1942), in Noble E. Cunningham, Jr., *The Jeffersonian Republicans, The Formation of Party Organization 1789–1801* (1957), and, brilliantly, by the late Joseph Charles, in his *Origins of the American Party System* (1956)— originally a series of articles in the *William and Mary Quarterly* (Vol. XII, Nos. 2–4, 1955). See also Oscar and Mary Handlin, "Radicals and Conservatives in Massachusetts after Independence," *New England Quarterly,* XVII (September 1944), where the authors deny "the mossy conception of two-party continuity." L. D. White, *The Federalists* (1948) is a good administrative study, bringing out the embarrassing importance of every tiny decision that Washington had to make.

In foreign policy, the standard works are *Jay's Treaty* (1923) and *Pinckney's Treaty* (1926), both by the doyen of American diplomatic historians, S. F. Bemis. In *Entangling Alliance* (1958) Alexander DeConde is critical and stimulating in his view of Washington as President, but the book is ill organized. Of the involved politics in the West, the best studies are by A. P. Whitaker, *The Spanish-American Frontier* (1927) and *The Mississippi Question 1795–1803* (1934), and by T. P. Abernethy, *From Frontier to Plantation in Tennessee* (1932), supplemented now by W. H. Masterton's admirable portrait of the elusive *William Blount* (1954). Of the first President's "role" in history, as seen in retrospect, there are many studies, most of them ephemeral. Three of permanent value are Dixon Wecter, *The Hero in America* (1941); William A. Bryan, *George Washington in American Literature 1775–1865* (1952); and C. P. Nettels,

"The Washington Theme in American History," *Proceedings of the Massachusetts Historical Society,* LXVIII (1952).

The revival of interest in American conservatism has brought an all-too-long-delayed interest to the presidency of John Adams. He has always been esteemed, but rather as thinker and crank than as man of affairs. The new interest has been in his presidency and in his later, rather than his earlier, ideas. C. N. Walsh's study, *The Political Science of John Adams* (1915), is far from satisfactory as analysis and deals largely with Adams as revolutionary. C. D. Bowen, in her popular and "fictional" but accurate *John Adams and the American Revolution* (1949), does not come beyond 1776. Chinard's biography *Honest John Adams* (1933) is, like all he writes, good on the man and his European experiences, but less incisive on domestic party issues.

A new edition of Adams' *Correspondence* is being prepared by L. H. Butterfield. Until it is completed, C. F. Adams' edition of his *Works* (10 vols., 1850–56), containing the all-too-revealing diary and the unreliable but fascinating autobiography, needs supplementing by *The Warren-Adams Letters* (1917, 1925) and the delightful *Adams–Jefferson Correspondence,* well edited by Lester J. Cappon (1959). A short selection of the Adams' writings—father and son—can be found in Adrienne Koch and W. J. Peden (ed.), *The Selected Writings of John and John Quincy Adams* (1946). The best picture of the man as thinker, however, is to be found in Zoltan Haraszti, *John Adams and the Prophets of Progress* (1952), which draws on Adams' marginal comments in some hundred of the three thousand books he had in his library. The comments are not only revealing but explosive. At times they are incoherent: "Thou Louse, Flea, Tick, Wasp or whatever vermin thou art!" It is well to have John Adams brought to life.

Recent secondary studies have drawn on this material to supply a corrective to the views made fashionable in the New Deal period by Claude Bowers. Jefferson and Adams are now seen to be much closer to each other than before; Jefferson is seen as politician to be less important than Madison in the years 1794–1797 (a view confirmed by Brant and by Noble Cunningham); and Adams is seen as a far more balanced exponent of Federalism than Hamilton. This was detected some years ago by Merle Curti in his *The Growth of American Thought* (1943), by A. B. Darling, *Our Rising Empire 1763–1803* (1940), and by Richard Hofstadter, *The American Political Tradition and the Men Who Made It* (1949). The extent of the split among Federalists on the Alien and Sedition acts is well analyzed by J. C. Miller, *Crisis in Freedom, The Alien and Sedition Acts* (1951) and by James M. Smith in *Freedom's Fetters* (1956), the first of what promises to be an excellent two-volume analysis. For the presidency as a whole there are two admirable recent assessments: Manning J. Dauer, *The Adams Federalists* (1953), while preoccupied with the attempt to study the period by using modern techniques—and also some modern jargon—offers an original and searching analysis of the Federalist party; and Stephen Kurtz, *The Presidency of John Adams* (1957) provides a very welcome and lucid account of the four-year "reign." One of the best studies of the whole period is John C. Miller's *The Federalist Era* (1960).

Many of the lesser figures of these years—some of whom, like Elbridge Gerry or Matthew Lyon, are as colorful as J. A.—still cry out for biographers. S. E. Morison's essays on Gerry and the irascible brothers Ames, collected as Part II of his essays *By Land and By Sea* (1954), offer a model of how history can be written.

CHAPTER 10

American society in 1800 is ruthlessly portrayed by Henry Adams in the opening chapters of his *History of the United States* (9 vols., 1889–91) and engagingly portrayed by Van Wyck Brooks in the opening chapters of *The World of Washington Irving* (1944). John H. Powell's *Bring Out Your Dead* (1950) is a vividly drawn study of Philadelphia in the grip of yellow fever.

Descriptions of this, and other less natural Gothic features, make dramatic the novels of Charles Brockden Brown. There is an excellent biography of Brown by Harry R. Warfel (1949), and a good study of *The Connecticut Wits* by Leon Howard was published in 1942. The best short guide to the literature and the literary figures of 1790–1800 is in Robert Spiller, Willard Thorp, *et al., The Literary History of the United States* (3 vols., 1948). If Parrington's *Main Currents in American Thought* (3 vols., 1927–30) is now thought old-fashioned as well as incomplete, it is at its best on political writing—in which (alone, some might feel) the late eighteenth century was strong. It was, Parrington said. a *saeculum politicum.* The Age of Reason and of deism is still the most secular-minded of all the Christian centuries, not excluding our own.

The ideas of the Jeffersonian circle are brilliantly studied in Daniel Boorstin, *The Lost World of Thomas Jefferson* (1948). Along with this should be read Jefferson's own writings, especially his *Notes on Virginia,* the *Letters* of Benjamin Rush, edited by L. H. Butterfield (2 vols., 1951), and Mark Van Doren (ed.), *The Travels of William Bartram* (1928). N. B. Fagan, *William Bartram, Interpreter of the American Landscape* (1933), emphasizes Bartram's literary influence rather than his scientific attainments; Francis Harper's edition of Bartram's *Travels* (1958) is a superb corrective. See also Brooke Hindle, *The Pursuit of Science in Revolutionary America 1735–1789* (1956). All biographical studies of Tom Paine are, of course, far more sympathetic than were the final contemporary verdicts on him. There is a good recent study of him by A. O. Aldridge, *Man of Reason* (1959). Moncure Conway's study of 1892 (2 vols.) is still urbane reading; Philip S. Foner's edition of *The Complete Writings of Thomas Paine* (2 vols., 1945) is prefaced by an admirable biographical essay; H. H. Clark has made a useful selection from Paine's writings for his study of Paine (*American Writers Series,* 1944). Dixon Wecter comes as close to accuracy as perhaps can be done in "Hero in Reverse," *Virginia*

Quarterly Review, XVIII (1942). See also Herbert M. Morais, *Deism in Eighteenth-century America* (1934). In *Ethan Allen* (1939), John Pell tells a vivid story to match a picturesque and colorful career. Unlike its successors, this founding family of the Green Mountain state was neither laconic, taciturn, nor "canny"; Vermont has been living down their memory ever since.

For art see C. C. Sellers, *Charles Willson Peale* (2 vols., 1947); Virgil Barker, *American Painting* (1951); James T. Flexner, *America's Old Masters; First Artists of the New World* (1939), and Oliver Larkın, *Art and Life in America* (1949).

Like Washington and Franklin, America itself was seen by Europe through a glass darkly. The marvels of nature as described by Bartram greatly impressed Coleridge—as J. L. Lowes demonstrates in *The Road to Xanadu* (1930); the New World helped to produce the imagery of "The Ancient Mariner." America became not fact but stereotype and myth—and, indeed, mirage. The European view of America—as reflected not only by Lafayette and Crèvecoeur but by Brissot and Mably, Raynal and Chastellux—was brilliantly described in 1957 by Durand Echeverria in *Mirage in the West.* To the émigrés, cast on American shores by the French Revolution, this it turned out to be. But Stephen Girard and Dupont de Nemours found its gold substantial and not illusory. A similar, if less exciting study, is by W. Stark, *America: Ideal and reality: The United States of 1776 in contemporary European philosophy* (1947). Then, as now, there were both admirers and critics—in Europe as at home. In his *The Age of the Democratic Revolution,* Vol. 1 (1959), R. R. Palmer argues that the New World was portent and promise of the changes that were to come in Europe. Not all will agree that he proves his case in his first volume. But this debate, like that aroused by Becker and by Beard, did not begin in 1913. It began in 1763, and continues still.

Index

Adams, Abigail, 149
Adams, Henry, 240
Adams, John, 15, 66, 79, 82, 83, 87, 88, 91, 95, 99, 145, 152, 156, 168, 188, 215, 244
  biographers of, 219
  character of, 219–21
  foreign policy, 222–24, 226–28
  and Hamilton, 229–34
  as President, 217–36
Adams, John Quincy, 227, 244
Adams, Samuel, 60, 66, 68, 83, 96, 97, 104, 156, 174
Adet, Pierre, 212, 222
Administration of Justice Act, 68
Admiralty, British, 30, 119–20
Alabama, 162
Albany Plan, 20, 42, 44
Alien Act, 225
Allegiance and Treason Resolves, 95
Allen, Ethan, 91, 159, 246
Allen, James, 94, 146
Alsop, George, 9
American Prohibitory Act, 99
Ames, Fisher, 189, 224, 241
Amherst, Jeffrey (Baron Amherst), 5, 49, 109, 124
Anburey, Lieutenant Thomas, 121, 122
Andrews, John, 86

Annapolis, 165
Anti-Federalists, 174, 200, 204, 209, 233
Aristocracy, colonial, 8
Army, American, 90, 92, 98, 128–34
  British colonial, 41–42, 45, 47, 58, 61, 66, 69, 73–74
  British, during War, 108–28
Arnold, Benedict, 91, 117, 129
Articles of Confederation, 156
Asbury, Bishop Francis, 246
Associated Loyalists, Board of, 100
Atkin, Edmund, 44
Attucks, Crispus, 61

Bache, Sarah Franklin, 253
Bancroft, George, 37
Bank of the United States, 199, 200
Barbary pirates, 159
Bard, Samuel, 249
Barré, Isaac, 27, 69
Barrington, William Wildman (2nd Viscount), 58, 75, 106, 120
Barton, Benjamin Smith, 248
Bartram, John, 193
Bartram, William, 249
Bass, Robert, 107
Beard, Charles A., 177–80, 183
Becker, Carl, 93, 178
Beckford, William, 24

Beckley, John, 172
Bedford, John Russell (4th Duke), 72, 77
Belcher, Governor Jonathan, 29
Benezet, Anthony, 149
Berkeley, Bishop George, 237
Bernard, Governor Francis, 31, 54, 76
Bill of Rights, 173, 175
Bingham, Mrs. William, 253
Bishop of London, 30
Blackstone, Sir William, 33, 48
Bland, Richard, 81
Blount, William, 163
Bollan, William, 47, 48, 101
Boone, Daniel, 10, 65, 163
Boonesboro, 163
Boorstin, Daniel, 181
Boston, 60, 61, 68
Boston Massacre, 61
Boston Tea Party, 67
Botetourt, Norborne Berkeley, Lord, 84
Bouquet, Colonel Henry, 44, 47, 58
Bowles, William Augustus, 162
Bowman, Allen, 129
Bownas, Samuel, 18
Braddock, General Edward, 41, 44, 112
Brandywine, 112
Brant, Joseph (Thayendanegea), 128, 161
Braxton, Carter, 93
Bridenbaugh, Carl, 20
Brooke, John, 24, 25
Brown, Charles Brockden, 150, 248
Brown, John, 67
Brown, Robert E., Jr., 179–80, 187
Brown University, 13
Brown, W. H., 250
Buckland, William, 9
Bull, Governor William, 82
Bunker Hill, 92, 110, 112
Burke, Edmund, 23, 37, 70, 77
Burr, Aaron, 197, 217, 229, 234

Bute, John Stuart (3rd Earl), 24
Burgoyne, General John, 107, 112, 113, 116–18, 120
Butler, Pierce, 167
Butterfield, L. H., 219
Byrd, William, 11, 17, 19

Cabinet, Presidential, 198–99, 221
Cabot, George, 224
Callender, James T., 196
Camden, Charles Pratt (1st Earl), 101
Canada, 1, 76, 117
Carleton, General Guy, 49, 76, 107, 112, 117, 118
Carlisle Commission, 124, 136
Carpenter's Hall (Philadelphia), 87
Carr, Dabney, 82
Cavendish, General Lord Frederick, 110
Charles, Joseph, 195
Charleston, 60, 68
Chastellux, François Jean, Marquis de, 18, 238
Chatham, 1st Earl of; see Pitt
Cherokee Indians, 44, 65, 102
Cherry Valley, 128
Chisholm v. Georgia, 217
Choiseul, Etienne François, Duc de, 135
Circular Letter of 1768, 60
Clark, George Rogers, 130, 156, 205
Clinton, George, 175, 207
Clinton, Sir Henry, 107, 116, 124
Cobbett, William, 193, 196
Cod fisheries, 1, 3
Coercive Acts, 68, 136
Colden, Cadwallader, 194
Colonies, American, in 1763, 1, 2
    administration of, 28–32
    defense, 40
    differences among, 12–21
    frontier, 9–10
    government, 4–6
    population, 11

society, 6–9
Concord Bridge, 92
Congress, First Continental, 87–89
  Second Continental, 91–92
Connecticut, 4, 44
Constitution of 1787, adoption of,
    173–76
  assessed, 176–87
  compromises, 169–91
  Convention, 165–68
  document, 171–73
Constitutions, state, 145–46
Continental Association, 87
Conway, Henry Seymour, 27
Cooke, George, 56
Cornstalk, 66, 163
Copley, J. S., 8, 193
Cornwallis, General Charles, 107,
    116, 117, 126
Correspondence, committees of, 67,
    68, 82, 86
Corwin, E. S., 179
Cowpens, Battle of, 132, 134
Crawford, William, 102
Creek Indians, 161–62, 198
Cresap, Thomas, 47
Crèvecoeur, Hector St. John de, 239
Croghan, George, 58, 76
Crosskey, W. W., 181
Crown Point, 91
Cruger, Henry, 27
Cumberland Gap, 162
Currency Act, 39
Customs, Commissioner of, 30, 36,
    38, 39, 60, 80
Customs Commissioners, Board of,
    60
Cutler, Reverend Manasseh, 161

Dartmouth, William Legge (2nd
    Earl), 29, 65, 78, 84, 102, 106
Dartmouth College, 13
De Chartres, Fort, 3
Declaration of Causes of Taking Up
    Arms, 92

Declaration of Independence, 95–
    96, 100
Declaration of Rights and Griev-
    ances (1765), 55
Declaration of Rights and Griev-
    ances, 89
Declaratory Act, 57, 71
DeConde, Alexander, 195
Deism, 246
De Lancey, James, 93
Delaware, 4
Delaware Indians, 66
Democracy, in colonies, 7–8, 10–11
  in state constitutions, 145–46
Democratic Republicans; see Anti-
    Federalists
Dennie, Joseph, 250
Detroit, 3
Devonshire, William Cavendish
    (4th Duke), 23
Dickerson, O. M., 38
Dickinson, John, 55, 62, 80, 88, 91,
    93, 94, 97, 167, 186
Dinwiddie, Governor Robert, 5, 41,
    48
Douglas, David, 8
Duane, James, 88
Duane, William, 197
Duer, William, 153
Dulany, Daniel, 80, 94
Dunlap, William, 248, 251
Dunmore, John Murray (4th Earl),
    66, 91, 94, 102, 145
Dunmore's War, 163
Dupont de Nemours, 203
Dwight, Timothy, 150, 238, 246
Dyer, Eliphalet, 47

East India Company, 67
Eden, William, 136
Egremont, Sir Charles Wyndham
    (2nd Earl), 45, 46, 49
Electoral college, 171
Eliot, Jared, 193
Ellis, Henry, 45

Episcopal Church, during Revolution, 83
Estaing, Vice-Admiral Count d', 135
Evans, Oliver, 151

Fairfax, Thomas (6th Lord), 7, 146
Fallen Timbers, Battle of, 208
Faneuil, Benjamin, 68
Farewell Address (Washington), 211–12
Farrand, Max, 166
Fauchet, Claude, 212, 222
Federalism, 170, 174, 199–210
Federalism, "High," 223–34
Federalist Papers, 175
Feke, Robert, 193
Fenno, John W., 201, 206
Ferguson, Patrick, 123
Fiske, John, 157, 177
Fitch, John, 151, 190, 249
Florida, 1, 4, 42, 139
Forbes, General John, 49
Fort Stanwix, Treaty of, 65, 102
France, losses in 1763, 1
    role in American Revolution, 124, 136–39
Franklin, Benjamin, 1, 10, 21, 26, 37, 39, 50, 52–54, 56, 58, 64, 65, 71, 72, 81, 82, 84, 96, 138, 142, 173
Franklin, William, 84, 100
Franklin, "state" of, 163
Freeman, Douglas Southall, 195
French and Indian War, 20
French Revolution, 202–8
    Adams' difficulties with, 222–24, 226–29
Freneau, Philip, 150
Fries Rebellion, 226
Frontier, 9–10, 16, 41
    defense of, 43–45, 58, 102
Fuller, Rose, 56

Gadsden, Christopher, 140

Gage, General Thomas, 48, 49, 61, 69, 73–75, 90, 97, 107, 108, 110
Gallatin, Albert, 207
Galloway, Joseph, 88, 89, 97, 104
Gaspee, 66
Gates, General Horatio, 111, 130
Gazette of the United States, 207
General Court of Massachusetts, 60
Genêt, Edmond Charles, 205–8, 212, 222
George III, 22, 70
Georgia, 7, 17, 19, 55
Germain, George Sackville, Lord, 29, 49, 106, 113, 118–22
Germantown, 112
Gerry, Elbridge, 171, 222
Giles, William, 207
Glassford, John, 56
Gloucester, 12
Glover, John, 130
Golden Hill, Battle of (1770), 61
Governors, colonial, 5, 84
Government, colonial, 5–6
Grafton, Augustus Henry Fitzroy (3rd Duke), 59, 63
Graves, Admiral Thomas, 110, 120
Green Mountains, 141
Greene, General Nathanael, 129, 130
Greenhough, Horatio, 196
Greenville, Treaty of, 161
Grenada, 2, 45
Grenville, George, 23, 25, 42, 45, 52, 53, 58, 72
Grenville, William Wyndham, Baron, 222
Grey, Major General Charles, 121
Guadeloupe, 1

Haldimand, General Sir Frederick, 47, 76, 161
Halifax, 3, 39, 60, 68, 108
Halifax, George Montague Dunk (2nd Earl), 28, 29, 41, 43, 49
Hamilton, Dr. Alexander, 16

Hamilton, Alexander, 108, 166, 172, 174–75, 178
  and Adams, 229–34
  as Secretary of the Treasury, 198–210
Hanbury, Capel, 38, 56
Hancock, John, 8, 38, 61, 66, 82, 96, 174, 207
Hard Labour, Treaty of, 102
Harper, L. A., 38
Harper, Robert Goodloe, 224, 227
Harrison and Barnard, 38
Harrower, John, 9
Hartford Wits, 248
Hartley, David, 138
Hartz, Louis, 180, 186
Harvard College, 13, 246
Harvey, General Edward, 120, 125
Hastings, Francis Rawdon, Lord, 108
Hawley, Joseph, 60, 94
Hays' Tavern (Williamsburg), 83
Henderson, Judge Richard, 163
Henry, Patrick, 54, 81, 82, 88, 96, 140, 200
Hessians, 127
Hillsborough, Wills Hill (2nd Viscount), 29, 31, 64, 74, 84
Hood, Admiral Samuel, 61
Hopkins, Esek, 136
Hopkinson, Francis, 250
Hosack, David, 249
Houdon, Jean Antoine, 196
Howe, Sir William (5th Viscount), 96, 107–19, 125
Hudson Bay Territory, 1
Hudson Valley, 15
Hughes, Ensign Thomas, 121, 125
Hughes, John, 53
Hulton, Henry, 76
Hutchinson, Governor Thomas, 54, 61, 67, 68, 82

Illinois, 64, 157
Illinois–Wabash Company, 156

Imperialism, western American, 44
  British, 2, 30–50
Indentured servants, 9
Independence, American, forces for, 96–100
Indian superintendencies, 44, 46, 64–65
Indiana Company, 156
Indians, 43, 44, 64
  in American Revolution, 127–28, 138
  after 1783, 161, 162
Ingersoll, Jared, 52, 53
"Intolerable" Acts (1774), 68
Iron Act (1750), 34
Iroquois Indians, 44, 102, 161
Irving, Washington, 194

Jackson, Richard, 27, 32, 52, 53
Jackson, William, 166
Jameson, J. Franklin, 178
Jay, John, 88, 105, 138, 156, 197, 209
Jay, Mrs. John, 253
Jay Treaty, 209–10
Jefferson, Thomas, 18, 20, 81, 82, 89, 96, 148, 151, 160, 198, 201–4, 206, 210, 220, 245–48
Jenkinson, Charles (1st Earl of Liverpool), 71
Jensen, Merrill, 157
Jenyns, Soame, 48, 101
Johnson, Sir John, 146
Johnson, Sir William, 44, 65, 76
Johnston, Gideon, 19
Johnstone, William, 27
Jones, John Paul, 137
Judiciary Act, 197

Kalm, Peter, 16
Kaskaskia, 3
Kemble, Stephen, 154
Kentucky, 65, 162, 210
Kentucky and Virginia Resolutions, 226
Keppel, Admiral Augustus, 110

King, Rufus, 167, 224, 226
Knox, Henry, 129, 150, 199, 202, 210
Knox, William, 27, 30, 49, 58, 71

Labrador, 3
Lafayette, Marquis de, 131, 204
Lamb, Sergeant Roger, 107
Land claims of states, 156
Lansing, John, 166, 174
League of Armed Neutrality, 137
Lee, General Charles, 111, 132
Lee, Charles (Attorney-General), 221
Lee, Major Henry ("Light-horse Harry"), 130, 204
Lee, Richard Henry, 82, 88, 95, 96
Lee, William, 72, 77
L'Enfant, Major Pierre Charles, 150
Leonard, Daniel, 83, 100
Letters from a Farmer in Pennsylvania, 62
Lewis, Andrew, 66, 163
Lexington, 91
Liberty, 61
"Liberty, Sons of," 28, 67, 78, 80
Liston, Robert, 196, 222, 227, 241
Liston, Henrietta, 196
Livingston, Robert, 142, 147
Lochaber, Treaty of, 102
Logan, Dr. George, 227
Loudoun, John Campbell (4th Earl), 5, 41
Louisiana, 1
Louisburg, 3; see also Pepperrell
Loyalism, 96, 124–26, 143, 146, 153–55
Lyon, Matthew, 207, 226

McCulloch, Henry, 146
McDonald, Forrest, 180
McDougall, Alexander, 82
McGillivray, Alexander, 162
McHenry, James, 167, 210, 221, 228
Mackenzie, Colonel Frederick, 110, 111

Mackintosh, Ebenezer, 80
Maclay, William, 198, 200, 220
Maclean, Colonel Allan, 115
MacPherson, John, 8
Madison, James, 165, 166, 172, 175, 176, 192, 194, 200, 204, 206
Maine, 7
Mansfield, William Murray (1st Earl), 48, 71, 81
Marblehead, 12
Marshall, John, 222, 234, 236
Martin, Governor Josiah, 143
Martin, Luther, 167
Martinique, 1
Maryland, 4, 9, 156
Maseres, Francis, 101
Mason, George, 81
Massachusetts, 5, 6, 19, 54, 60, 66, 68, 88, 89, 155, 156
Massachusetts Government Act (1774), 69
Masterman, George, 57
Mayhew, Jonathan, 83
Mein, John, 99
Mercer, George, 53, 56
Merchants, American, 62, 86, 93, 104
    British, attitude in 1774, 72
    British, and repeal of Stamp Act, 56
    West Indian, 27, 57, 72
Middle Colonies, 14, 35
Militia, 134
Minutemen, 90
Miquelon, 1
Miranda, Francisco de, 215, 226
Mobs, power of, 28, 74, 76, 80, 93, 100
Mobile, 4
"Mohawk River Indians," 28, 68
Mohawk Valley, 15, 161
Molasses Act (1733), 35, 38, 80
Monroe, James, 222
Moore, Governor Sir Henry, 77
Morgan, Daniel, 10, 130, 134
Morgan, Edmund, 54, 164

Morgan, John, 194
Morris, Gouverneur, 93, 167, 204, 222, 225, 241
Morris, Robert, 167
Morse, Jedediah, 150, 243
Mount Vernon Conference, 160, 165
Mulgrave, Constantine, 119
Murray, Governor James, 3
Murray, Captain Sir James, 113
Murray, William Vans, 227, 228

Namier, Sir Lewis, 22
Nantucket, 12
Natchez, 4
National Debt, British, 41, 42
National Gazette, 207
Nationalism, growth of, 82, 150, 212, 240, 242
Naturalization Act, 225
Navigation Acts, 34–38
Navy, American, 136
Negroes; *see* Slavery
"Neptune, Sons of," 80
New Bedford, 12
New England, 7, 8, 12, 159
New England Restraining Act, 90
New Hampshire, 159
New Jersey, 44
New Jersey Plan, 169
New Smyrna, 4
New York, 7, 15, 28, 44, 55, 59, 60, 68, 174
Neutrality Proclamation, 203–4, 206
Newcastle, Thomas Pelham-Holles (1st Duke), 24, 28
Newfoundland, 1, 2, 3
Nonimportation, 55, 62, 87–88
North, Frederick (2nd Earl of Guilford), 24, 28
North Carolina, 10, 85–86, 144, 175
Northwest Ordinances, 160–61
Nova Scotia, 2, 3

Ohio Company of Virginia, 65, 161
Ohio Valley, 65, 66

Olive Branch petition, 91
Oswald, Richard, 26, 138
Otis, James, 19–20, 48, 54, 60, 80, 101

Paine, Thomas, 98, 104, 168, 201, 203, 213, 244
Palmer, R. R., 154
Panton and Leslie, 162
Pares, Richard, 23
Pargellis, Stanley, 41
Paris, Treaty of (1763) 1 (1783), 138–39
Paterson, William, 167
Pawtucket, 66
Paxton Boys, 142
Peale family, 196, 248
Pennsylvania, 4, 15, 16, 19, 85, 141–42, 144, 146
Pensacola, 4
Pepperrell, Sir William, 7, 146
Philadelphia, 16, 60, 68, 85, 142, 190
  Aurora, 207
  "Patriotic Society," 80
  Philosophical Society, 247
Phillipse family, 146
Pickering, Timothy, 210, 221, 228
Pierce, William, views on Founding Fathers, 166–68
Pinckney, C. C., 167, 222
Pinckney, Charles, 167
Pinckney, Thomas, 210, 218
Pitt, William (1st Earl of Chatham), 1, 24–26, 33, 42, 49, 57–59, 70
Point Pleasant, 66, 163
Pontiac, Conspiracy of, 44, 141
Population, 11, 151–52, 190, 245
Postlethwayt, Malachi, 48
Pownall, John, 30, 45
Pownall, Thomas, 27, 30, 47, 49, 70, 101
Presidency, 171, 183
  of Adams, 234–36
  of Washington, 213–16

Press, role in Revolution, 82, 104
  in Washington's presidency, 207, 213
Proclamation Line (October 1763), 45–46, 58

Quartering Act, 59, 68
Quebec, 2, 3, 45, 55, 69, 103
Quebec Act (1774), 69
Quincy, Josiah, 18

Raleigh Tavern (Williamsburg), 62
Ramsay, David, 238
Randolph, Edmund, 174, 199, 202, 210
Randolph, Sir John, 153
Rationalism, 245–48
Rawdon, Lord; see Hastings
Rawdon's Volunteers, 126
Reed, Joseph, 70
Reeve, Judge Tapping, 246
Reeve, William, 57
Regulator movement, 85–86, 142–43, 162
Republicanism, 148
Revenue Act (1764), 39, 51, 57
Revolution, American; see War of Independence
Rhode Island, 4, 7, 19, 66, 135, 159, 175
Riedesel, Baron Friedrich Adolph von, 123
Riedesel, Baroness von, 116
Riots; see Mobs
Rittenhouse, David, 247
Rivington, James, 82, 99, 155
Robertson, James, 65, 162
Rochambeau, Jean Baptiste de Vimeur, Comte de, 135
Rockingham, Charles Watson-Wentworth (2nd Marquis), 24, 26, 56–58, 102
Rodney, Admiral, 139
Rogers, Robert, 123
Rossiter, Clinton, 181

Rowson, Susanna, 150, 250
Royal American Regiment, 127
Royal Greens, 126
Royal Welch Regiment, 107, 123
Rule of 1756, 208
Rush, Benjamin, 149, 247
Rutledge, Edward, 13
Rutledge, John, 85, 170

Sackville, Lord George; see Germain
St. Augustine, 4
St. Leger, Lt. Col. Barry, 161
St. Lorenzo, Treaty of, 210
St. Pierre, 1
Saintes, Battle of the, 139
Salem, 69
Sandwich, John Montagu (4th Earl), 119–20
Saratoga, 112, 118
Sayre, Stephen, 73
Schlesinger, Arthur, Sr., 178
Schuyler, General Philip, 108, 198, 225
Schuyler, R. L., 179
Scott, John Morin, 142
Search, right of, 208
Sears, Isaac, 80
Secretary of State for American Affairs, 31
Sectionalism, in colonial period, 13–20
  after 1783, 140–45, 191–92
  Washington's view of, 214
Sedgwick, Theodore, 224, 225
Sedition Act, 225
Serle, Ambrose, 127
Servitude, indentured, 9
Sevier, John, 65, 162
Shawnee Indians, 103, 163
Shays' Rebellion, 143
Shelburne, William Petty (2nd Earl), 25, 26, 45, 49, 58, 63–64, 138
Sherman, Roger, 167, 168
Shippen, William, 194

Shirley, Governor William, 38, 48

Silliman, Benjamin, 249

Simcoe, J. G., 122

Slavery, 17, 149

Smibert, John, 193

Smith, Elihu Hubbard, 248

Smuggling, 38–39

"Sons of Liberty," 28, 67, 79, 80

"Sons of Neptune," 80

South, characteristics of, 17–20, 36

Southwest, 161–63, 209

South Carolina, 10, 17, 18, 87, 146

Spain, 1, 138

Sparks, Jared, 194

Stamp Act, 52–58

Stamp Act Congress, 55

Staple Act of 1663, 34

Statute of Virginia for Religious Freedom, 148

Steuben, Baron Friedrich von, 131

Stewart, Lazarus, 142

Stiles, Ezra, 238

Stirling, William A. ("Lord"), 130

Stoddert, Benjamin, 227

Stuart, Charles, 108, 110, 116

Stuart, Gilbert, 150, 193, 248

Stuart, John, 44, 128

Suffolk Resolves, 89

Suffrage, 6–7, 146–48

Sugar Act, 39

Sullivan, General John, 108, 129

Talleyrand, Charles Maurice, 222, 227

Tarleton, Lieutenant Colonel Banastre, 107, 117, 126

Tea Party, Boston (1773), 67

Tennessee, 162–63, 210

Theater, 148, 151, 251

Thomson, Charles, 9

Thayendanegea (Joseph Brant), 128, 161

Thornton, Matthew, 9

Ticonderoga, 91

Tobacco, 17

Tooke, Horne, 73

Tory Rangers, 126

Townshend, Charles, 49, 59–61, 63, 72, 102

Tracy, Uriah, 224

Trade and Plantations, Board of, 28, 30, 32

Transylvania, 163

Treaty-making, 198

Trecothick, Barlow, 27, 56, 72

Trumbull, John, 243, 250, 252

Tryon, Governor William, 84, 142

Turnbull, Dr. Andrew, 4

Turner, Frederick Jackson, 162, 241

Tyler, Royall, 148

Uhlandorf, Bernard A., 107

United Empire Loyalists, 100, 155

Valley Forge, 134

Van, Charles, 77

Vandalia, 65

Van Rensselaer family, 147

Van Schaak, Peter, 154

Van Tyne, C. H., 126, 140

Vergennes, Charles Gravier, Comte de, 136, 138

Vermont, 141, 164

Vice-Admiralty Courts, 38, 60

Vincennes, 3

Virginia, 5, 8, 17, 20, 39, 44, 54, 55, 62, 146, 156

    Gazette, 82, 91

    Plan (1787), 168

War of Independence, American, causes, 50, 70–86, 96–105

    reasons for American victory, 128–38

    reasons for British defeat, 110–28

    seapower in, 118–19, 136–37

    sources for study, 107–8

Ward, General Artemas, 129

Warren, Charles, 179

Warren, Joseph, 92

Warren, Mercy Otis, 149
Washington, George, 8, 17, 21, 38, 90, 92, 98
  biographies of, 194
  character, 194–96
  as commander, 128–35
  as Federalist, 185, 207
  foreign policy, 202–10
  as President, 194–216
Watauga, 65, 162
Waterhouse, Benjamin, 194
Waxhaws, 144
Wayne, General Anthony, 130
Webster, Noah, 150
Weems, "Parson" Mason, 194
Wentworth, Sir John, 71, 84, 146
Wentworth, Paul, 27
West, Benjamin, 150, 193, 252
West Indies, British, 2, 36
  French, 39
West Indian merchants, 27, 57, 72
Western frontier, 9–11, 40–48, 58, 64, 102, 138, 142–43, 160–64, 191–92
Wharton, Samuel, 65
Wharton project, 65

Wharton Baynton Morgan Company, 102
Whately, Thomas, 52, 63
Whig Party (Old Whigs), 23–24
Whiskey Rebellion, 143, 207–8
Whitney, Eli, 249
Wilkes, John, 24, 33, 60, 70, 81
Willcox, William, 107, 116
Williams, Israel, 86
Wilson, James, 81, 89, 95, 167
Winthrop, John, 194
Wolcott, Oliver, 210, 221, 229, 234
Woodmason, Reverend Charles, 144
Woolman, John, 18
Worthington, John, 86
Wright, Sir James, 7, 71, 84, 100, 146
Wyoming Valley, 128, 140

XYZ Affair, 222

Yale College, 13, 150, 246
Yates, Robert, 166, 174
Yorktown, 116
Youghiogheny, 102

ESMOND WRIGHT, Professor of Modern History at the University of Glasgow since 1957, is becoming increasingly well known on both sides of the Atlantic as an authority in the field about which he has written in *Fabric of Freedom*.

Born in England in 1915, Mr. Wright graduated from the University of Durham and was Commonwealth Fund Fellow and John White Stevenson Prizeman at the University of Virginia, at which school he earned his M.A. degree.

During World War II he served in the British Army, chiefly in the Middle East, and left the service as a lieutenant colonel. He joined the faculty of the University of Glasgow in 1946. Professor Wright has also been visiting professor at the University of Tennessee, Johns Hopkins, and the University of Minnesota.

Mr. Wright's books include *A Short History of Our Own Times* (1951), *Washington and the American Revolution* (1957), and *Fabric of Freedom* (1961). He is at work on books about Benjamin Franklin and General Burgoyne.

AMERICAN CENTURY SERIES

WHEN ORDERING, please use the Standard Book Number consisting of the publisher's prefix, 8090-, plus the five digits following each title. (Note that the numbers given in this list are for paperback editions only. Many of the books are also available in cloth.)

The Hoosier School-Master by Edward Eggleston (0001-6)
The Magnificent Ambersons by Booth Tarkington (0002-4)
The Harbor by Ernest Poole (0003-2)
The Higher Learning in America by Thorstein Veblen (0007-5)
The Shame of the Cities by Lincoln Steffens (0008-3)
Company K by William March (0009-1)
The Influence of Seapower upon History by Alfred T. Mahan (0010-5)
A Daughter of the Middle Border by Hamlin Garland (0011-3)
How the Other Half Lives by Jacob Riis (0012-1)
Barren Ground by Ellen Glasgow (0014-8)
Hospital Sketches by Louisa May Alcott (0015-6)
A Traveler from Altruria by William Dean Howells (0016-4)
The Devil's Dictionary by Ambrose Bierce (0017-2)
Moon-Calf by Floyd Dell (0018-2)
The Big Rock Candy Mountain by Wallace Stegner (0019-9)
Life on the Mississippi by Mark Twain (0021-0)
Troubadour by Alfred Kreymborg (0022-9)
The Iron Heel by Jack London (0023-7)
The Grandissimes by George W. Cable (0025-3)
The Autocrat of the Breakfast Table by Oliver Wendell Holmes (0026-1)
The Jeffersonian Tradition in American Democracy by Charles Wiltse (0028-8)
The Narrative of Arthur Gordon Pym by Edgar Allan Poe (0029-6)
A Connecticut Yankee in King Arthur's Court by Mark Twain (0030-X)
Theodore Roosevelt and the Progressive Movement by George E. Mowry (0031-8)
The Autobiography of an Ex-Coloured Man by James Weldon Johnson (0032-6)
Jack London: Short Stories (0033-4)
Jefferson by Albert Jay Nock (0034-2)
Hemingway and His Critics ed. by Carlos Baker (0036-9)
The Best of Simple by Langston Hughes (0039-3)
American Social Thought ed. by Ray Ginger (0040-7)
William Dean Howells ed. by Rudolf and Clara Marburg Kirk (0041-5)
Walt Whitman ed. by Floyd Stovall (0042-3)
Thomas Paine ed. by Harry Hayden Clark (0043-1)
American Moderns by Maxwell Geismar (0044-X)
Edgar Allan Poe ed. by Hardin Craig and Margaret Alterton (0046-6)
Jonathan Edwards ed. by C. H. Faust and T. H. Johnson (0047-4)
Indian Tales by Jaime de Angulo (0049-0)
A Time of Harvest ed. by Robert E. Spiller (0050-4)
The Limits of Language ed. by Walker Gibson (0051-2)
Sherwood Anderson: Short Stories ed. by Maxwell Geismar (0052-0)
The World of Lincoln Steffens ed. by Ella Winter and Herbert Shapiro (0053-9)
Mark Twain on the Damned Human Race ed. by Janet Smith (0054-7)
Man Against Myth by Barrows Dunham (0056-3)
Something in Common and Other Stories by Langston Hughes (0057-1)
Writers in Transition: Seven Americans by H. Wayne Morgan (0058-1)
The Lincoln Nobody Knows by Richard N. Current (0059-8)
The Disinherited by Jack Conroy (0060-1)
Eisenhower As President ed. by Dean Albertson (0061-X)
Thoreau: People, Principles, and Politics ed. by Milton Meltzer (0064-4)
The Big Sea by Langston Hughes (0065-2)
The Golden Age of Homespun by Jared van Wagenen, Jr. (0066-0)
The Senate Establishment by Joseph S. Clark and Other Senators (0067-9)

I Wonder As I Wander by Langston Hughes (0068-7)
Science in Nineteenth-Century America ed. by Nathan Reingold (0069-5)
The Course of the South to Secession by Ulrich Bonnell Phillips (0070-9)
American Negro Poetry ed. by Arna Bontemps (0071-7)
Horace Greeley by Glyndon G. Van Deusen (0072-5)
David Walker's Appeal ed. by Charles M. Wiltse (0073-3)
The Sentimental Years by E. Douglas Branch (0074-1)
Henry James and the Jacobites by Maxwell Geismar (0075-X)
The Reins of Power by Bernard Schwartz (0076-8)
American Writers in Rebellion by H. Wayne Morgan (0077-6)
Policy and Power by Ruhl Bartlett (0078-4)
Wendell Phillips on Civil Rights and Freedom ed. by Louis Filler (0079-2)
American Negro Short Stories ed. by John Henrik Clarke (0080-6)
The Radical Novel in the United States: 1900-1954 by Walter B. Rideout (0081-4)
A History of Agriculture in the State of New York by Ulysses Prentiss Hedrick (0082-2)
Criticism and Fiction by William Dean Howells and *The Responsibilities of the Novelist* by Frank Norris (0083-0)
John F. Kennedy and the New Frontier ed. by Aïda DiPace Donald (0084-9)
Anyplace But Here by Arna Bontemps and Jack Conroy (0085-7)
Mark Van Doren: 100 Poems (0086-5)
Simple's Uncle Sam by Langston Hughes (0087-3)
Stranger at the Gates by Tracy Sugarman (0088-1)
Waiting for Nothing by Tom Kromer (0089-X)
31 New American Poets ed. by Ron Schreiber (0090-3)
Documents of Upheaval ed. by Truman Nelson (0092-X)
Black Pow-Wow by Ted Joans (0093-8)
Half a Man by M. W. Ovington (0094-6)
Collected and New Poems: 1924-1963 by Mark Van Doren (0095-4)
From Plantation to Ghetto (Revised) by August Meier and Elliott Rudwick (0096-2)
Tambourines to Glory by Langston Hughes (0097-0)
Afrodisia by Ted Joans (0098-9)
Natural Process ed. by Ted Wilentz and Tom Weatherly (0097-7)
The Free World Colossus (Revised) by David Horowitz (0107-1)

THE MAKING OF AMERICA
Fabric of Freedom: 1763-1800 by Esmond Wright (0101-2)
The New Nation: 1800-1845 by Charles M. Wiltse (0102-0)
The Stakes of Power: 1845-1877 by Roy F. Nichols (0103-9)
The Search for Order: 1877-1920 by Robert H. Wiebe (0104-7)
The Urban Nation: 1920-1960 by George E. Mowry (0105-5)

AMERICAN PROFILES
Thomas Jefferson: A Profile ed. by Merrill D. Peterson (0200-0)
Franklin D. Roosevelt: A Profile ed. by William E. Leuchtenburg (0201-9)
Alexander Hamilton: A Profile ed. by Jacob E. Cooke (0202-7)
Mark Twain: A Profile ed. by Justin Kaplan (0203-5)
Theodore Roosevelt: A Profile ed. by Morton Keller (0204-3)
Woodrow Wilson: A Profile ed. by Arthur S. Link (0205-1)
John C. Calhoun: A Profile ed. by John L. Thomas (0206-X)
Ralph Waldo Emerson: A Profile ed. by Carl Bode (0207-8)
William Jennings Bryan: A Profile ed. by Paul W. Glad (0208-6)
Martin Luther King, Jr.: A Profile ed. by C. Eric Lincoln (0209-4)
George Washington: A Profile ed. by James Morton Smith (0210-8)
Jonathan Edwards: A Profile ed. by David Levin (0212-4)
Benjamin Franklin: A Profile ed. by Esmond Wright (0214-0)